Individual Criminal Responsibility for the Financing of Entities Involved in Core Crimes

Studies in International Criminal Law

VOLUME 3

The titles published in this series are listed at *brill.com/sicl*

Individual Criminal Responsibility for the Financing of Entities Involved in Core Crimes

By

Laura Ausserladscheider Jonas

BRILL
NIJHOFF

LEIDEN | BOSTON

Cover illustration: Untitled watercolour, 2011, Edward Matwijkiw (1937–2012), reproduced with kind permission of the family.

Library of Congress Cataloging-in-Publication Data

Names: Ausserladscheider Jonas, Laura, author.
Title: Individual criminal responsibility for the financing of entities involved in core crimes / by Laura Ausserladscheider Jonas.
Description: Leiden ; Boston : Brill Nijhoff, [2022] | Series: Studies in international criminal law, 2666-903X ; volume 3 | Based on author's thesis (doctoral - University of Pretoria, 2021) | Includes bibliographical references and index.
Identifiers: LCCN 2021044556 (print) | LCCN 2021044557 (ebook) | ISBN 9789004470927 (hardback) | ISBN 9789004470934 (ebook)
Subjects: LCSH: International crimes–Finance–Law and legislation. | Accomplices (International law)
Classification: LCC KZ7096 .A97 2022 (print) | LCC KZ7096 (ebook) | DDC 345/.0235–dc23/eng/20211015
LC record available at https://lccn.loc.gov/2021044556
LC ebook record available at https://lccn.loc.gov/2021044557

Typeface for the Latin, Greek, and Cyrillic scripts: "Brill". See and download: brill.com/brill-typeface.

ISSN 2666-903X
ISBN 978-90-04-47092-7 (hardback)
ISBN 978-90-04-47093-4 (e-book)

This book is printed on acid-free paper and produced in a sustainable manner.

To the victims of core crimes.
Every line of this book has been written with you in mind.
May this horrendous part of history never be repeated.

True peace is not merely the absence of tension: it is the presence of justice. Without justice, there can be no peace.
He who passively accepts evil is as much involved in it
as he who helps to perpetuate it.

MARTIN LUTHER KING, JR

Contents

PART 2
Complicity – Internationally and Nationally

PART 3
Determination of the Rules

Foreword

In this book, Individual Criminal Responsibility for the Financing of Entities Involved in Core Crimes, Dr Laura Ausserladscheider Jonas addresses a uniquely important subject, and does so in a thoughtful, scholarly and methodical way.

I begin first with the importance of the topic. War crimes, crimes against humanity, genocide and the crime of aggression – those crimes that we consider to be core crimes – are often facilitated by financial and other resources. They could, in many instances, not be perpetrated without the provision of financial assistance in some way or another (whether the provider of the finances is aware or not). If the goal of international criminal law is, in addition to ending impunity, to prevent the commission of these crimes, it is necessary to identify how and under what circumstances those who provide financing to entities involved in the commission of core crimes can be held responsible under international law. That is the purpose of Dr Ausserladscheider Jonas's book.

The book examines the basis for criminal liability in international criminal law for persons who finance entities that perpetrate core crimes. While it might seem obvious that such persons ought to be held responsible under international law, the rules are less than clear. In particular, there is no agreement on whether liability exists under international law for these individuals, and more importantly, if there is liability, under what circumstances such liability exists.

It is to these two questions that Dr Ausserladscheider Jonas dedicates her efforts in this book. To determine the minimum standard of liability of these individuals, the work analyses the legal rules relating to complicity in international criminal law and seeks to determine whether there are minimum standards of liability for aiders and abettors.

International criminal law, the study area under which this research is situated, is the meeting point of two areas of law: criminal law and international law. In this book, Dr Ausserladscheider Jonas skilfully navigates these two areas, illustrating expertise in both, and as a result she stays true to the methodology of both areas. She penetrates into criminal law concepts like complicity, aiding and abetting, *mens rea*, and *dolus eventualis*. She addresses these (and other) concepts from both a general standpoint as well as from the perspective of their understanding under the Rome Statute of the International Criminal Court.

Yet, to try to find the general rules of international law, the work turns to and employs the methodology and sources of public international law. The general rule for identifying the appropriate standard of liability for financing entities involved in the commission of core crimes is, according to the book, general principles of law within the meaning of Article 38(1)(c) of the Statute of the International Court of Justice. Tangentially, I might add that Dr Ausserladscheider Jonas avoids the "recognised by civilised nations" debate by simply referring to recognition by the international community of States and relying on the generally accepted method for identifying general principles of law, namely the search for domestic law principles.

For (domestic) criminal lawyers this method might seem somewhat counter-intuitive. An assessment of the domestic laws of more than twenty States might seem to undermine the depth of the analysis. Yet, the search for general principles of law within the meaning of Article 38(1)(c) of the Statute of the International Court of Justice requires a search to determine whether there are common traits or commonalities across legal systems generally. Such an assessment cannot be conducted by a traditional comparative study of two or three States, where depth is prioritised over breadth. Yet, even with its breadth – twenty States from every region and legal tradition and also across languages – the book is still able to provide rich account of the nuances of standards of liability in those legal systems.

With this book, Dr Laura Ausserladscheider Jonas has produced a significant and scholarly work on an important subject. I am very pleased to be associated with the production of this book, and I wholeheartedly recommend the book to scholars of international criminal law.

Dire Tladi
Professor of International Law
SARChI Chair of International Constitutional Law
University of Pretoria

Acknowledgements

This book is based on my doctoral thesis, and was inspired by the course on International Criminal Law taught by Judge Theodor Meron at the University of Oxford in the 2015/2016 academic year. As with all works of this kind, it depended on a great deal of assistance and encouragement.

First and foremost, I would like to thank Professor Dire Tladi, my LLD supervisor, for his direction and advice on the dissertation and this book, as well as his warm support and guidance. I owe him a great deal. I feel privileged to have had the honour of being his student.

I owe an intellectual debt to many, particularly to Judge Meron, who taught me International Criminal Law, for his rigour and inspiration. I am also extremely grateful to all who discussed drafts, chapters, and ideas with me and who read entire drafts and for whose comments it is vastly better: Professor Eugenio Raúl Zaffaroni, Professor Gabriel Pérez Barberá, Professor Luís Greco, Professor Vladimir Aras, Professor Shizhou Wang, Professor Moisés Moreno Hernández, Professor Ramón Ragués I Vallès, Professor Khalid Ghanayim, Professor Mordechai Kremnitzer, Professor Adham Hashish, Professor Gleb Bogush, Professor Willem Gravett, Dr. Sylvia Tellenbach, Dr. Angela Hefti, Karyn Kenny, Dr. Ebba Lekvall, Cannelle Lavite, Philippe Kuhn, Jessica Allemman, Dr. Yolandi Meyer, Dr. Eduardo Kapapelo, Esther Earbin, Ankita Shanker, as well as all the women in the Alas Women Network.

This project would not have seen the light without the generosity of the SARChI Chair at the University of Pretoria. I am also in dept to the Swiss Federal Office of Justice for allowing me to take a leave of absence from my intensive and rewarding job, as well as for their financial contribution. I am also thankful to the Swiss Institute of Comparative Law, in particular Sadri Saieb, Dr. Karim El Chazli, and Michele Baccherassi, and to the Max Planck Institute for Foreign and International Criminal Law (now renamed Max Planck Institute for the Study of Crime, Security and Law), in particular Dr. Johanna Rinceanu, and Dr. Jan-Michael Simon, where I received scholarships to effectuate research stays as a guest doctoral researcher.

Finally, I am deeply grateful to my family for their love and support. To Kenny Jonas and Creed Ausserladscheider Jonas, whose unconditional love and support carry me every day. I am forever thankful. They are my soul.

Figures and Maps

Figures

Maps

PART 1

A Theory of International Criminal Law

CHAPTER 1

Introduction

1 Introduction

War crimes, crimes against humanity, genocide and the crime of aggression (hereinafter, 'core crimes')[1] could in many instances not be perpetrated without financial assistance. Holding those accountable who finance entities that commit core crimes would therefore contribute to the project of fighting impunity by removing the tools that contribute to the commission of those crimes. This book examines the basis for criminal liability in international criminal law for persons who finance entities that perpetrate core crimes. Despite the need for clear rules, neither international courts nor scholars agree upon (i) whether liability exists for individuals who finance entities that commit core crimes; and (ii) if so, the circumstances under which such liability exists.

To determine the minimum standard of liability, this work analyses the legal rules relating to complicity in twenty selected national jurisdictions in Africa, Asia, Europe, Latin America, North America and Oceania. This comparative analysis aims to determine whether there are general principles of law recognised by the community of States[2] on the minimum standard of liability for aiders and abettors.

---

1 The term 'core crimes' is derived from Antonio Cassese and Paola Gaeta, *Cassese's International Criminal Law* (Oxford University Press 2013). These terms are also used by others, see for example Terje Einarsen, *The Concept of Universal Crimes in International Law* (Opsahl Academic EPublisher 2012).

2 By 'general principles of law recognised by the community of States', I mean general principles of law within the meaning of Art 38(1)(c) of the ICJ Statute. This book uses the term 'community of States' rather than 'civilized nations', as the latter term portrays, in my view, a colonial perspective of the world. This work rejects the binary representation that is prevalent in international criminal law, namely the dichotomy between western countries and other countries. Consequently, the relevant national laws that this work analyses (when available) is the legislation, customary law, and jurisprudence of the community of States, thereby including Africa, Asia, Europe Latin America, North America and Oceania. See also International Law Commission, 'Second Report of the Special Rapporteur on General Principles of Law, Marcelo Vázquez-Bermúdez, UN Doc. A/CN.4/741' (2020) in particular paragraphs 176–7. An approach similar to the persective adopted in this work has been discussed in Julio A Barberis, *Formación Del Derecho Internacional* (Editorial Ábaco de Rodolfo Depalma 1994) 244; Christian Tomuschat, *International Law : Ensuring the Survival of Mankind on the Eve of a New Century: General Course on Public International Law, Volume 281* (Brill | Nijhoff 1999) 337; Francesco Capotorti, *Cours Général de Droit International Public, Volume 248* (Brill

 | DOI:10.1163/9789004470934_002

Therefore, this work proposes a normative framework for assessing legal rules relating to complicity, and it advances a normative argument as to how legal rules should be structured concerning the criminal responsibility of individuals who finance entities that commit core crimes. It is my thesis that not only individuals who perpetrate core crimes should be held criminally liable, but also those who substantially assist in the commission of these crimes, including through their financial assistance.

I proceed from the premise that access to financial resources facilitates the commission of core crimes. Thus, one of the underlying objectives is to establish whether current international criminal law could be used as a tool to impede the flow of financial resources to perpetrators of core crimes by obstructing, or at least disrupting, the procurement of the financial means to commit these crimes. My ultimate objective is to contribute to safeguarding international peace and security and the protection of human lives.[3]

I argue that an individual who finances an entity that perpetrates a core crime should be held criminally liable under customary international criminal law as an aider and abettor. Significantly, the International Criminal Court ('ICC') cannot, under the current framework of Article 25 of the Rome Statute, hold an individual liable for knowingly and intentionally assisting the perpetration of the crime by the principal if she does not act with the purpose of facilitating the offence.[4] However, I believe that other international tribunals applying general principles recognised by the community of States should hold an aider and abettor liable if she fulfils the material and mental elements of the offence, notably if she substantially contributes to the perpetration of the offence by the principal, and if she acts with at least wilful blindness and *dolus eventualis*.[5] An accused acts with wilful blindness if she deliberately shuts her eyes in order to avoid criminal liability. She acts with *dolus eventualis* when she is aware of the danger of her conduct, she foresees the possibility of the harmful consequences occurring, she does not wish for it, but she nevertheless consciously allows those consequences.[6] Based on the comparative analysis, I do

| Nijhoff 1994) 118; Pierre-Marie Dupuy, *L'Unité de l'Ordre Juridique International, Volume 297* (Brill | Nijhoff 2002) 179–80; as Dupuy noted in footnote 301, 'Ces nations étaient tellement civilisées, au moment de l'adoption de cette expression, contemporaine du Traité de Versailles, qu'elles venaient de s'entre-tuer pendant quatre ans dans la boue des tranchées!'

3 Emil Dall, Tom Keatinge and Andrea Berger, 'Countering Proliferation Finance: An Introductory Guide for Financial Institutions' (2017) 3, available at <https://rusi.org/sites/default/files/201704_rusi_cpf_guidance_paper.1_0.pdf%0D> accessed 12 September 2018.

4 See Chapter 4, section 4.1.

5 See Chapter 4, section 4.2, and Chapter 6, sections 2 and 3.

6 See Chapter 6, sections 2 and 3.

not argue that enough acceptance exists in practice for the wilful blindness doctrine to become a general principle of law recognised by the community of States. Rather, I recognise that currently the minimum level of knowledge necessary for criminal liability is active knowledge, and I encourage the implementation of the wilful blindness doctrine in future international instruments as an extension of the knowledge requirement. *Dolus eventualis*, as a form of intent, constitutes a general principle of law recognised by the community of States, because it is widely recognised as a sufficient level of intent for criminal liability at the international and national level. Furthermore, this recognition respects the principles of international criminal law, notably because it is foreseeable that the term 'intent' encompasses *dolus directus*, *dolus indirectus* and *dolus eventualis*.

Anchored by the normative framework, I aim to clarify the basis for individual criminal liability for persons who finance entities that perpetrate core crimes. The objective of this book is to clarify the rules to enable international courts and tribunals to identify the extent to which individual criminal liability attaches to the financing of core crimes, as well as the legal basis for such liability.

By clarifying the criminal liability of individual who finance entities that perpetrate core crimes, I also seek to clarify the mental elements of the mode of liability of aiding and abetting. This is achieved through a thorough analysis of the applicable rules in the international arena, as well as through the comparative analysis, which aims to be truly international in its scope.

2 Structure of the Research

This work is divided into three parts. Part 1 (Chapters 1 to 3), Chapter 1 (the present Chapter) is a general introduction. Chapter 2 provides an overview of the nature and sources of international criminal law and examines some fundamental principles of international criminal law. These principles are those with which any *actus reus* and *mens rea* requirements and general principles of law recognised by the community of States must comply. Chapter 3 considers the *actus reus* and *mens rea* requirements in international criminal law. Part 1 provides the normative framework against which the findings and conclusions of this work are to be tested.

Part 2 (Chapters 4 and 5) examines the *actus reus* and *mens rea* elements of aiding and abetting in international criminal law and in national jurisdictions. Chapter 4 analysis the mode of liability of aiding and abetting as understood at the ICC and in customary international law. It thus determines the applicable law in the international arena. Chapter 5 offers a comparative analysis of the knowledge and intent requirements of aiding and abetting at the national level in twenty selected jurisdictions. Chapters 4 and 5 together are a critique of the lack of clarity of the mental elements of aiding and abetting at the international level, and constitute an analytical account of this mode of liability in international criminal law and in national jurisdictions. The purpose of this analysis is to determine the existence of general principles of law.

In Part 3 (Chapters 6 and 7), Chapter 6 places the findings from Chapters 4 and 5 within the normative framework developed in Part 1, by verifying that a large number and a variety of domestic legal systems recognise the legal principles distilled from Chapters 4 and 5. The aim is to determine whether these principles meet the requirements to be general principles of law recognised by the community of States according to Article 38(1)(c) of the Statute of the International Court of Justice ('ICJ Statute'). In fact, I utilise the analysis in Chapter 4 of the applicable legal principles in international criminal law and the knowledge gleaned from the comparative analysis in Chapter 5 to determine, within the normative framework developed in Part 1, what the current law on aiding and abetting is in international criminal law. Chapter 6 also conducts a compatibility test, which serves to ensure that the developed general principles of law recognised by the community of States are capable of existing within the broader framework of international law. Finally, Chapter 7 draws the conclusion.

3 Scope of the Research

This book focuses on the participation of individuals who finance entities involved in the commission of core crimes. It thus becomes necessary to define the terms 'individual criminal liability', 'entities', 'core crimes', 'participatory conduct', 'punishable complicity', 'financing', and 'responsibility, accountability and liability'.

3.1 *Individual Criminal Liability*

This work focuses on the international criminal liability of individuals. Thus, it does not include a detailed discussion of the criminal liability of other actors, such as states or corporations, although parallels with the criminal liability of such other actors may be drawn.

In fact, the law of state responsibility belongs to a separate branch of international law, and it neither implies nor is dependent upon the legal responsibility of individuals.[7] Also, the international community has not yet recognised corporate criminal responsibility under international law.[8]

Individuals are the subjects of international criminal law.[9] The Nuremberg trials contributed significantly to the development of the concept of individual criminal responsibility under international law.[10] Indeed, the Nuremberg Tribunal famously declared:[11]

> Crimes against international law are committed by men, not by abstract entities, and only by punishing individuals who commit such crimes can the provisions of international law be enforced.

The statutes of the two *ad hoc* Tribunals, the International Criminal Tribunal for the former Yugoslavia ('ICTY') and the International Criminal Tribunal for Rwanda ('ICTR'), respectively, reaffirmed the legal principles with regard to individual criminal responsibility under international law.[12] Another major contribution to the evolution of the concept of individual criminal responsibility was the adoption of the *Draft Code of Offences Against the Peace and Security of Mankind*, prepared by the International Law Commission ('ILC'), which generally views individual criminal liability similarly than the Nuremberg principles.[13] Finally, the Rome Statute of the International Criminal Court ('Rome

7 André Nollkaemper, 'Concurrence between Individual Responsibility and State Responsibility in International Law' (2003) 52 The International and Comparative Law Quarterly 615.

8 Andrew Clapham, 'Extending International Criminal Law Beyond the Individual to Corporations and Armed Opposition Groups' (2008) 6 Journal of International Criminal Justice 899, 899. See also generally ICJ, 'Report of the ICJ Expert Legal Panel on Corporate Complicity in International Crimes' (*International Commission of Jurists* 2008) available at <https://www.icj.org/report-of-the-international-commission-of-jurists-expert-legal-panel-on-corporate-complicity-in-international-crimes/> accessed 12 September 2018. See however draft Article 6(8) of the 'Fourth Report on Crimes against Humanity, Sean D. Murphy, 18 February 2019, A/CN.4/725'.

9 Andrew Clapham, 'The Role of the Individual in International Law' (2010) 21 European Journal of International Law 25, 27. See also the 'International Law Commission, Draft Code of Offences against the Peace and Security of Mankind, 1954' (2005), where the principle of individual responsibility for crimes under international law was recognized.

10 IMT *Trial of the Major War Criminals before the International Military Tribunal, Judgment of 1 October 1946*. On the Tokyo Tribunal, see Bernard Victor Aloysius Röling and Antonio Cassese, *The Tokyo Trial and Beyond: Reflections of a Peacemonger* (Polity Press 1993).

11 IMT *Trial of the Major War Criminals before the International Military Tribunal, Judgment of 1 October 1946* 447.

12 Statute of the International Criminal Tribunal for the Former Yugoslavia 2002; Statute of the International Criminal Tribunal for Rwanda 1994.

13 The 1996 *Draft Code of Crimes* is the result of several decades of work by the ILC since its adoption of the 1954 Draft Code of Offences Against the Peace and Security of Mankind.

Statute') confirmed the establishment of individual criminal responsibility. It states that: 'A person who commits a crime [...] shall be individually responsible and liable for punishment'.[14] It also notes that: 'No provision in this Statute relating to individual criminal responsibility shall affect the responsibility of States under international law'.[15]

A core crime usually is committed by a plurality of offenders, each of whom plays a different role in the orchestration of the crime. This plurality of offenders generally means that there are individuals behind the scenes, notably individuals who finance these crimes. To determine individual criminal responsibility it becomes indispensable to assess of the role played by the person who finances entities involved in the commission of core crimes.

3.2 *Entities*

This work focuses primarily on the question of whether an individual who finances an 'entity' (also referred to as 'mixed entity', 'organisation' or 'mixed organisation') could be held criminally liable for the core crimes committed by such an entity.

A 'mixed entity' is defined in accordance with the meaning of this term in the *Perisic* case,[16] *i.e.* an organisation that is simultaneously implicated in both criminal and legitimate (non-criminal) activities. For example, in *Perisic* the ICTY held that the Army of Republika Srpska ('VRS') constituted a 'mixed entity'. Certain members of VRS undoubtedly participated in the perpetration of core crimes in Srebrenica and Sarajevo, while others respected international humanitarian law. The VRS was therefore neither a wholly criminal nor a wholly law-abiding organisation.

My research focuses on mixed entities because, as noted in the War Report 2013:[17]

> It is hard, if not impossible, to think of a conflict where no crimes were ever committed. Likewise, it is difficult to think of a conflict where nothing but crimes (at international law) were carried out [...]. [Therefore,] as soon as a group carries out at least some actions—however small in number—that are consistent with [international humanitarian law],

14 Article 25 paragraph 2 of the Rome Statute of the International Criminal Court 1998 (last amended 2010).

15 ibid, Article 25 paragraph 4.

16 ICTY *Prosecutor v Perisic, Appeals Chamber Judgment* (IT-04-81-A).

17 Stuart Casey-Maslen (ed), *The War Report: Armed Conflict in 2013* (Oxford University Press 2014) 526.

> even in a vast and endless sea of criminality, then such a group should fall into the category of the VRS in Perisic; that is, a mixed organization.

In the case of a mixed entity it becomes necessary to distinguish between financial aid that contributed to the general war effort and legal military action on the one hand, and aid provided for the commission of criminal activities on the other.[18]

3.3 *Core Crimes*

As stated at the outset, this book focuses on core crimes, *to wit* war crimes, crimes against humanity, genocide, and the crime of aggression.

Core crimes have four constitutive elements.[19] Firstly, they violate rules of customary international law. Secondly, the international community, as a whole, adheres to the legal rules that repress the commission of these crimes. Thirdly, core crimes are of concern to the international community; thus there exists a universal interest in prohibiting these crimes. Finally, because of the gravity of these crimes, if state officials of a state committed core crimes in their official capacities it has been argued that the state is barred from claiming immunity from the civil and criminal jurisdiction of foreign states in whose territory such core crimes were committed.[20]

In sum, the gravity and scale of these crimes shock the conscience of humanity.[21] Core crimes:[22]

> [D]efy boundaries in a very real way: [they are] cases which by their magnitude so threaten our sense of humanity that they belong to a sort of 'world heritage of pain'.

The international community considers war crimes, crimes against humanity and genocide to be the worst of all crimes. As Bassiouni notes, it is accepted

---

18 ICTY *Prosecutor v Perisic, Appeals Chamber Judgment* (*IT-04-81-A*).

19 Cassese and Gaeta (n 1) 20.

20 Note that if a head of state of government, foreign minister, or diplomatic agent commits core crimes while still serving, then she enjoys complete personal immunity as long as she is in office. These were discussed in the ICJ *Case Concerning the Arrest Warrant of 11 April 2000 (Democratic Republic of the Congo v Belgium), 14 February 2002*; Cassese and Gaeta (n 1) 20.

21 Rome Statute of the International Criminal Court 1998 (last amended 2010) 2nd recital of the preamble.

22 Frederic Megret, 'In Defence of Hybridity: Towards a Representational Theory of International Criminal Justice' (2005) 38 Cornell International Law Journal 725, 737.

that war crimes, crimes against humanity, and genocide constitute *jus cogens* crimes.[23]

3.4 *Participatory Conduct (Complicity)*

International criminal law holds individuals liable, not only for committing core crimes, but also for attempting, assisting in, facilitating, or aiding and abetting the commission of such crimes.[24] Direct participation, conspiracy (as mode of liability), and complicity were the first recognised modalities of criminal responsibility in international law.[25]

As a derivative form of participation, the participatory conduct of the accomplice is tied to the wrongdoings of the principal actor.[26] Jackson states:[27]

> Complicity is a particular way of contributing to wrongdoing. In reflecting this, legal systems should hold accomplices responsible for their own contribution to the principal's wrong, rather than for the wrong of their principal.

This is a conceptually coherent and normatively desirable approach to participation in wrongdoing, which also avoids the principled objections to imputational responsibility. It allows for a balance between the accused's individual contribution to the commission of the crime, and the collective nature of core crimes. Because rules of complicity take a variety of forms that differ in their source, content, and structure, certain questions regarding the content and structure of these rules must be addressed.[28]

Financing a crime consists of a derivative form of participation in the crime. This work provides an analysis of legal rules of complicity, including their source, content and structure. This essentially derivative character of the act of financing explains the exclusion of certain forms of responsibility.[29]

---

23 Cherif M Bassiouni, 'International Crimes: Jus Cogens and Obligatio Erga Omnes' (1996) 59 Law and Contemporary Problems 63, 68; Cassese and Gaeta (n 1).

24 International Committee of the Red Cross Advisory Service on International Humanitarian Law, 'General Principles of International Criminal Law' (2014) available at <https://www.icrc.org/en/document/general-principles-international-criminal-law-factsheet> accessed 12 September 2018.

25 Elies van Sliedregt, *Individual Criminal Responsibility in International Law* (Oxford University Press 2012).

26 Sanford Kadish, 'Complicity, Cause and Blame: A Study in the Interpretation of Doctrine' (1985) 73 California Law Review 323, 337.

27 Miles Jackson, *Complicity in International Law* (Oxford University Press 2015) 22.

28 ibid 87.

29 See Chapter 4, section 3.

This book does not address in detail the conduct of all the parties involved in the commission of a crime (namely direct perpetration, co-preparation, joint criminal enterprise ('JCE'), instigation, ordering, contributing to a group acting with a common purpose, planning, conspiracy, incitement and command responsibility). The principal mode of liability that I explore in this work is the derivative form of liability of aiding and abetting. This mode of liability, which finds extensive application in national as well as international courts and tribunals,[30] is the mode applicable to an individual who finances an entity that perpetrates core crimes.[31]

3.5 *Punishable Complicity*

It is necessary to distinguish an action – which itself is not punishable but can become punishable if done with the view to committing an offence, such as financing – from an action that is *per se* dangerous, but in principle permissible. Examples of the former include providing money or a vehicle, which actions are in and of themselves not punishable. The latter, however, are dangerous actions – such as putting weapons of war, the production and export of which are lawful, in circulation – which actions are permissible under lawful circumstances.

In the case of dangerous but permissible actions, the widely accepted doctrine of objective (fair) attribution or imputation prevails.[32] According to this doctrine the conduct that is dangerous *per se* (such as putting weapons of war in circulation) is considered to be a permissible risk.[33] This doctrine limits accomplice liability to those acts of assistance or contribution which either create a risk/harm, or increase an existing risk/harm, under circumstances in which that risk/harm is legally prohibited and therefore constitutes an illegal risk/harm.[34] The attributory nexus is therefore interrupted in

30 ICTY *Prosecutor v Tihomir Blaškić, Appeals Chamber Judgment* (*IT-95-14-A*); ICTY *Prosecutor v Vidoje Blagojevic and Dragan Jokic, Appeals Chamber Judgment* (*IT-02-60-A*); ICTY *Prosecutor v Perisic, Trial Chamber Judgment* (*IT-04-81-T*).

31 See Chapter 4, section 3.

32 Kai Ambos, 'Complicity in War Crimes through (Legal) Arms Supplies?' available at <https://www.ejiltalk.org/complicity-in-war-crimes-through-legal-arms-supplies/?fbclid=IwAR1XQooWW4onE7NcHt1EhdoXPPtdqbtxvnpvj43UScvU88cNmHVMgxhUHaY> accessed 20 January 2020.

33 Andrew von Hirsch, 'Extending the Harm Principle: "Remote" Harms and Fair Imputation' in Andrew Simester and Anthony Terry Hanmer Smith (eds), *Harm and Culpability* (Oxford University Press 1996) 259 ss.

34 Kai Ambos, *Treatise on International Criminal Law Volume 1: Foundations and General Part* (Oxford University Press 2013) 165.

cases of dangerous but permissible actions, because the risk/harm is legally permissible.

Acts that do not require authorisation to be lawful, such as financing an entity, fall outside the scope of this theory. Therefore, in the case of an individual donating money to an entity that commits core crimes, the nexus between the donation and the perpetration of a crime is not interrupted.

3.6 *Financing*

Financing generally consists of the action of providing funding to a person or enterprise.[35] However, this book focuses specifically on the action of providing monetary means to *entities* involved in the commission of core crimes, which involvement has a substantial effect on, or substantially contributes to, the perpetration of those crimes.

This work focuses on assistance through the provision of monetary contributions, and it does not address the provision of weapons, armed forces or any other kind of contribution. Thus, in the context of this work, 'financing' means making a *substantial* financial contribution to entities that commit these crimes. The question of whether the funding is 'substantial' must be determined on a case-by-case basis.[36]

In *Aleksovski* the ICTY explained that 'substantial' assistance could 'consist of providing the means to commit the crime'.[37] Moreover, in *Vasiljevic*, in discussing the substantial nature of the contribution, the tribunal stated that, '[t]he act of assistance need not have caused the act of the principal offender, but it must have had a substantial effect on the commission of the crime by the principal offender'.[38] Similarly, the provision of funds does not need to have caused the act of the principal; it is sufficient for it merely to have had a substantial effect on the perpetration of the crime by the principal.[39] In addition, the sums

---

35 *Oxford English Dictionary* (2018) defines 'financing' as 'to furnish with finances or money'.

36 For a detailed discussion on the notion of 'substantial effect/contribution', see Chapter 4, section 4.2.3.1.

37 ICTY *Prosecutor v Zlatko Aleksovski, Trial Chamber Judgment* (IT-95-14/1-T) 62; ICTY *Prosecutor v Radislav Krstic, Appeals Chamber Judgment* (IT-98-33-A) 137–144.

38 ICTY *Prosecutor v Vasiljević, Trial Chamber Judgment* (IT-98-32-T) 70.

39 See also ICTY *Prosecutor v Anto Furundzija, Trial Chamber Judgment* (IT-95-17/1-T) 234; 'The position under customary international law seems [...] to be best reflected in the proposition that the assistance must have a substantial effect on the commission of the crime.' When discussing the mode of liability of aiding and abetting, the Tribunal also stated in ICTY *Prosecutor v Tihomir Blaškić, Trial Chamber Judgment* (IT-95-14-T) 285 that '[p]roof that the conduct of the aider and abettor had a causal effect on the act of the principal perpetrator is not required'.

required to fund the perpetration of core crimes are not always substantial. Rather, the focus is on the impact of the defendant's financial assistance *vis-à-vis* the commission of the core crime as even limited financial involvement could have the requisite substantial effect on the commission of the crime.

3.7 *Responsibility, Accountability and Liability*

Individuals are responsible for their participatory conduct in the commission of a crime. The Oxford English Dictionary defines 'responsibility' as 'the state or fact of being accountable; liability, accountability for something'.[40] It also defines 'accountability' as 'the quality of being accountable; liability to account for and answer for one's conduct, performances of duties [...]; responsibility'.[41] Finally, 'liability' is defined as 'the condition of being liable or answerable by law or equity'.[42]

Both 'responsibility' and 'accountability' seem to include an element of blameworthiness that flow from the violation of an obligation, while 'liability' seems to be more focused on the legal consequences of violating an obligation. Fischer and Tognazzini note that: '[A]ccountability refers to the interaction between the agent and the moral community to which she belongs'.[43]

However, Kool argues that:[44]

> Politicians, academics and practitioners from different (legal(-philosophical)) backgrounds [have come to the conclusion that the] interpretation and application of the concepts of responsibility, accountability and

40 *Oxford English Dictionary* (n 35).

41 ibid.

42 ibid.

43 John Martin Fischer and Neal A Tognazzini, 'The Physiognomy of Responsibility' (2011) 82 Philosophy and Phenomenological Research 381. See also generally R Jay Wallace, *Responsibility and the Moral Sentiments* (Harvard University Press 1998); Gary Watson, 'Two Faces of Responsibility' (1996) 24 Philosophical Topics 227; Thomas M Scanlon, *Moral Dimensions: Permissibility, Meaning, Blame* (Harvard University Press 2008).

44 Renée SB Kool, '(Crime) Victims' Compensation: The Emergence of Convergence' (2014) 10 Utrecht Law Review 14, 25–6. It is important to note that according to Kool, ' "legitimate victims" policy, however, can lead towards a penalization of the civil law, or in reverse, to a civilization of the criminal law', because 'subscribing to the legitimacy of the pursuit of victims' compensation and the related need for procedural justice has resulted in the fact that the interpretation and application of the concepts of responsibility, accountability and liability with regard to crime-related tort are – albeit within a certain perspective – converging.' Kool concludes that, 'such an effect is hard to avoid, given the close relationship between crime and crime-related tort'.

> liability with regard to crime-related tort are – albeit within a certain perspective – converging.

In fact, scholars in the field of international criminal law also use these terms interchangeably. For example, the terms 'mode of liability' and 'mode of responsibility' generally refer to the same concept. The same reasoning seems to apply to 'accountability', which is generally used to mean 'responsibility' and 'liability'.[45]

Therefore, because the differences between these terms are often unclear and seem to be insignificant, and because most scholars seem to use them interchangeably, for purposes of simplicity I, too, use the terms 'responsibility', 'accountability' and 'liability' interchangeably.

4 Rationale for This Research

A clarification of the rules of international criminal law in this area is necessary for three reasons: (i) it will help to resolve the current legal uncertainties; (ii) international courts and tribunals need a clear determination of the *actus reus* and *mens rea* elements of aiding and abetting; and (iii) it will contribute to ending the circle of impunity.

4.1 *Legal Uncertainty*

Firstly, in international criminal law the basis for individual criminal liability for financing the commission of core crimes is unclear. On the one hand, courts at both the international and national levels have handed down conflicting judgments regarding the constitutive elements of the mode of liability of aiding and abetting. On the other hand, most legal scholars have focused on the validity of the so-called 'specific direction' requirement.[46] In-depth analyses have not been done on either the legality of financing entities that commit core crimes or the individual criminal responsibility for providing such financing.

Because the requirements for criminal liability under both national and international law have never been determined, it is unclear what behaviour might be punishable, resulting in legal uncertainty. There are numerous areas

45 See generally Robert Cryer *et al*, *An Introduction to International Criminal Law and Procedure* (3 ed, Cambridge University Press 2014); Cassese and Gaeta (n 1).

46 The 'specific direction' requirement has been overwhelmingly rejected and is discussed in detail in Chapter 4, section 4.2.3.1.

where disagreements have arisen in the law of aiding and abetting.[47] The question of responsibility for financing is one of a 'number of open issues and questions' that need to be addressed, which 'yearn for clarity' and for which '[s]crutiny and analysis' is required.[48] To remedy this lack of clarity, the prohibited behaviour of an individual who finances an entity that perpetrates core crimes, including the possible modes of liability, must clearly be circumscribed so as to clarify the elements of the potential crime and the modes of liability. This book aims at filling this *lacuna*. In other words, an individual should have legal certainty about the circumstances under which she could face criminal liability for financing an entity involved in the perpetration of core crimes.

4.2 *All International Courts and Tribunals*

Secondly, all international, hybrid and *ad hoc* tribunals and courts, such as the Residual Mechanism for International Criminal Tribunals ('MICT'), the Syrian International, Impartial and Independent Mechanism, the Independent Investigative Mechanism for Myanmar, and the Kosovo Specialist Chambers & Specialist Prosecutor's Office, as well as future international tribunals need a clear determination of the *actus reus* and *mens rea* elements of the mode of liability of aiding and abetting. It is thus necessary to clarify the rules to enable judges in all international criminal courts and tribunals to adopt a unified approach in determining the liability of a person who finances an entity that perpetrates core crimes.

4.3 *End the Cycle of Impunity*

Thirdly, one of the fundamental purposes of international criminal law is to protect human life and to end impunity.[49] It is trite that the perpetration of core crimes generally requires financial resources. Holding responsible those individuals who finance entities that perpetrate core crimes might play a significant role in preventing the commission of those crimes, and in ending the cycle of impunity. Clear principles of legal liability might also disincentivise the financing of core crimes, thereby contributing to the reduction of these crimes by denying perpetrators the financial resources necessary to commit them.

---

47 See Chapter 4, section 4.2.3.

48 Manuel J Ventura, 'Aiding and Abetting' in Jérôme de Hemptinne, Robert Roth and Elies von Sliedregt (eds), *Modes of Liability in International Criminal Law* (2019) 175.

49 See generally, Chirs Jenks and Guido Acquaviva, 'Debate: The Role of International Criminal Justice in Fostering Compliance with International Humanitarian Law' (2014) 96 International Review of the Red Cross 775.

5 Methodology

This book discusses the criminal responsibility of individuals who finance entities that are involved in the commission of core crimes by analysing whether international criminal law allows for the extension of liability to these individuals. Because 'there are competing positions on the normal threshold of *mens rea* that triggers criminal responsibility for core crimes in the international arena',[50] the assessment that I undertake in this research is based on current treaties, rules of customary international law, general principles of law recognised by the community of States, international and national jurisprudence, and the study of leading scholars in the field to determine what exactly the elements are of the mode of liability of aiding and abetting.

The comparative perspective is added for three reasons. The first and main reason is that primary sources of international criminal law are either silent or contain omissions regarding the determination of individual criminal liability for the financing of core crimes. A comparative analysis is therefore necessary to identify general principles of law recognised by the community of States, as defined in Article 38(1)(c) of the ICJ Statute.

Article 38(1)(a) – (d) of the ICJ Statute requires courts to determine the applicable law by applying treaty law or customary international law, general principles of law recognised by the community of States, and 'judicial decisions and the teachings of the most highly qualified publicists of the various nations, as subsidiary means for the determination of rules of law'. General principles of law recognised by the community of States fill a gap[51] and can be derived from a wide and representative comparative analysis of national legal systems, which principles must be generally recognised by the analysed national legal systems.[52]

Primary sources of international criminal law contain an omission concerning the determination of the criminal responsibility of individuals who finance core crimes. At first glance it is unclear whether the general principles of law recognised by the community of States set forth a minimum standard

50 Sara Porro, *Risk and Mental Element: An Analysis of National and International Law on Core Crimes* (Stämpfli 2014) 131.

51 International Law Commission, 'Record on General Principles of Law, A/CN.4/SR.3489, 25 September 2019'; International Law Commission, 'Record on General Principles of Law, A/CN.4/SR.3493, 31 October 2019'; International Law Commission, 'Record on General Principles of Law, A/CN.4/SR.3492, 2 October 2019'; International Law Commission, 'Record on General Principles of Law, A/CN.4/SR.3490, 30 September 2019'.

52 International Law Commission, 'Second Report of the Special Rapporteur on General Principles of Law, Marcelo Vázquez-Bermúdez, UN Doc. A/CN.4/741' 7.

of knowledge and intent regarding the criminal liability of an aider and abettor. I therefore have recourse to the jurisprudence of both international and national courts and tribunals to determine whether general principles of law recognised by the community of States could be derived from a general consensus. In other words, general principles of law recognised by the community of States are derived from an analysis of the applicable law in the international arena and from a comparative analysis of the national laws concerning the minimum standard of knowledge and intent required for the criminal liability of an aider and abettor.

A comparative analysis for the purpose of establishing the existence of general principles should 'cover as many national legal systems as possible to ensure that a principle has effectively been recognised by the community of States'.[53] Regarding the meaning of a principle being recognised in national legal systems generally, Special Rapporteur Vázquez-Bermúdez notes that:[54]

> The above position does not mean, however, that one must consult every single national legal systems of the world in order to identify a general principle of law. This would make the identification of general principles of law extremely burdensome, if not impossible. Rather, a more pragmatic approach appears in practice, where States and international courts and tribunals have sought to carry out wide and representative comparative analyses, covering different legal families and regions of the world.

This approach has been endorsed by state practice, where one can find numerous cases recognising the requirement that a principle must be generally accepted in national legal systems. Importantly, the recognition of general principles of law recognised by the community of States is neither 'a matter of mathematical calculation', nor does it mean that it needs to be recognised by the entire community of States.[55] In most cases courts and tribunals have carried out rather limited comparative analysis, which were deemed sufficient to establish the existence of general principles of law recognised by the community of States.[56]

---

53 ibid 8.

54 ibid 9–10.

55 ibid footnote 59.

56 For example, in ICTY *Prosecutor v Dusko Tadic, Appeals Chamber Judgment* (*IT-94-1-A*), the Appeals Chamber relied on one common law jurisdiction (United Kingdom) and four civil law jurisdictions (China, France, Germany, Russia); ICTR, *Prosecutor v Alfred Musema, Judgment and Sentence* (*ICTR-96-13-T*) 186–91; ICC, *Situation on the registered vessels of the Union of the Comoros, the Hellenic Republic and the Kingdom of Cambodia,*

Much of the literature adopts an analogous approach and has, for example, noted that 'one of the conditions for the identification of a general principle is its presence in a large number and variety of domestic legal systems'.[57] Thus, general principles of law recognised by the community of States cannot be deemed to exist if rules across national legal systems are fundamentally different.[58] Furthermore, as observed by the International Law Association:[59]

> [I]t is also not enough to 'identify' a general principle among the main legal systems if there is not enough geographical representation, e.g. a general principle shared by Civil Law countries in Europe should also be identified in other Civil Law countries located in different geographical areas and belonging to different civilizations.

As stated above, the comparative analysis includes the legal rules relating to complicity in twenty selected jurisdictions in Africa, Asia, Europe, Latin America, North America and Oceania, and include both common law and civil law jurisdictions, countries with both Western and non-Western traditions, countries that are both economically developed and economically developing, as well as countries with a variety of religious traditions (including Christian, Hindu, Jewish, Muslim, and secular traditions).[60] I have taken into consideration materials available in a multitude of languages, such as Arabic, English, French, German, Italian, Portuguese, Russian, Spanish, and Turkish.[61] Importantly, in some States, I encountered accessibility difficulties, which either made it impossible to analyse the law of a particular State, or only allowed me to access a limited number of sources.[62] Thus, this comparative

Decision on the 'Application for Judicial Review by the Government of the Union of Comoros', Pre-Trial Chamber I (ICC-01/13) 107; less commonly, in some cases the number of analysed jurisdictions was significantly higher. See for example ICTY *Prosecution v Delalic et al, Appeals Chamber Judgment* (IT-96-21-A) 584-89; ICTY *Prosecutor v Pavle Strugar, Appeals Chamber Judgment* (IT-01-42-A) 52–4; ICTY *Prosecutor v Anto Furundzija, Trial Chamber Judgment* (IT-95-17/1-T) 180.

57 Jaye Ellis, 'General Principles and Comparative Law' (2011) 22 European Journal of International Law 949, 955.

58 International Law Commission, 'Second Report of the Special Rapporteur on General Principles of Law, Marcelo Vázquez-Bermúdez, UN Doc. A/CN.4/741' 21.

59 International Law Association, 'Report of the Study Group on the Use of Domestic Law Principles in the Development of International Law, Report of the Seventy-Eighth Conference' (2018) paragraph 214.

60 See Chapter V.

61 I had recourse to the services of translators to interpret documents written in Arabic, Portuguese, Russian, and Turkish.

62 For example, in Malawi, I only had access to a limited number of sources.

analysis is limited by the online and print accessibility of certain academic texts and judicial decisions and by language barriers that I encountered in certain jurisdictions.[63] The purpose of this diversity in jurisdictions analysed is to emphasise the representativity of States, which in turn speaks to the quality of the comparative analysis. In short, my approach has been wide and representative, as suggested by Special Rapporteur Vázquez-Bermúdez.[64]

Furthermore, for a general principle recognised by the community of States 'to be elevated to a general principle of law in the sense of 38(1)(c) of the ICJ Statute, that principle must be compatible with the fundamental principles of international law' identified in Part 1, Chapter 2.[65] Thus, this work tests the results of the analysis of the applicable international rules and of the comparative analysis against the principles of international criminal law to determine their compatibility with the fundamental principles of international criminal law.[66] The purpose of this test is 'to ensure that a legal principle is not only recognised by the community of States as just, but also as capable of existing within the broader framework in international law'.[67]

International criminal law generally consists of customary legal rules that are identified, clarified and spelled out by courts.[68] Academic literature notes the increasing significance of comparative criminal law to equip international law with 'general principles of law' as identified in domestic criminal law systems.[69] In the words of Bassiouni, 'such a degree of cross-fertilisation between international and national criminal law contributes to the harmonisation of substantive and procedural laws both at the national and international levels'.[70]

63 Many of the online and print texts I have referred to in this work were consulted in the libraries of the Swiss Institute of Comparative Law and the Max Planck Institute for Foreign and International Criminal Law (now renamed as the Max Planck Institute for the Study of Crime, Security and Law).

64 International Law Commission, 'Second Report of the Special Rapporteur on General Principles of Law, Marcelo Vázquez-Bermúdez, UN Doc. A/CN.4/741' 15.

65 ibid 23.

66 See Chapter 6, sections 2.2 and 3.2.

67 International Law Commission, 'Second Report of the Special Rapporteur on General Principles of Law, Marcelo Vázquez-Bermúdez, UN Doc. A/CN.4/741' 23.

68 Cassese and Gaeta (n 1) 30.

69 For support of this position, see notably Kai Ambos, 'Remarks on the General Part of International Criminal Law' (2006) 4 Journal of International Criminal Justice 660, 661–2; Iryna Marchuk, *The Fundamental Concept of Crime in International Criminal Law: A Comparative Law Analysis* (Springer Science & Business Media 2013) 2–3.

70 M Cherif Bassiouni, *International Criminal Law: Sources, Subjects and Contents, Volume 1* (3 ed, Brill | Nijhoff 2008) 6.

Only the thoughtful incorporation of general principles identified from many legal systems across the world can compellingly demonstrate that international criminal law is rooted in 'generally accepted standards rather than national idiosyncrasies or aberrations'.[71] As Bassiouni recognises, the most challenging aspect in the application of the comparative method is 'attempting to reconcile, let alone combine, legal concepts pertinent to different legal systems under the umbrella of international criminal law'.[72] The use of comparative law is about 'hybridisation inspired by pluralism', and not about the 'transplantation of one dominant model' into international criminal law.[73] Thus, only the existence of *lacunae* in the primary sources of international criminal law can rationalise a careful application of general principles of law derived from a comparative analysis of national laws.

In sum, the national legal systems that are most frequently examined are those of Germany, France, England and Wales, the United States of America, Italy, and Canada.[74] To refer systematically to the same national legal systems runs counter to a pluralist conception of international law. I have therefore selected national legal systems in accordance with 'historical titles' (meaning countries, the legal systems of which, have had a significant influence on the legal systems of other countries), and according to a geographically equitable distribution. The inclusion of other national legal systems in this research allows for the general principles of law derived from national legal systems to enjoy greater legitimacy, because of the effective demonstration of their worldwide recognition by nations. Because a clear trend among national courts can be established, it demonstrates the existence of general principles recognised by the community of States regarding the minimum standard of intent and the absence of general principals with regard to the knowledge requirement.

The second reason for a comparative analysis is that forms of responsibility under international criminal law are largely modelled on domestic criminal law and they are interpreted by judges who were educated in their own national legal systems. Domestic criminal law has thus been an important source for drafting provisions of individual responsibility in international

71 Robert Cryer, *Prosecuting International Crimes: Selectivity and the International Criminal Law Regime* (Cambridge University Press 2005) 173.

72 Cherif M. Bassiouni, *The Legislative History of the International Criminal Court: Introduction, Analysis, and Integrated Text, Volume 1* (Brill | Nijhoff 2005) 158.

73 Mireille Delmas-Marty, 'Comparative Criminal Law as a Necessary Tool for the Application of International Criminal Law' in A Cassese (ed), *The Oxford Companion to International Criminal Justice* (Oxford University Press 2009) 99.

74 Fabián O Raimondo, *General Principles of Law in the Decisions of International Criminal Courts and Tribunals* (Brill | Nijhoff 2008) 194.

criminal law.[75] The field of international criminal law is the product of the world's major legal systems (*i.e.* Germany, France, England and Wales and the United States) cooperating to combat international crimes. This cooperation resulted in the jurisprudence of international criminal courts and tribunals being a fusion of criminal laws from various domestic legal systems. However, the *ad hoc* Tribunals and the ICC[76] have incorporated national approaches to international criminal law through a technical transposition of concepts, rather than a careful comparison of the similarities and differences between the different legal systems. This has resulted in many inconsistencies and *lacunae* in the jurisprudence relating to the definition and interpretation of the fundamental concept of a 'crime' in international law.[77]

Additionally, judges in international tribunals and courts understand these incorporated legal notions, such as 'aiding and abetting', which originated in domestic criminal law,[78] from the perspective of their respective domestic laws, which may cause – and indeed has caused – confusion.[79] Because national courts have to some extent dealt with the same issues as those encountered by international courts and tribunals, Cassese states:[80]

> [G]iven the characteristics of ICL one should set great store by national or international judicial decisions. They may prove of crucial importance, not only for ascertaining whether a rule of customary international law has evolved, but also as a means to establish the most appropriate interpretation.

Thus, instead of attempting to introduce legal concepts from one's own national jurisdiction into international criminal law, it is advisable to rather engage in a comprehensive comparative analysis that might reveal the existence of commonly shared 'universal values' across many legal jurisdictions.[81] As Delmas-Marty advocated, the use of comparative law should promote 'progressive reconciliation between international and domestic law'.[82]

75 Van Sliedregt (n 25) 65.
76 Articles 22 to 33 of the Rome Statute lay down a foundation for 'general principles' of international criminal law.
77 Marchuk (n 69) 1.
78 Van Sliedregt (n 25) 89.
79 ibid.
80 See generally, Cassese and Gaeta (n 1) 18.
81 George P Fletcher, *The Grammar of Criminal Law: American, Comparative, and International, Volume 1* (Oxford University Press 2007) 4–5.
82 Delmas-Marty (n 73) 103.

The third reason for a comparative analysis is that I desire to integrate non-Western legal traditions into the globalised understandings of the adequacy of the rules of international criminal law.[83] Most of the architects of international criminal law have been Western lawyers or those trained in the West.[84] In order for international criminal law to become truly international, it is necessary to incorporate all the main legal traditions from Africa, Asia, Europe, Latin America, North America and Oceania.[85]

In conclusion, the use of a comparative methodology allows for a determination and definition of the mode of liability of aiding and abetting which international criminal law can apply to hold an individual liable who finances an entity that perpetrates core crimes. This methodology also has the benefit of resulting in a more homogenous interpretation of the rules of international criminal law, as well as being more inclusive.

---

83 Kai Ambos, *La Parte General Del Derecho Penal Internacional : Bases Para Una Elaboración Dogmática* (Duncker & Humboldt 2005). The autor argues that the limitation of national legal systems to Romano-Germanic and the Common Law legal families is due in the main to the language limitations of Western authors, not to their unwillingess to consider other conceptions.

84 See generally Antony Anghie and Bhupinder S Chimni, 'Third World Approaches to International Law and Individual Responsibility in Internal Conflicts' (2003) 2 Chinese Journal of International Law 77.

85 Statistics Division of the United Nations Secretariat, *Standard Country or Area Codes for Statistical Use* (United Nations Publications 1999) 13–22, available at <https://unstats.un.org/unsd/publication/SeriesM/Series_M49_Rev4(1999)_en.pdf> accessed 11 March 2019. Antarctica, despite being a region according to the Statistics Division of the United Nations, is omitted because it is not subject to the jurisdiction of any particular nation. Article 4 of the Antarctic Treaty of 1959 402 UNTS 71 stipulates that there is in that region an absence of a specific body of law governing criminal actions; however, all members of the Antarctic Treaty may exercise territorial jurisdiction. As noted by Seganish, 'there exists multiple sets of rules depending upon where the act occurs and whether the country which has jurisdiction decides to assert its right to prosecute such activity.'; W Michael Seganish, 'Criminal Law In Antarctica: Law West Of The Pecos Revisited' (2016) 1 Journal of Business & Economics Research 13, 14.

CHAPTER 2

Current State of International Criminal Law

1 Introduction

To interpret current rules of international criminal law, I firstly provide a brief explanation of the nature and the impact of international criminal law; secondly, I analyse its sources; and thirdly, I discuss its main principles. Section 2 shows that, at present, the nature of international criminal law as it has emerged through its brief history, plays a considerable role in the way in which the rules of international criminal law are established and interpreted.

To determine the circumstances under which an individual who finances an entity that perpetrates core crimes could be held criminally liable, tribunals must have recourse to the sources of international criminal law. These sources, which are based on Article 38 of the ICJ Statute, and which are discussed in section 3, are treaty-based sources, customary international law, general principles of law recognised by the community of States, judicial decisions of international and national courts, and legal scholarship.

As shown in section 4, the main principles of international criminal law provide general rules about the proper interpretation of norms, and how the formation of new rules of international criminal law might occur. These principles include those of legality, specificity, non-retroactivity, *favor rei*, and the prohibition of analogy. These principles are of the utmost importance because it is against these principles that the results of this research are to be tested.

2 The Nature of International Criminal Law

International law governs the rights and responsibilities of states,[1] while criminal law, including international criminal law, is concerned with prohibiting violations committed by individuals and punished by a state.[2] Cryer notes that '[t]he development of a body of international criminal law which imposes responsibilities directly on individuals and punishes violations

1 Ian Brownlie, *Oppenheim's International Law: Peace, Volume 1* (Longman 1992) 5–7.
2 Glanville Williams, 'The Definition of Crime' (1955) 8 Current Legal Problems 107.

 DOI:10.1163/9789004470934_003

through international mechanisms is relatively recent'.[3] In the twentieth century individuals were also recognised as subjects of international law.[4] However, it was only with the horrors of the Nazi regime that the notion of the international criminal responsibility of the individual emerged.[5] The victorious powers in World War II demanded the creation of international courts.[6] This represented the first major milestone in the development of international criminal law. Today, the nature of international criminal law plays a significant role in the way the rules of international criminal law are interpreted and developed.

After World War II the principle of international criminally liability for core crimes – as enumerated in the Charter of the International Military Tribunal at Nuremberg and applied by the Nuremberg Tribunal and the Tokyo Tribunal – were affirmed by the United Nations General Assembly.[7] In the mid-1990s, the United Nations created the *ad hoc* Tribunals for the former Yugoslavia and Rwanda.[8] These developments marked the first time in history that criminal tribunals of a truly international character were set up to prosecute core crimes. International criminal law was then crystallised with the drafting and subsequent entry into force in 2002 of the Rome Statute, as well as the establishment of the ICC. Scholars now accept that '[t]he collective nature of crimes under international law does not absolve us of the need to determine individual responsibility'.[9] These milestones reaffirmed the status of the principles of international criminal law as customary law. It is the development of international criminal law that made it possible for individuals to be held accountable, not only nationally, but also by international tribunals and courts.

3 Robert Cryer *et al*, *An Introduction to International Criminal Law and Procedure* (3 ed, Cambridge University Press 2014) 1.

4 ibid; Ole Spiermann, 'Twentieth Century Internationalism in Law' (2007) 18 The European Journal of International Law 785, 786.

5 Gerhard Werle and Florian Jessberger, *Principles of International Criminal Law* (3 ed, Oxford University Press 2014) 1.

6 ibid 2.

7 ibid.

8 United Nations, 'Security Council Resolution 827/1993' (1993); United Nations, 'Security Council Resolution 955/1994' (1994).

9 Gerhard Werle, 'Individual Criminal Responsibility in Article 25 ICC Statute' (2007) 5 Journal of International Criminal Justice 953, 953; Jann Kleffner, 'The Collective Accountability of Organized Armed Groups for System Crimes' in Andre Nollkaemper and Harmen van der Wilt (eds), *System Criminality in International Law* (Cambridge University Press 2009) 238–269.

3 Sources of International Criminal Law

To determine under which circumstances an individual who finances the commission of core crimes could be held criminally liable, and what the exact nature of such liability would be, tribunals must have recourse to the sources of international criminal law.

Because international criminal law is part of general international law, it follows that the sources of law pertaining to international criminal law are derived from public international law. International criminal courts and scholars agree that these sources are listed in Article 38 of the ICJ Statute.[10]

Pursuant to Article 38 of the ICJ Statute, the sources of international criminal law are as follows:[11]

1. The primary sources, which encompass treaty rules and customary international law rules;
2. The supplementary sources, which consist of general principles of law common to national legal systems, particularly those related to criminal matters; and
3. Lastly, as subsidiary means for determining international criminal law, judicial decisions and the teachings of the most highly qualified publicists of the various nations.

---

10 Article 38 (1) of the Statute of the International Court of Justice ('ICJ Statute') 1945 is generally recognised as a definitive statment of the sources of international law, and states as follows: 'The Court, whose function is to decide in accordance with international law such disputes as are submitted to it, shall apply: a. international conventions, whether general or particular, establishing rules expressly recognized by the contesting states; b. international custom, as evidence of a general practice accepted as law; c. the general principles of law recognized by civilized nations; d. subject to the provisions of Article 59, judicial decisions and the teachings of the most highly qualified publicists of the various nations, as subsidiary means for the determination of rules of law'. It is important to note that this list is not exhaustive. See ICTY *Prosecutor v Mucić et al, Trial Chamber Judgment* (*IT-96-21-T*) 414; Bruno Simma and Andreas Paulus, 'Le Rôle Relatif Des Différentes Sources Du Droit International Public: Dont Les Principles Généraux Du Droit' in Hervé Ascensio, Emmanuel Decaux and Alain Pellet (eds), *Droit Pénal International* (11 ed, Pedone 2000) 55; Cassese and Gaeta (n 1) 18; Kai Ambos, *La Parte General Del Derecho Penal Internacional: Bases Para Una Elaboración Dogmática* (Duncker & Humboldt 2005) 35; As noted by Mark Eugen Villiger, *Customary International Law and Treaties: A Manual on the Theory and Practice of the Interrelation of Sources* (2 ed, Kluwer Law International 1997) the ICJ recognises other sources of international law, such as the decisions of international organisations and jus cogens.

11 Antonio Cassese and Paola Gaeta, *Cassese's International Criminal Law* (Oxford University Press 2013) 9.

As shown below,[12] primary sources of international criminal law contain *lacunae* regarding the liability of individuals who finance the commission of core crimes. This work therefore relies on general principles of law recognised by the community of States as expounded in Article 38(1)(c) of the Statute of the ICJ, as well as subsidiary sources of international criminal law, to determine the liability of those individuals. Because the general principles of law recognised by the community of States do not at first blush clearly set out the requirements for the criminal liability of an individual who finances the perpetration of core crimes, I conduct a comparative analysis of the applicable national law in twenty States regarding the minimum standard of knowledge and intent required for the criminal liability of aiders and abettors. This comparative analysis aims at determining whether general principles of law recognised by the community of States could be identified regarding the minimum standard of knowledge and intent for an aider and abettor to be held criminally liable.

Establishing the existence of general principles of law recognised by the community of States can be achieved by showing that there is consensus amongst the community of States that rise to the level of general principles. Then, to ensure the compatibility of the general principles thus developed, the results from the comparative analysis are tested against the principles of international criminal law so that these findings might be applied by international criminal courts.

3.1 *Primary Sources: Treaties and Customary International Law*

Treaty-based sources of international criminal law include: the 1907 Hague Regulations,[13] the London Charter of the International Military Tribunal (1945),[14] the 1949 Geneva Conventions and their additional protocols,[15] the Genocide Convention[16] and the Rome Statute.[17]

12 See Chapter 4, section 4.2.3.1.

13 International Conferences (The Hague), Hague Convention (IV) Respecting the Laws and Customs of War on Land and Its Annex: Regulations Concerning the Laws and Customs of War on Land, 18 October 1907.

14 United Nations, Charter of the International Military Tribunal - Annex to the Agreement for the Prosecution and Punishment of the Major War Criminals of the European Axis ('London Agreement'), 8 August 1945.

15 Protocol Additional to the Geneva Conventions of 12 August 1949, and Relating to the Protection of Victims of International Armed Conflicts (Protocol I) 1977.

16 UN General Assembly, Convention on the Prevention and Punishment of the Crime of Genocide, 9 December 1948.

17 Cryer *et al* (n 3) 6, 7; Cassese and Gaeta (n 11) 11. As an exception to other international criminal courts' statutes, the Rome Statute provides a provision on sources. Indeed, Article 21 creates a hierarchy of sources. The primary sources are: the Statute; the Elements of Crimes and the Rules of Procedure and Evidence. The secondary sources are: applicable

Additionally, primary sources of international criminal law include the sources of some international courts.[18] United Nations Security Council resolutions 827 (2003) and 955 (2004) brought into being the ICTY and ICTR, respectively. These resolutions, adopted by the Security Council pursuant to its powers under Chapter VII of the United Nations Charter, find their binding force in Article 25 of the Charter. The Special Court for Sierra Leone ('SCSL') was established by an agreement between the United Nations and the Government of Sierra Leone pursuant to Security Council resolution 1315 (2000).[19] The Statute of the Special Tribunal for Lebanon is set forth in an agreement between the United Nations and Lebanon, which entered into force pursuant to United Nations Security Council resolution 1757 (2007).

These treaty sources are incomplete regarding determining the liability of individuals who finance core crimes. Except for the Rome Statute, none of the treaties lay down the *actus reus* and *mens rea* requirements of the mode of liability of aiding and abetting, which applies to the conduct of an individual who finances an entity involved in core crimes.[20] The Rome Statute, in Article 25 (Individual Criminal Responsibility) and Article 30 (Mental Element), does set forth the elements of the mode of liability of aiding and abetting, however, as described below,[21] this source also contains *lacunae*. The conduct of an individual who finances an entity that perpetrates core crimes, is also not explicitly covered by any mode of liability at the ICC.[22]

Moreover, it is trite that customary international law consists of two elements: (i) *opinio juris*, which is the conviction that a certain State practice is law; and (ii) general international practice, as supported by case law, treaty provisions, the views of State officials, and the convergence of the community of States.[23] The disadvantage of customary international law is that it might be challenging to determine its content because of difficulties in establishing

treaties; and the principles and rules of international law. Finally there are the general principles derived from national law.

18 International criminal courts are bound by the principle of speciality, meaning that they must first and foremost apply the statutes specific to them.

19 Although international courts must first and foremost apply the statutes specific to them, they often refer, even if only implicitly, to other international treaties.

20 See Chapter 4, section 4.

21 See Chapter 4, section 4.1.1.

22 See Chapter 4, section 4.1.1.2.

23 Article 38 of the Statute of the International Court of Justice 1945; Article 30 of the Rome Statute of the International Criminal Court 1998 (last amended 2010); International Law Commission, 'Draft Conclusions on Identification of Customary International Law, U.N. Doc. A/73/10, 30 April-1 June and 2 July-10 August 2018' (2018).

State practice; it has also been criticised as being too vague.[24] The definition of aiding and abetting according to customary international law is uncertain. The minimum level of intent and knowledge must be clarified.[25]

Therefore, reliance on primary sources of international criminal law is not sufficient to determine the content and extent of the complicity rules applicable to individuals who finance entities that commit core crimes.

3.2 *Supplementary Sources*

General principles of law recognised by the community of States (also referred to as general principals of law recognised by civilized nations, or general principles of law common to national legal systems) 'may be derived, with all due caution, from national laws'.[26] Under Article 38(1)(c) of the ICJ Statute, a court may apply 'general principles of law recognised by civilized nations', which this work refers to as 'the community of States'.[27] General principles of law have played a significant role in the development of international criminal law, as several general principles of law applied by international criminal courts and tribunals have become convention and customary rules of international criminal law.[28]

My research relies on general principles of law because primary sources of law do not define with clarity under which circumstances an individual who finances an entity involved in the perpetration of core crimes, could be held liable. To rectify omissions or reinforce legal reasoning, international criminal courts and tribunals have relied heavily on general principles of law because of 'the underdeveloped nature of international criminal law, the imprecision of many of its legal rules, the need to make compelling legal arguments, and the existence of relevant domestic criminal law analogies'.[29]

The ICTY Trial Chamber in *Furundzija* stated that:[30]

> [R]eliance upon national legislation is justified, subject to the following conditions: (i) [...] international courts must draw upon the general

---

24 Vladimir-Djuro Degan, 'On the Sources of International Criminal Law' (2005) 4 Chinese Journal of International Law 45, 67.

25 See Chapter 4, section 4.2.3.2.

26 Iryna Marchuk, *The Fundamental Concept of Crime in International Criminal Law: A Comparative Law Analysis* (Springer Science & Business Media 2013) 112.

27 See Chapter 1, footnote 2.

28 Fabián O Raimondo, *General Principles of Law in the Decisions of International Criminal Courts and Tribunals* (Brill | Nijhoff 2008) 191.

29 ibid 74.

30 ICTY *Prosecutor v Anto Furundzija, Trial Chamber Judgment* (IT-95-17/1-T) 178.

> concepts and legal institutions common to all the major legal systems of the world [not only that of common law or civil law states]. This presupposes a process of identification of the common denominators in these legal systems so as to pinpoint the basic notions they share; (ii) [...] account must be taken of the specificity of international criminal proceedings when utilising national law notions. In this way a mechanical importation or transposition from national law into international criminal proceedings is avoided, as well as the attendant distortions of the unique traits of such proceedings.

The recourse to general principles of law is aimed at filling legal *lacunae*, interpreting existing legal rules (emerging from primary sources), and corroborating a decision based on what has been found by numerous other courts and tribunals that have adopted a similar approach.[31] Lauterpacht notes that recourse to general principles of law should only take place if the settlement of a given legal issue cannot be achieved without difficulty in individual cases, by filling the *lacuna* with 'logical deduction from existing rules of international law or of analogy to them'.[32]

The determination of whether a legal principle is a general principle of law applicable in international criminal law is determined by drawing from previous decisions of international courts and tribunals – these decisions being one of the recognised means of determining legal rules and principles.[33] The existence, content, and scope of general principles may also be established by means of comparative law.[34] Raimondo argues that the comparative method is a two-fold process, consisting of the vertical operation and the horizontal operation.[35] The vertical operation comprises abstracting legal rules from national legal systems with the aim of deriving an underlying principle; while the horizontal operation consists of verifying that the majority of nations recognise the legal principles derived through the vertical operation by means of a comparison of national legal systems. Thus, in this work I derive general principles from an analysis of the applicable law concerning the minimum

31 Raimondo (n 28) 44.

32 Hersch Lauterpacht, *Private Law Sources and Analogies of International Law: With Special Reference to International Arbitration* (Longmans, Green and Co 1927) 85.

33 Raimondo (n 28) 45.

34 See generally International Law Commission, 'Second Report of the Special Rapporteur on General Principles of Law, Marcelo Vázquez-Bermúdez, UN Doc. A/CN.4/741'.

35 Raimondo (n 28) 45–57.

standard of knowledge and intent of an aider and abettor in the international arena and from a comparative analysis of the national laws.[36]

This work examines the relevant national rules of the community of States in Asia, Africa, Europe, Latin America, North America and Oceania. As stated, the aim of this approach is to include a wide range of the world's legal systems and geographical regions.[37] As Raimondo states:[38]

> Comparative law research conducted on the basis of equitable geographic distribution will make it clear that not only are the solutions offered by the main legal families of the world taken into account, but also that the general principles of law thus derived are the expression of the community of States rather than an oligarchic international society.

When deriving general principles of law recognised by the community of States from national laws, I do not mechanically seek to find mere coincidences among legal rules, but rather I aim to determine common denominators among legal rules by identifying the *ratio legis* and the fundamental principles that are common within different national legal systems.[39] In fact, what matters is the existence of a common legal principle.[40] Kolb[41] and Raimondo[42] correctly observe that the content of the general principles of law are broad, allowing them to be flexible enough to serve as a means of dynamic interpretation of legal rules, as well as a means of developing the law.

3.3 *Other Subsidiary Sources Derived from National Laws*

Recourse to judicial decisions of international and national courts and to legal scholarship are means of determining international criminal law.[43] The ICTY

36 For a detailed discussion on the way this work uses general principles, see Chapter 1, section 6.

37 International Law Commission, 'Second Report of the Special Rapporteur on General Principles of Law, Marcelo Vázquez-Bermúdez, UN Doc. A/CN.4/741' 15.

38 Raimondo (n 28) 55–56.

39 Paul Reuter, *Droit International Public* (Presses Universitaires de France 1958) 118.

40 Michael Akehurst, 'Equity and General Principles of Law' (1976) 25 International and Comparative Law Quarterly 801, 814.

41 Robert Kolb, 'Principles as Sources of International Law: (With Special Reference to Good Faith)' (2006) 53 Netherlands International Law Review 1, 9.

42 Raimondo (n 28) 50.

43 As noted by Gerhard Werle and Florian Jessberger, *Principles of International Criminal Law* (3 ed, Oxford University Press 2014) 65: 'The function of national courts in determining international criminal law is twofold. First, as expressions of opinio juris and as state practice, they may confirm or create customary law and contribute to the formation of

and the ICTR have referred to both domestic and international case law[44] and have drawn on the writings of the most highly qualified publicists of the various nations.[45] Reference to court decisions and the teaching of the most qualified publicists enables one to determine the existence, content, and scope of general principles of law. It is worth noting that scholarly writings on their own have not facilitated the establishment of general principles of law. It is only when scholarly writings have been combined with analyses of the relevant legislation or judicial decisions, for example, that they have played a role in determining general principles of law.

4 General Principles of International Criminal Law

General principles of international criminal law are inherent to the international legal system. Therefore, identifying these principles does not require an in-depth comparative survey of the community of States.[46] They include principles specific to international criminal law, such as the principles of legality, specificity, non-retroactivity, *favor rei,* and the prohibition of analogy.[47] These principles provide general rules with regard to the proper interpretation of norms, and how the formation of new rules of international criminal law might occur. However, they do not provide clarity as to the criminal liability of individuals who finance entities that are involved in the perpetration of core crimes.[48]

In this work I use general principles of international criminal law to determine the results of the analysis of the applicable international law and of the comparative analysis' compatibility with these principles. As seen below,[49]

general principles of law. Second, national court decisions can serve as aids in recognizing law, helping to determine the content of norms of international criminal law.' On the authoritative nature of national decisions, see also James Crawford, *Brownlies's Principal of Public International Law* (8 ed, Oxford University Press 2012).

44 ICTY *Prosecutor v Dusko Tadic, Appeals Chamber Judgment* (*IT-94-1-A*) 255–70.

45 ICTY *Prosecutor v Radislav Krstic, Appeals Chamber Judgment* (*IT-98-33-A*) 10; ICTY *Prosecutor v Milomir Stakic, Trial Chamber Judgment* (*IT-97-24-T*) 519.

46 Gerhard Werle, 'Individual Criminal Responsibility in Article 25 ICC Statute' (2007) 5 Journal of International Criminal Justice 953 953; Jann Kleffner, 'The Collective Accountability of Organized Armed Groups for System Crimes' in Andre Nollkaemper and Harmen van der Wilt (eds), *System Criminality in International Law* (Cambridge University Press 2009) 238–69.

47 Cassese and Gaeta (n 11) 15, 23–37.

48 For a discussion on the principles of international criminal law, see Chapter 2, section 3.1.

49 See Chapter 2, section 4.1.

there are gaps in the sources of international criminal law regarding the individual criminal liability of individuals who finance the commission of core crimes. To resolve this issue I use the general principles of international criminal law enumerated above to test the general principles drawn from the analysis of the applicable rules, both internationally and nationally (Chapter VI).

4.1 *Principle of Legality*

The principle of legality, also known as the doctrine of *nullum crimen, nulla poena sine lege*, states that no one may be punished for an action or omission that did not violate a law in existence at the time of perpetration.[50] This principle was described by Franz von Liszt as:[51]

> [T]he bulwark of the citizen against the state's omnipotence; they protect the individual against the ruthless power of the majority, against the Leviathan. However paradoxical it may sound the Criminal Code is the criminal's *magna carta*. It guarantees his right to be punished only in accordance with the requirements set out by the law and only within the limits laid down in the law.

The principle of legality was famously at issue at Nuremberg during the trial of *Göring and others*. The German defence counsel objected to the Tribunal's jurisdiction, arguing that the Tribunal was violating the prohibition against *ex post facto* law.[52] The Tribunal, adopting the substantive justice approach[53] to the principle of legality, held that:[54]

> To assert that it is unjust to punish those who in defiance of treaties and assurances have attacked neighbouring states without warning is

50 Protocol Additional to the Geneva Conventions of 12 August 1949, and Relating to the Protection of Victims of International Armed Conflicts (Protocol I) 1977; Cassese and Gaeta (n 11).

51 Franz von Liszt, 'Die Deterministischen Gegner Der Zweckstrafe' (1893) 13 Zeitschrift für die gesamte Strafrechtswissenschaft 325, 357 (an English translation of some excerpts from this paper has been published in 5 JICL [2007], 1009-13).

52 IMT *France and ors v Göring (Hermann) and ors, Judgment of 1 October 1946.*

53 Cassese and Gaeta (n 11) 25 note regarding the doctrine of substantive justice that it 'punishes acts that harm society deeply and are regarded as abhorrent by all members of society, even if these acts were not prohibited as criminal when they were performed'.

54 IMT *Trial of the Major War Criminals before the International Military Tribunal, Judgment of 1 October 1946.* (emphasis added). It is important to note that some of the Tribunal's interpretations, notably the fact that crimes against peace were already prohibited at the time of perpetration, are questionable. However, they fall beyond the scope of the work.

> obviously untrue, for in such circumstances the attacker must know that he is doing wrong, and so far from it being unjust to punish him, *it would be unjust if his wrong were allowed to go unpunished.*

Although it is subject to several significant qualifications, at present the principle of legality is strictly applied at the international level. This shift occurred because after World War II states signed and ratified a number of significant human rights treaties,[55] which affirmed the principle of legality as a legal standard for national courts. The *nullum crimen sine lege* principle therefore became an inherent part of an individual's basic human rights. Additionally, the principle of legality was laid down, albeit implicitly, in the Statutes and case law of the ICTY and ICTR.[56] This principle is also well recognised in several international treaties and by the international community.[57]

The principle of legality consists of four underlying principles: (i) specificity; (ii) non-retroactivity; (iii) the ban on analogy and extensive interpretation; and (iv) *favor rei.*

---

55 For example, see Article 15 of the International Covenant on Civil and Political Rights 1966.

56 ICTY *Prosecutor v Mucić et al, Trial Chamber Judgment* (*IT-96-21-T*) 402–7; ICTY *Prosecutor v Goran Jelisic, Trial Chamber Judgment* (*IT-95-10-T*) 61; ICTY *Prosecutor v Hadzihasanovic and Kubura, Appeals Chamber Judgment* (*IT-01-47-A*) 32–6; ICTY *Prosecutor v Dusko Tadic, Appeals Chamber Judgment* (*IT-94-1-A*).

57 The principle of legality is enshrined in Article 15 of the International Covenant on Civil and Political Rights. The Rome Statute also contains a specific provision on the principle of legality in Article 22. To understand this principle in international criminal law, one must first distinguish between the principle of legality in civil and common law systems, as this principle is not uniformly applied. Civil law systems tend to uphold the doctrine of strict legality, whereas common law systems tend to be a mix between the doctrines of legality and substantive justice. On the one hand, under the doctrine of strict legality a person may only be held criminally liable if, at the moment of the commission of the act, the act was regarded as a criminal offence under applicable law. The criminal offences must have been enumerated in written law – *nullum crimen sine legal scripta.* Moreover, the doctrine of strict legality is associated with the principle of specificity, the principle of non-retroactivity, and the prohibition of analogy, which are discussed in more detail below. On the other hand, according to the doctrine of substantive justice: '[T]he legal order must primarily aim at prohibiting and punishing any conduct that is socially harmful or causes danger to society, whether or not that conduct has already been legally criminalised at the moment it is taken.' Common law jurisdictions typically adopt a hybrid approach to these two doctrines. Indeed, common law offences result from, among other things, decisions of courts and consequently may lack the requirements of rigidity and certainty characteristics of written legislation. Also, common law offences are not strictly subject to the principle of non-retroactivity, as exemplified in *R v R* [1991] UKHL 1, where the court held that marriage could no longer be a defence for a husband's rape of his wife.

4.2 *Principle of Specificity*

The principle of specificity, also known as *nullum crimen sine lege stricta*, means that the definition of the prohibited act must be as detailed as possible.[58] The objective and subject elements of the crime must be described in such a way that they clearly circumscribe the prohibited conduct. Cassese explains:[59]

> [T]he contribution of courts to giving precision to law, not infrequent even in civil law systems, and quite normal in common law countries, becomes of crucial importance at the international level. [...] For the time being, international criminal rules still make up a body of law in need of legal precision and some major refinement on the level of definitions and general principles.

Some current rules of international criminal law lack clarity in their scope and purport, and thus do not seem to fulfil the requirements of the principle of specificity. For example, crimes against humanity in the ICTY and ICTR Statutes is defined as encompassing 'other inhumane acts'.[60] Moreover, the crimes of 'rape', 'torture', 'persecution' and 'enslavement' are not defined in these statutes. The judicial definition of 'rape' has also changed over time and has depended on the panel or court hearing the case. Finally, the modes of liability of aiding and abetting (as defined in customary international law) are not clearly defined, again raising an issue of a lack of legal certainty.[61]

4.3 *Principle of Non-Retroactivity*

A corollary to the principle of liability is the principle of non-retroactivity, which is defined as requiring rules of criminal law to cover acts committed only after the enactment of these rules unless they are favourable to the accused.[62] This interpretation of the principle of non-retroactivity was only accepted after World War II. Crimes against peace and crimes against humanity were introduced during the Nuremberg trials. In so doing, the Tribunal applied *ex*

---

58 International Committee of the Red Cross Advisory Service on International Humanitarian Law, 'General Principles of International Criminal Law' (2014) available at <https://www.icrc.org/en/document/general-principles-international-criminal-law-factsheet> accessed 12 September 2018; Cassese and Gaeta (n 11).

59 Cassese and Gaeta (n 11) 28–9.

60 Article 5 of the Statute of the International Criminal Tribunal for the Former Yugoslavia; Article 3 of the Statute of the International Criminal Tribunal for Rwanda.

61 See Chapter 4, section 4.2.3 for more detail.

62 Cassese and Gaeta (n 11) 28–9.

post facto law, as defence counsel rightly pointed out.[63] After the emergence of the *nullum crimen sine lege* principle as a general rule, the principle of non-retroactivity also started being applied in international criminal law. This principle is currently firmly embedded. It follows that, at present, courts may only apply existing rules of criminal law. This does not mean, however, that judges are barred from refining and elaborating upon existing rules of criminal law.[64] The ICTY noted in *Aleksovski* that the *nullum crimen sine lege* principle:[65]

> [D]oes not prevent a court, either at the national or international level, from determining an issue through a process of interpretation and clarification as to the elements of a particular crime; nor does it prevent a court from relying on previous decisions which reflect an interpretation as to the meaning to be ascribed to particular ingredients of a crime.

As mentioned, international criminal law consists of customary rules and the decisions of judges. Thus, in contemplating the nature of international criminal law one should reconcile the principle of non-retroactivity with the inherent characteristics of international criminal law.[66] This interpretation seems to have been confirmed by the European Court of Human Rights ('ECtHR'). In *Cantoni v France*,[67] the court stated that, for criminal law to be able to keep up with the *nullum crimen* principle, it must meet the requirements of accessibility and foreseeability.[68] When a rule of criminal law is laid down in vague terms, there may exist 'grey areas at the fringes of the definition'.[69] The court explained that:[70]

> [T]he scope of the notion of foreseeability depends to a considerable degree on the content of the text in issue, the field it is designed to cover and the number and status of those to whom it is addressed [...]. A law may still satisfy the requirement of foreseeability even *if the person concerned has to take appropriate legal advice to assess, to a degree that is reasonable in the circumstances, the consequences which a given action*

63 IMT *Trial of the Major War Criminals before the International Military Tribunal, Judgment of 1 October 1946.*

64 Cassese and Gaeta (n 11) 30.

65 ICTY *Prosecutor v Zlatko Aleksovski, Appeals Chamber Judgment* (*IT-95-14/1-A*) 127.

66 Cassese and Gaeta (n 11) 30.

67 ECtHR *Cantoni v France* (*Judgment of 15 November 1996*).

68 ECtHR *Kononov v Latvia* (*Judgment of 17 May 2010*) 185, 235 and ff.

69 ECtHR *Cantoni v France* (*Judgment of 15 November 1996*) 32.

70 ibid 35 (emphasis added).

> *may entail* [...]. This is particularly true in relation to persons carrying on a professional activity, who are used to having to proceed with a high degree of caution when pursuing their occupation. They can on this account be expected to take special care in assessing the risks that such activity entails.

Cassese rightly infers from the reasoning of the ECtHR that, firstly, 'while interpretation and clarification of existing rules [are] always admissible, adaptation is only compatible with legal principles subject to stringent requirements'.[71] Secondly, the evolutive adaptation of criminal prohibitions by courts must fulfil certain requirements:[72]

> [T]he extension of such legal ingredients of an offence as *actus reus*, in order to cover conduct previously not clearly considered as criminal must: *i*) be in keeping with the criminal rules relating to the subject matter, more specifically with the rules defining 'the essence of the offence'; *ii*) conform with, and indeed implement fundamental principles of ICL or at least general principles of law; and *iii*) be reasonably foreseeable by the addressees.

These requirements mean that the extension of the legal ingredients of a crime, if consonant with or even required by general principles of criminal law, could be reasonably anticipated by the accused, even though an adaptation might work to her detriment. Consequently, courts can adapt provisions of existing criminal offences to changing social conditions; however, they cannot create new criminal offences with new legal ingredients (such as a novel *actus reus* or *mens rea*). For example, a lawful adaptation could result from the court broadening the *actus reus* or lowering the threshold of the subjective element, such as from *dolus indirectus* to *dolus eventualis*, or from active knowledge to wilful blindness.

Cassese also points out that the adaptation process must presuppose the 'existence of a broad criminal prohibition' (such as the proscription of murder), as well as 'no clear-cut and explicit enumeration, in the law, of the acts embraced by this definition'.[73] Because the line between 'adaption' (which is permitted) and 'analogy' (which is prohibited) is sometimes blurred, Cassese

---

71 Cassese and Gaeta (n 11) 31.

72 ibid 31–2.

73 ibid 32.

warns courts to proceed with great caution, and to determine whether the 'adaption' under discussion is legally warranted on a case-by-case basis.[74]

Another example of 'adaptation' of existing law can be seen in the *Tadic*[75] and *Hadzihasanovic* Appeals Chamber Judgments.[76] In the *Tadic* case, the Appeals Chamber held unanimously that some customary rules of international law were applicable in an internal armed conflict, despite the fact that, prior to this decision, the International Committee of the Red Cross (ICRC) and many States and commentators had stated that violations of humanitarian law in a non-international armed conflict did not amount to war crimes, because these crimes could only be committed in the context of an international armed conflict.[77] Indeed, the ICTY in *Tadic* decided that:[78]

> A State-sovereignty-oriented approach has been gradually supplanted by a human-being-oriented approach [...]. It follows that in the area of armed conflict the distinction between interstate wars and civil wars is losing its value as far as human beings are concerned. Why protect civilians from belligerent violence, or ban rape, torture or the wanton destruction of hospitals, churches, museums or private property, as well as proscribe weapons causing unnecessary suffering when two sovereign States are engaged in war, and yet refrain from enacting the same bans or providing the same protection when armed violence has erupted "only" within the territory of a sovereign State? If international law, while of course duly safeguarding the legitimate interests of States, must gradually turn to the protection of human beings, it is only natural that the aforementioned dichotomy should gradually lose its weight.

The ICTY thus clearly 'adapted' existing law to correspond to modern-day reality.

Likewise, in *Hadzihasanovic*, the ICTY decided that individuals could be held liable under the mode of liability of command responsibility in an internal armed conflict.[79] This interpretation was novel and constitutes another example of judicial adaptation of existing rules.

---

74 ibid 31–2.
75 ICTY *Prosecutor v Dusko Tadic, Appeals Chamber Judgment* (IT-94-1-A).
76 ICTY *Prosecutor v Hadzihasanovic and Kubura, Appeals Chamber Judgment* (IT-01-47-A).
77 ICTY *Prosecutor v Dusko Tadic, Appeals Chamber Judgment* (IT-94-1-A).
78 ibid 97.
79 ICTY *Prosecutor v Hadzihasanovic and Kubura, Appeals Chamber Judgment* (IT-01-47-A) 31 ff.

4.4 *Principle of the Ban on Analogy and Extensive Interpretation*

The principle of legality also includes the principle against analogy and extensive interpretation. This implies that courts cannot broaden surreptitiously, by way of interpretation, the scope and purport of rules of criminal law to circumstances that had not been specifically envisaged by those rules.

However, the prohibition of analogy and extensive interpretation needs to be interpreted in light of three qualifications. Firstly, international criminal law only prohibits the so-called *analogia legis*, while it does allow the so-called *analogia juris*. The former occurs when a rule of criminal law is extended to cover a matter that is not addressed by the law. The latter concerns the regulation of a matter:[80]

> [N]ot covered by a specific provision or rule, by resorting to general principles of [international criminal law], or to general principles of criminal justice, or to principles common to the major legal systems of the world.

Thus, courts can resort to the interpretation of existing rules when they aim to spell out or clarify an existing prohibition that was already laid down in either customary law or treaties.

Secondly, certain rules of criminal law require judicial officers to resort to the use of analogy, notably when customary law or treaty rules include the penalisation of 'other inhumane acts'.[81] To solve this issue, judges may have recourse to the *ejusdem generis* canon of statutory interpretation.[82] According thereto, if a law lists specific classes of persons or things, and then refers to them in general, judges may interpret these general statements as only applicable to the same kind of persons or things as those specifically listed.

Thirdly, rules of international criminal law might invite a judge to use a logical approach in interpreting them, which is permissible if the rules apply to general principles. For example, this might be the case when a judge has to consider a new weapon that does not fall under any of the prohibited weapons lists because of its novel features. If that new weapon is inherently indiscriminate or causes unnecessary suffering, the judge is entitled to use a logical approach in prohibiting it.

80 Cassese and Gaeta (n 11) 34.

81 For example, Article 5(i) of the Statute of the International Criminal Tribunal for the Former Yugoslavia, under crimes against humanity, 'other inhumane acts' are prohibited.

82 Cassese and Gaeta (n 11) 34.

4.5 *Principle of* Favor Rei

The principle of *favor rei* is closely linked to the prohibition on analogy and thus the principle of legality. *Favor rei* entails that, when faced with conflicting interpretations of a rule, judges must adopt the construction that favours the accused. In the case of *Flick*, the Nuremberg Tribunal held that 'if from credible evidence two reasonable inferences may be drawn, one of guilt and the other of innocence, the latter must be taken'.[83] This principle was confirmed by the ICTY in the *Stakic* case.[84]

5 Conclusion

The development of international criminal law has made it possible for individuals to be held accountable, not only nationally, but also by international tribunals and courts for actions that are collective in nature. This is particularly important in the context of the financing of core crimes, because financial resources are a means of enabling the commission of crimes. Thus, not only individuals who perpetrate core crimes, but also those who substantially assist in the perpetration of these crimes, should be held criminally liable.

Furthermore, the general principles of international criminal law allow us to test the results of the analysis of the applicable international law and of the comparative analysis to determine if they are compatible with these principles. The principles dealt with in this Chapter are also those which any *actus reus* or *mens rea* requirement must comply with.

Finally, to determine the applicable set of rules involved in holding an individual who finances an entity criminally liable, I analysed the sources of international law according to Article 38 of the ICJ Statute. This Chapter demonstrates that treaties and customary international law rules are incomplete in determining the criminal liability of individuals who finance the perpetration of core crimes. Supplementary sources are also vague because clear general principles of law recognised by the community of States cannot be deduced.

In Chapter 3, I discuss the *actus reus* and *mens rea* requirements in international criminal law in broad terms, as these requirements are applicable to every crime and mode of liability. The aim of the following Chapter is to provide the tools to better understand the *actus reus* and *mens rea* of the mode of liability of aiding and abetting.

83 IMT *Flick et al, Judgment of 22 December 1947*.

84 ICTY *Prosecutor v Milomir Stakic, Trial Chamber Judgment* (IT-97-24-T).

CHAPTER 3

Actus Reus and *Mens Rea* in International Criminal Law

1 Importance of Defining *Actus Reus* and *Mens Rea*

In this Chapter, I briefly discuss the *actus reus* and *mens rea* requirements in international criminal law in general terms, because this allows us to better understand the *actus reus* and *mens rea* of a specific crime or mode of liability.

International crimes differ from domestic crimes because of the collective nature of international crimes, and the way in which these crimes are committed.[1] Generally, international crimes are not committed by single individuals but by several people, such as a group, militia or other collection of individuals.[2] To hold an individual liable for financing an entity involved in the perpetration of core crimes, international criminal law has developed a system of modes of liability broadly inspired by national legal systems. To be held criminally liable, an individual needs to meet all the criteria for the *actus reus* and *mens rea* requirements of the crime and mode of liability.

According to the Constitutional Court of South Africa (O'Regan J), the requirement of *mens rea* is one of the fundamental principles of democratic societies. It is therefore imperative to define it and determine its elements:[3]

> The striking degree of correspondence between different legal systems in relation to an element of fault in order to establish criminal liability reflects a fundamental principle of democratic societies: as a general rule people who are not at fault should not be deprived of their freedom by the state. This rule is the corollary of another rule which the same comparative exercise illustrates: when a person has committed an unlawful act intentionally or negligently, the state may punish them. Deprivation of liberty, without established culpability, is a breach of this established

1 Jann Kleffner, 'The Collective Accountability of Organized Armed Groups for System Crimes' in Andre Nollkaemper and Harmen van der Wilt (eds), *System Criminality in International Law* (Cambridge University Press 2009).

2 Aron Naumovich Traĭnin, *Hitlerite Responsibility under Criminal Law* (Hutchinson & Co 1945).

3 *S v Coetzee and Others* (*CCT50/95*) [*1997*] *ZACC 2; 1997* (*4*) *BCLR 437; 1997* (*3*) *SA 527* 176.

 | DOI:10.1163/9789004470934_004

rule. Where culpability is established, and the conduct is legitimately deemed unlawful, then no such breach arises.

Additionally, it is necessary to differentiate between the *actus reus* and *mens rea* requirements of a crime, because as stated in the maxim, *actus non facit reum, nisi mens sit rea*, an act does not make a person guilty unless her mind is guilty.[4]

In this Chapter, section 2 provides a general definition of the *actus reus* requirement in customary international law, which is also applicable at the ICC. Section 3 defines the *mens rea* requirement, first at the ICC level, and then as understood in customary international law. It is necessary to differentiate between the *mens rea* requirement at the ICC and in international criminal law, because these two systems differ. The definition of the *mens rea* elements at the ICC does not reflect the commonly agreed-upon definition of *mens rea* in international criminal law.

2 *Actus Reus*

The definition of the *actus reus* requirement in customary international law is similar to its definition at the ICC. The *actus reus* requirement of an offence is divided into three elements: (i) the conduct; (ii) the consequences; and (iii) the circumstances.[5]

Firstly, the conduct can be defined as an act or an omission, for example the prohibition against murder as an element of crimes against humanity. In other words, it is the behavioural element of a crime that requires an action or an omission of some kind.

Secondly, the consequences are the result of the act or omission. Between the conduct and consequences there must be a causation *nexus*.[6] This *nexus* is of particular significance in the case of financing entities involved in the perpetration of core crimes. Without a *nexus* between the funds and the perpetrated crimes, the individual who provided the financing cannot be held liable.[7] In international criminal law, the main theory regarding causation in

4 Bryan Garner, *A Dictionary of Modern Legal Usage* (2 ed, Oxford University Press 1995) 21.
5 Albin Eser, 'Mental Element - Mistake of Fact and Mistake of Law' in Antonio Cassese, Paola Gaeta and John RWD Jones (eds), *The Rome Statute of the International Criminal Court: A Commentary, Volume 1* (Oxford University Press 2002).
6 Antonio Cassese and Paola Gaeta, *Cassese's International Criminal Law* (Oxford University Press 2013) 38.
7 For greater detail on the substantial contribution requirement, see Chapter 4 section 4.2.3.1.

complicity is the theory of 'substantial contribution/effect', *i.e.* a 'substantial contribution' to the principal's act is required.[8] However, 'substantial contribution' is an imprecise concept. As Reggio puts it: 'In the end, the identification of the relevant proximate causes among the many causes will depend upon several aspects, including policy decisions.'[9]

Lastly, the circumstances are:[10]

> [A]ny objective or subjective facts, qualities or motives with regard to the subjects of the crime (such as the perpetrator and any accomplices), the object of the crime (such as the victims or other impaired interests), or any other modalities of the crime (such as means or time and place of commission).

For example, the forcible movement of a civilian population from one place to another, which forms part of crimes against humanity, is the circumstance required by the rule.

3 *Mens Rea*

Put simply, the mental element in international criminal law could be defined as the intent or negligence of a person regarding her actions. The person carrying out the conduct needs to have the necessary 'state of mind; that is, a psychological element required by the legal order for the conduct to be blameworthy and consequently punishable'.[11] There can be no criminal responsibility without *mens rea*. Thus, the absence of, or defect in, *mens rea* precludes the imposition of criminal responsibility. Marchuk states:[12]

> The cornerstone of criminal law is the principle of culpability that requires a guilty state of mind on the part of an individual.

---

8 Andrea Reggio, 'Aiding and Abetting in International Criminal Law: The Responsibility of Corporate Agents and Businessmen for Trading with the Enemy of Mankind' (2005) 5 International Criminal Law Review 623, 671.

9 ibid.

10 Eser (n 5) 919.

11 Cassese and Gaeta (n 6) 39.

12 Iryna Marchuk, *The Fundamental Concept of Crime in International Criminal Law: A Comparative Law Analysis* (Springer Science & Business Media 2013) 112.

When determining the various forms that the *mens rea* requirement might take in international criminal law, two problems arise. Firstly, with the exception of the *Elements of Crimes* of the ICC, most substantive rules concerning international crimes do not specify the subjective element required for each specific offence.[13] In the case of individuals who finance entities involved in the perpetration of core crimes, this means that it is unclear what types of *mens rea* (*e.g.*, *dolus directus*, *dolus indirectus*, *dolus eventualis*, active knowledge, or wilful blindness) lead to criminal responsibility.[14] Even the *Elements of Crimes* of the ICC, which are designed to set out the categories of crimes over which the ICC may exercise jurisdiction, are not aimed at codifying, restating or contributing to the development of customary international law.[15]

Secondly, there exists no customary international law norm that sets out a general definition of the various types of *mens rea*.[16] International courts and tribunals have from time to time differed in their definitions of the subjective elements. Thus, at the international level, there are no clear definitions of the subjective elements.

3.1 Mens Rea *at the ICC*

The Rome Statute is the only international instrument that provides a general definition of the mental element of international crimes, and it sets out a description of the terminology used. Article 30(1) provides that: 'A person shall be criminally responsible and liable for punishment for a crime within the jurisdiction of the Court only if the material elements are committed with intent and knowledge.'[17] The Rome Statute further clarifies that:[18]

> A person has intent where: (a) In relation to conduct, that person means to engage in the conduct; (b) In relation to a consequence, that person means to cause that consequence or is aware that it will occur in the ordinary course of events.

In addition, '"[k]nowledge" means awareness that a circumstance exists, or a consequence will occur in the ordinary course of events.'[19] However, the

13 International Criminal Court, 'Elements of Crimes' (2011).
14 For an in-depth discussion of this problem, see Chapter 4, section 4.2.3.2.
15 Cassese and Gaeta (n 6) 43.
16 For a definition of these terms, see Chapter 4, section 4.2.3.2.
17 Article 30 paragraph 1 of the Rome Statute of the International Criminal Court 1998 (last amended 2010).
18 ibid, Article 30 paragraph 2.
19 ibid, Article 30 paragraph 3.

definitions in Article 30 of the Rome Statute are not representative of customary international law norms.[20]

Article 30 does not contain other mental elements for core crimes. However, one can argue that *dolus eventualis*, recklessness and negligence are not disregarded, because intent and knowledge are implied 'unless otherwise provided'.[21] Provisions such as Article 28(a)(i), which allows for the liability of superiors, and Article 8(2)(xxvi), which holds those who conscript or enlist children responsible for war crimes, envisage the 'culpable negligence' and 'should have known' standard, respectively. Therefore, when a substantive provision of the Rome Statute does not specify the mental element required for a crime, intent and knowledge can be inferred to be the required substantive provisions. These required mental elements might in some cases be higher than those set out in customary international law. For example, with regard to aiding and abetting, Article 25(3)(c) of the Rome Statute requires that the accomplice's conduct must be committed with 'the purpose of facilitating the commission' of the crime, while it has been suggested that, according to customary international law, only knowledge might be necessary.[22] The requirement set out in the Rome Statute is therefore higher than that provided for by customary international law. According to the ordinary meaning of Article 25(3)(c) of the Rome Statute, it can thus be argued that it is not possible to hold an individual liable for aiding and abetting, unless she had the knowledge and acted with the purpose of providing an entity with the financial means to commit core crimes.[23]

3.2 Mens Rea *in Customary International Law*

Customary international law applies to all international criminal courts and tribunals which are bound by it if their statutes do not regulate a particular matter differently.[24] The Appeals Chamber in *Hadžihasanović* noted that, 'to hold that a principle was part of customary international law, it has to be satisfied that State practice recognized the principle on the basis of supporting

20 See Chapter 4, section 4.1.

21 Article 30 of the Rome Statute of the International Criminal Court 1998 (last amended 2010).

22 See also SCSL *Prosecutor v Charles Ghankay Taylor, Appeals Chamber Judgment* (*SCSL-03-01-A*) 436; ICTY *Prosecutor v Tihomir Blaškić, Appeals Chamber Judgment* (*IT-95-14-A*); ICTY *Prosecutor v Tihomir Blaškić, Trial Chamber Judgment* (*IT-95-14-T*); ICTY *Prosecutor v Anto Furundzija, Trial Chamber Judgment* (*IT-95-17/1-T*) (n 39).

23 For a detailed discussion of the *mens rea* element of aiding and abetting at the ICC, see Chapter 4, section 4.1.

24 Cassese and Gaeta (n 6) 43.

opinio juris'.[25] The ICC is not bound by the customary international law definition of an aider and abettor's *mens rea*, because Article 25(3)(c) and Article 30 of the Rome Statute mandate the ICC to apply a definition which differs from customary international law.

In international criminal law, substantive rules regarding crimes often do not specify the *mens rea* element required for each specific offence.[26] However, several international treaties contain provisions describing the subjective elements of international crimes which have become customary international law.[27] In fact, '[w]hile there is international customary law which is not laid down in conventions, some of the major conventional humanitarian law has become part of customary international law'.[28] This is notably the case in the following examples: Article 2 of the Genocide Convention lays down that genocide, as an international crime, requires the accused to have the special '*intent* to destroy, in whole or in part, a national, ethnical, racial or religious group';[29] Article 1 of the Convention Against Torture provides that: '"Torture" means any act by which severe pain or suffering, whether physical or mental, is *intentionally* inflicted on a person for such purposes';[30] and Article 85, paras 3 and 4, of the First Additional Protocol states that grave breaches must be committed *wilfully*.[31] The ICRC Commentary explains that the word 'wilfully' implies that:[32]

25 ICTY *Prosecutor v Hadzihasanovic and Kubura, Appeals Chamber Judgment* (*IT-01-47-A*) 12. For a more detailed discussion on customary international law, see Chapter 4, section 4.2.

26 Cassese and Gaeta (n 6) 39.

27 International Law Commission, 'Draft Conclusions on Identification of Customary International Law, U.N. Doc. A/73/10, 30 April-1 June and 2 July-10 August 2018' (2018) conclusion 10 stipulates that '[f]orms of evidence of acceptance as law (opinio juris) include, but are not limited to: [...] treaty provisions [...]'.

28 United Nations Secretary-General, 'Report of the Secretary-General Pursuant to Paragraph 2 of Security Council Resolution 808' (1993) 33.

29 Article 2 of the Convention on the Prevention and Punishment of the Crime of Genocide, 9 December 1948. See also for example ICJ, *Case Concerning Application of the Convention on the Prevention and Punishment of the Crime of Genocide (Croatia v Serbia), Judgment, 3 February 2015* at paragraphs 132-148; ICJ *Application of the Convention on the Prevention and Punishment of the Crime of Genocide (Bosnia and Herzegovina v Serbia and Montenegro), Judgment, 27 February 2007* at paragraphs 186-91, and in particular paragraph 187, where the ICJ stated that this 'special intent' meant 'intent to destroy the protected group'.

30 Article 1 of the Convention Against Torture and Other Cruel, Inhuman or Degrading Treatment or Punishment, 10 December 1984.

31 Article 85, paragraphs 3 and 4 of the Protocol Additional to the Geneva Conventions of 12 August 1949, and Relating to the Protection of Victims of International Armed Conflicts (Protocol I) 1977.

32 Claude Pilloud and others, 'Commentary on the Additional Protocols of 8 June 1977 to the Geneva Conventions of 12 August 1949' (1987) 27 International Review of the Red Cross 119, paragraph 3473.

> The accused must have acted consciously and with intent, i.e., with his mind on the act and its consequences, and willing them ('criminal intent' or 'malice aforethought'); [this] encompasses the concepts of 'wrongful intent' or 'recklessness', viz., the attitude of an agent who, without being certain of a particular result, accepts the possibility of it happening.

Thus, intent, wilfulness and recklessness are specifically required by several treaty provisions, thereby automatically excluding any other subjective frame of mind such as negligence or wilful blindness. However, the above examples notwithstanding, the identification of a clear subjective element in international treaty provisions remains the exception. As explained in the next Chapter, regarding aiding and abetting in international criminal law, certain elements of the *mens rea* requirement are generally agreed upon at the *ad hoc* and hybrid Tribunals, while others need clarification.[33]

4 Conclusion

To be perpetrated, a crime requires illegal conduct, also referred to as *actus reus* (*i.e.* the contribution to a core crime by financing the entity involved in its commission), and a mental element, also referred to as *mens rea* (*i.e.* the knowledge and intent to contribute to the principal's crimes). The *actus reus* element of a crime consists of: (i) conduct; (ii) consequences; and (iii) circumstances. In case of the financing of an entity involved in the commission of core crimes, this means that an individual: (i) provides funds to an entity; (ii) these funds substantially contribute to the perpetration of the crime by the principal; and (iii) with these funds, the principal, for example, forcibly transfers the local population, which amounts to a crime against humanity. The specific *actus reus* elements of the behaviour of an individual who finances entities involved in the commission of core crimes (*i.e.* aider and abettor) are discussed in the next Chapter.

In the context of the *mens rea* element of a crime, criminal liability can only arise when the individual who finances the commission of core crimes carries out this behaviour with a culpable frame of mind. It is, however, not easy to identify the various forms of the mental element in international criminal law. Certain *mens rea* elements of an individual who finances the commission

33 For greater detail about the contested *mens rea* elements of aiding and abetting, see Chapter 4, section 4.2.3.

of core crimes are generally agreed upon by the *ad hoc* and hybrid Tribunals, while others need clarification.[34] It thus becomes necessary to have recourse to general notions of *mens rea* common to most domestic legal systems, to clarify the subjective element of aiding and abetting.[35]

The following Chapter provides an in-depth discussion of the objective (*actus reus*) and subjective (*mens rea*) elements of aiding and abetting in international criminal law. There I rely on primary, secondary and subsidiary sources of international criminal law to present a definition of aiding and abetting at the ICC and in customary international law. It provides the *actus reus* and *mens rea* elements upon which there is a general agreement and highlights the ones which need clarification.

34 See Chapter 4, sections 4.2.2 and 4.2.3.

35 This is done in the comparative analysis in Chapter 5.

PART 2

Complicity – Internationally and Nationally

CHAPTER 4

Culpability in International Criminal Law with Regard to Aiding and Abetting

1 Introduction

International criminal courts and tribunals impose criminal liability on any person who 'commits' a crime.[1] This raises the questions of who can be considered to have 'committed' a crime, and under which circumstances a person – who has not 'committed' but has participated in the commission of a crime – could be held accountable for her conduct. This is particularly important in the case of an individual who finances an entity that is involved in the perpetration of core crimes, as that individual does not commit any crimes herself.

A crime can be committed by one or multiple main perpetrators, with or without the support of accomplices. The Appeals Chamber of the ICTY explained in *Tadic*:[2]

> Most of these crimes do not result from the criminal propensity of single individuals but constitute manifestations of collective criminality: the crimes are often carried out by groups of individuals acting in pursuance of a common criminal design. Although some members of the group may physically perpetrate the criminal act (murder …), the participation and contribution of the other members of the group is often vital in facilitating the commission of the offence in question. It follows that the moral gravity of such participation is often no less – or indeed no different – from that of those actually carrying out the acts in question.

To hold an individual liable for her conduct, it is necessary to determine her degree of participation in a crime. This Chapter argues that an individual who finances the commission of core crimes cannot be held criminally liable under any mode of liability at the ICC – not even aiding and abetting – because of her

1 See for example Article 7 (1) of the Statute of the International Criminal Tribunal for the Former Yugoslavia; Article 6 (1) of the Statute of the International Criminal Tribunal for Rwanda.

2 ICTY *Prosecutor v Dusko Tadic, Appeals Chamber Judgment* (*IT-94-1-A*) 191.

 | DOI:10.1163/9789004470934_005

lack of purposeful assistance.[3] However, the same actions of the accused can trigger criminal responsibility for aiding and abetting in customary international law.[4] Aiding and abetting is the only mode of liability that is applicable to the conduct of a person who finances an entity which uses such financing to commit core crimes.[5] To determine the circumstances under which an accused could be held liable, it is necessary to clarify what the extent of the knowledge and intent requirements are through an analysis of the applicable international law and a comparative analysis of national laws.

2 Meaning of Aiding and Abetting

Aiding and abetting is a mode of liability that can be found in the founding documents of all modern international criminal statutes.[6] It is an accessorial mode of responsibility whereby a person is accused of having facilitated the commission of an offence which was committed by others. It consists of two forms of activity: 'aiding', which refers to the provision of practical or material assistance to the perpetrators of a crime; and 'abetting', which involves the provision of moral support or encouragement to the perpetrators of an offence.[7] For the sake of clarity, even though the actions of a person who finances an entity that perpetrates core crimes might amount to aiding, but not abetting, this work refers to this action as 'aiding and abetting', because this is the established use in international criminal law.

3 See Chapter 4, section 4.1.1.2. If an individual provides funds with the purpose of the principal using her funding to perpetrate core crimes, and all other *actus reus* and *mens rea* elements are met, she could be held liable as an aider and abettor at the ICC.

4 See Chapter 4, section 4.2.

5 See Chapter 4, section 4.2.

6 See Article 7(1) of the Statute of the International Criminal Tribunal for the Former Yugoslavia; Article 6(1) of the Statute of the International Criminal Tribunal for Rwanda; Article 25(3)(c) of the Rome Statute of the International Criminal Court 1998 (last amended 2010); Article 6(1) of the Statute of the Special Court for Sierra Leone; article 29 of the Extraordinary Chambers in the Courts of Cambodia Law. See also Article 29 of the Regulation on Panels with Exclusive Jurisdiction over Serious Criminal Offences (East Timor Tribunal); Article 10(2) of the Statute of the Extraordinary African Chambers; Article 16(1)(2) of the Law on Specialist Chambers and Specialist Prosecutor's Office (Kosovo Tribunal).

7 See for example ICTR *Prosecutor v Jean-Paul Akayesu, Trial Chamber Judgment* (*ICTR-96-4*) 484; ICTY *Prosecutor v Tihomir Blaškić, Trial Chamber Judgment* (*IT-95-14-T*) 284, footnote 510; ICTY *Prosecutor v Miroslav Kvocka et al, Trial Chamber Judgment* (*IT-98-30/1-T*) 254; ICTY *Prosecutor v Semanza, Trial Chamber Judgment* (*ICTR-97-20-T*) 384; ECCC *Prosecutor v Kaing Guek Eav, Trial Chamber Judgment* (*001/18-07-2007-ECCC/TC/E188*) 533; ICC *Prosecutor v Bemba et al, Trial Judgment* (*ICC-01/05-01/13-1989-Red*) 88–9.

The core element of liability for aiding and abetting has crystallised into customary international law.[8] However, as discussed below,[9] in recent years the determination of the *actus reus* and *mens rea* requirements of aiding and abetting have been at the core of heated debates among judges and scholars. Differing judicial interpretations of these requirements have literally meant the difference between verdicts of guilty and not guilty.[10] It is therefore crucial to determine and delineate the elements of aiding and abetting. It is firstly necessary to differentiate between aiding and abetting and other related concepts.

3 Related Concepts to Aiding and Abetting

In this section, I distinguish aiding and abetting from the concepts of direct commission, indirect commission, co-perpetration, JCE, instigation, ordering, contributing to a group acting with a common purpose, planning, conspiracy, incitement, and superior/command responsibility. This section shows that these other modes of liability are not applicable to the conduct of an individual who finances an entity involved in the perpetration of core crimes. I argue that only the mode of liability of aiding and abetting is applicable to the conduct of that individual.

3.1 *Direct Commission*

Direct commission is a form of individual perpetration of a crime, and it is a well-established form of liability in international criminal law. As the Appeals Chamber in *Tadic* stated, the commission is 'first and foremost the physical perpetration of a crime by the offender himself'.[11] The direct perpetrator is therefore the person who physically carries out all elements of the offence.[12] This approach was also adopted by the Extraordinary Chambers in the Courts

8 ICTY *Prosecutor v Dusko Tadic, Trial Chamber Judgment* (*IT-94-1-T*) 663–9; ICTY *Prosecutor v Anto Furundzija, Trial Chamber Judgment* (*IT-95-17/1-T*) 191–249; ECCC *Prosecutor v Kaing Guek Eav, Trial Chamber Judgment* (*001/18-07-2007-ECCC/TC/E188*) 475. See generally Wladyslaw Czaplinski, 'Customary International Law as a Basis of an Individual Criminal Responsibility' in Bartlomiej Krzan (ed), *Prosecuting International Crimes: A Multidisciplinary Approach* (Brill | Nijhoff 2019).

9 See Chapter 4, section 4.

10 See for example ICTY *Prosecutor v Perisic, Appeals Chamber Judgment* (*IT-04-81-A*); and SCSL *Prosecutor v Charles Ghankay Taylor, Appeals Chamber Judgment* (*SCSL-03-01-A*).

11 ICTY *Prosecutor v Dusko Tadic, Appeals Chamber Judgment* (*IT-94-1-A*) 188.

12 ICTR *Prosecutor v Renzaho, Trial Chamber Judgment* (*ICTR-97-31-T*) 739.

of Cambodia ('ECCC')[13] and the Special Tribunal for Lebanon ('STL').[14] Direct perpetration differs from aiding and abetting in the sense that an individual who finances the perpetration of core crimes does not herself carry out the crime; she does not do the *actus reus* of the offence.[15]

3.2 *Indirect Commission*

Indirect commission is a form of individual perpetration identified by the ICC in which the indirect perpetrator uses another person to physically commit the crime. According to Article 25(3) of the Rome Statute:[16]

> [A] person shall be criminally responsible and liable for punishment for a crime within the jurisdiction of the Court if that person: (a) commits such a crime, whether as an individual, jointly with another or *through another person, regardless of whether that other person is criminally responsible*.

Similar to direct perpetration (*i.e.* execution of the crime by the principal) and co-perpetration, indirect-perpetrators are not 'secondary parties/accomplices/accessories', but they are criminally liable as *principals* to the crime. The indirect perpetrator *uses* the direct perpetrator or co-perpetrator as 'a tool or an instrument for the commission of the crime'.[17] The direct perpetrator of the crime can be a 'non-innocent agent'[18] or an 'innocent agent',[19] but it is the indirect perpetrator who exercises control over the crime, because she knowingly directs the innocent or non-innocent agent as to whether and how a crime is committed.[20] In fact, she is the mastermind of an operation and controls the

13 ECCC *Prosecutor v Kaing Guek Eav, Trial Chamber Judgment* (001/18-07-2007-ECCC/TC/E188) 479–82.

14 STL *Interlocutory Decision on the Applicable Law: Terrorism, Conspiracy, Homicide, Perpetration, Cumulative Charging, Appeals Chamber Judgment* (STL-11-01/I/AC/R176bis/F0936) 216.

15 Flavio Noto, *Secondary Liability in International Criminal Law: A Study on Aiding and Abetting Or Otherwise Assisting the Commission of International Crimes* (Dike 2013) 12, 13.

16 Emphasis added.

17 ICC *Prosecutor v Katanga and Ngudjolo Chui, Decision on the Confirmation of Charges, Pre-Trial Chamber I* (ICC-01/04-01/07-717) 495.

18 In ibid 497. The Court held that 'in some scenarios it is possible for both perpetrators to be criminally liable as principals: the direct perpetrator for his fulfilment of the subjective and objective elements of the crime, and the perpetrator behind the perpetrator for his control over the crime via his control over the will of the direct perpetrator'.

19 As noted in ibid 495, the agent's 'innocence will depend upon the availability of acceptable justifications and/or excuses for his actions'.

20 ICC *Prosecutor v Lubanga, Appeals Chamber Judgment* (ICC-01/04-01/06-3121-Red) 469.

will of those who directly commit the offence.[21] By contrast, the commission of a crime does not lie in the hands of an individual who finances entities that are involved in the perpetration of core crimes, as that individual does not control the principal's crime. Also, indirect perpetration must fulfil all the subjective elements of the crime, which includes special intent, if required. The aider and abettor need not share the special intent of the principal.

In *Katanga and Ngudjolo Chui* the ICC held that indirect perpetration may also occur through control of an organisation.[22] This means that although the crime was committed by an agent, it is attributable to the mastermind of the organisation.[23] For liability to attach in this way the indirect perpetrator must 'control' an organisation, which:[24]

> [M]ust be based on hierarchical relations between superiors and subordinates. The organisation must also be composed of sufficient subordinates to guarantee that superiors' orders will be carried out, if not by one subordinate, then by another. These criteria ensure that orders given by the recognised leadership will generally be complied with by their subordinates.

An individual who finances an entity involved in the perpetration of core crimes does not fulfil these requirements, as she is not in functional control of an organisation.

3.3 *Co-Perpetration*

Co-perpetration is a form of joint commission which is based on the theory of joint control over the crime. This mode of liability finds application at the ICC and is foreseen in Article 25(3)(a) of the Rome Statute. It differs from aiding and abetting in significant ways. The Pre-Trial Chamber I of the ICC defined

21 For more detail on indirect participation, see notably Stefano Manacorda and Chantal Meloni, 'Indirect Perpetration versus Joint Criminal Enterprise: Concurring Approaches in the Practice of International Criminal Law?' (2011) 9 Journal of International Criminal Justice 159.

22 ICC *Prosecutor v Katanga and Ngudjolo Chui, Decision on the Confirmation of Charges, Pre-Trial Chamber I* (ICC-01/04-01/07-717) 501–3.

23 Robert Cryer *et al, An Introduction to International Criminal Law and Procedure* (3 ed, Cambridge University Press 2014) 353; Cryer refers to the mastermind as 'the controller' of the organisation.

24 ICC *Prosecutor v Katanga and Ngudjolo Chui, Decision on the Confirmation of Charges, Pre-Trial Chamber I* (ICC-01/04-01/07-717) 512.

co-perpetration in the *Lubanga Decision on the Confirmation of Charges* as follows:[25]

> [T]he concept of co-perpetration is originally rooted in the idea that when the sum of co-ordinated individual contributions of a plurality of persons results in the realisation of all the objective elements of a crime, any person making a contribution can be held vicariously responsible for the contributions of all the others and, as a result, can be considered as a principal to the whole crime.

The judges adopted the control theory approach to co-perpetration and they explained that the concept of co-perpetration is based on joint control over the crime:[26]

> [Co-perpetration] is rooted in the principle of the division of essential tasks for the purpose of committing a crime between two or more persons acting in a concerted manner. Hence, although none of the participants has overall control over the offence because they all depend on one another for its commission, they all share control because each of them could frustrate the commission of the crime by not carrying out his or her task.

Co-perpetration requires a plurality of persons and a common plan, while aiding and abetting does not.[27] Most significantly, co-perpetration requires each participant to provide an essential contribution to the commission of the crime, which contribution is indispensable for the success of the criminal endeavour. This means that without the contribution of each participant, the

---

25 ICC *Prosecutor v Lubanga, Decision on the Confirmation of Charges, Pre-Trial Chamber I* (*ICC-01/04-01/06-803-tEN*) 326.

26 ibid. See also Lachezar D Yanev, *Theories of Co-Perpetration in International Criminal Law* (Brill | Nijhoff 2018); ICC *Prosecutor v Lubanga, Trial Chamber Judgment* (*ICC-01/04-01/06-2842*); ICC *Prosecutor v Lubanga, Appeals Chamber Judgment* (*ICC-01/04-01/06-3121-Red*); ICC *Prosecutor v Bemba et al, Trial Judgment* (*ICC-01/05-01/13-1989-Red*); ICC *Prosecutor v Al Mahdi, Trial Chamber Judgment* (*ICC-01/12-01/15-171*).

27 ICC *Prosecutor v Lubanga, Decision on the Confirmation of Charges, Pre-Trial Chamber I* (*ICC-01/04-01/06-803-tEN*) 343; ICC *Prosecutor v Lubanga, Trial Chamber Judgment* (*ICC-01/04-01/06-2842*) 980-1; ICC *Prosecutor v Lubanga, Appeals Chamber Judgment* (*ICC-01/04-01/06-3121-Red*) 445; ICC *Prosecutor v Bemba et al, Decision on the Confirmation of Charges, Pre-Trial Chamber I* (*ICC-01/05-01/13-749*) 33; ICC *Prosecutor v Bemba et al, Trial Judgment* (*ICC-01/05-01/13-1989-Red*) 679, 802–3.

crime could not occur.[28] An individual who finances an entity that is involved in the commission of a core crime only aids the commission of the principal's crime; although her assistance is substantial, it is not essential. Thus, co-perpetration results in the criminal liability of the co-perpetrator as a principal, while aiding and abetting is an accessorial mode of liability.

3.4 *JCE*

A JCE is a form of joint commission in which a plurality of persons, acting pursuant to a common purpose, embark on a criminal activity that is either carried out jointly or by some members of the group. The members of this group act as principals; by contrast, 'the aider and abettor is always an accessory to a crime perpetrated by another person, the principal'.[29]

There are also important differences in the constitutive elements of these two modes of liability. Regarding the *actus reus*, the accused in the case of a JCE must have rendered a *significant* contribution to carrying out the common plan, whereas aiders and abettors at the *ad hoc* and hybrid Tribunals are held to a higher standard, inasmuch as they have to provide a *substantial* contribution.[30] Additionally, participants in a JCE must 'perform acts that in some way are directed to the furthering of the common plan or purpose',[31] whereas such a requirement does not exist for aiders and abettors.[32] An individual who finances an entity involved in the perpetration of core crimes does not perform acts that are directed toward the furthering of a common plan, but rather she substantially contributes monetarily to the principal's crime.

There are three forms of JCE and the *mens rea* elements in a JCE differ according to the category of common design under consideration. Regarding a

28 ICC *Prosecutor v Lubanga, Decision on the Confirmation of Charges, Pre-Trial Chamber I (ICC-01/04-01/06-803-tEN)* 346–7; ICC *Prosecutor v Lubanga, Trial Chamber Judgment* (*ICC-01/04-01/06-2842*) 999–1000; ICC *Prosecutor v Lubanga, Appeals Chamber Judgment* (*ICC-01/04-01/06-3121-Red*) 469, 473; ICC *Prosecutor v Bemba et al, Trial Judgment* (*ICC-01/05-01/13-1989-Red*) 679, 804; *ICC Prosecutor v Al Mahdi, Trial Chamber Judgment* (*ICC-01/12-01/15-171*) 19.

29 ICTY *Prosecutor v Dusko Tadic, Appeals Chamber Judgment* (*IT-94-1-A*) 229(i). See also ICTY *Prosecutor v Vidoje Blagojevic and Dragan Jokic, Appeals Chamber Judgment* (*IT-02-60-A*) 192; ICTY *Prosecutor v Vasiljević, Appeals Chamber Judgment* (*IT-98-32-A*) 102; ICTY *Prosecutor v Kvočka et al, Appeals Chamber Judgment* (*IT-98-30/1*) 92.

30 ICTY *Prosecutor v Dusko Tadic, Appeals Chamber Judgment* (*IT-94-1-A*) 229(iii); ICTY *Prosecutor v Sainovic et al, Appeals Chamber Judgment* (*IT-05-87-A*) 1649; ICTY *Prosecutor v Vidoje Blagojevic and Dragan Jokic, Appeals Chamber Judgment* (*IT-02-60-A*) 127; ICTY *Prosecutor v Popović et al, Appeals Chamber Judgment* (*IT-05-88*)1732.

31 ICTY *Prosecutor v Dusko Tadic, Appeals Chamber Judgment* (*IT-94-1-A*) 229(iii).

32 ibid 229(ii).

JCE I, members share the intent to perpetrate a crime. In a JCE II the accused must have personal knowledge of the system of ill-treatment, as well as the intent to further the commonly agreed-upon system. In the case of a JCE III, the intent 'to participate in and further the criminal activity or the criminal purpose of a group and to contribute to the joint criminal enterprise or in any event to the commission of a crime by the group' is required.[33] By contrast, under the jurisprudence of the ICTY and ICTR, aiders and abettors must possess the knowledge that their acts assist the commission of the crime by the principal.[34]

3.5 *Instigation*

Instigation, like aiding and abetting, is a form of participation in the perpetration of a crime. Despite some similarities between instigating and aiding and abetting, these two modes of liability differ in significant respects. Instigating is conduct that influences the decision of a principal perpetrator to commit a crime by 'urging, encouraging, or prompting' her to commit the crime.[35] Although it is not necessary to show that the instigation by the accused was indispensable to the commission of the crime, similar to aiding and abetting:[36]

> [I]instigating requires the *actus reus* to have a substantial effect on the perpetration of the crime. A finding that an accused's conduct had a 'substantial effect' for the purpose of aiding and abetting will therefore normally also satisfy the 'substantial effect' requirement for the purpose of instigating.

Nevertheless, instigation requires more than simply facilitating the perpetration of a crime; the instigator must prompt the perpetration of the offence. By contrast, it is sufficient for the aider and abettor's contribution to hinge on the principal's determination to commit the crime.[37] Thus, instigating requires a causal link between the act of instigating and the commission of the crime,

33 ibid 228.

34 ibid 229(iv).

35 ICTY *Prosecutor v Semanza, Trial Chamber Judgment* (*ICTR-97-20-T*) 381.

36 SCSL *Prosecutor v Moinina Fofana and Allieu Kondewa, Appeals Chamber Judgment* (*SCSL-04-14-A-829*) 84.

37 ICTY *Prosecutor v Orić, Trial Chamber Judgment* (*IT-03-68-T*) 271; ECCC *Prosecutor v Kaing Guek Eav, Trial Chamber Judgment* (*001/18-07-2007-ECCC/TC/E188*) 522.

whereas aiding and abetting does not to hold an individual liable who finances an entity involved in the perpetration of core crimes.[38]

Additionally, while instigation may under certain circumstances be direct and public, this is not a requirement.[39] The instigator must act, either with the intention that the crime be committed (direct *mens rea*) or 'with the awareness of the substantial likelihood that a crime will be committed in the execution of that instigation' (indirect *mens rea*).[40] In the case of aiding and abetting, however, the *ad hoc* and hybrid Tribunals have held that the aider and abettor must have knowledge that her act (or omission) assists, encourages or lends moral support to the perpetration of the offence.[41] In the case of an individual who finances an entity involved in the commission of core crimes, she must know that her monetary contribution assists the commission of the crime by the principal.

Instigation is only punishable when it leads to the commission of a crime. Therefore, instigating an inchoate offence does not constitute a criminally prohibited conduct.[42]

3.6 *Ordering*

Ordering, like aiding and abetting, is a form of participation in the commission of a crime. However, these forms of participation differ significantly.[43] The main difference lies in the fact that ordering includes an 'authority requirement', which entails that a 'person in a position of authority instructs another person to commit an offence'.[44] A relationship of authority thus exists between

---

38 SCSL *Prosecutor v Moinina Fofana and Allieu Kondewa, Appeals Chamber Judgment* (*SCSL-04-14-A-829*) 54.

39 ICTR *Prosecutor v Jean-Paul Akayesu, Appeals Chamber Judgment* (*ICTR-96-4*) 478.

40 ICTY *Prosecutor v Dario Kordic, Mario Cerkez, Appeals Chamber Judgment* (*IT-95-14/2-A*) 32.

41 At the ICC, a purposive standard is required. This standard will be discussed in Chapter 4, section 4.1.1.2.

42 Wibke Kristin Timmermann, 'Incitement in International Criminal Law' (2006) 88 International Review of the Red Cross 823, 839.

43 For example, international criminal law recognises that one can aid or abet by omission if the accused had a legal duty to act. However, this is not relevant in the scenario of financing an entity, because the perpetrator does not violate a duty to act. Furthermore, the *actus reus* requirement of ordering must necessarily precede the commission of the crime, whereas the *actus reus* requirement of aiding and abetting can occur during or after the commission of the crime. Again, this difference does not play a significant role in the context of the financing of an entity, because the provision of the funds takes place before the perpetration of the crimes.

44 ICTY *Prosecutor v Dario Kordic, Mario Cerkez, Appeals Chamber Judgment* (*IT-95-14/2-A*) 28; ICTR *Semanza v The Prosecutor, Appeals Chamber Judgment* (*ICTR-97-20-A*) 361; ICTR *Kalimanzira v Prosecutor, Appeals Chamber Judgment* (*ICTR-05-88-A*) 213.

the person who issues the order and the person who executes it. By contrast, between an individual who finances an entity involved in the perpetration of a core crime and the actual perpetrator of the crime, there is no authority requirement. The perpetrator does not even have to be aware of the contributing action of the individual who finances the entity that commits the core crime.[45]

3.7 *Contributing to a Group Acting with a Common Purpose*

Common purpose as a mode of liability is set forth in Article 25(3)(d) of the Rome Statute, and is a form of participation in group activities. It is a mode of liability exclusive to the ICC and it criminalises an action which '[i]n any other way contributes to the commission or attempted commission of [...] a crime by a group of persons acting with a common purpose'.[46] This mode of liability does not have an equivalent in the statutes of the *ad hoc* Tribunals, but it nonetheless bears similarities to JCE.[47]

Although both common purpose liability and aiding and abetting apply to persons who play an auxiliary role in the perpetration of an offence, there are nevertheless important differences between them. Most significantly, regarding the *actus reus* requirement, common purpose liability requires an agreement or common plan between a group of two or more people with respect to the perpetration of a crime.[48] Aiding and abetting neither requires such an agreement nor that the aid be given to a group of persons.

Moreover, under the jurisprudence of the *ad hoc* and hybrid Tribunals, aiding and abetting requires that the aid must have a substantial effect on, or substantially contribute to, the commission of the crime.[49] By contrast, common

---

45 ICTY *Prosecutor v Dusko Tadic, Appeals Chamber Judgment* (*IT-94-1-A*) 229(ii).

46 Article 25(3)(d) of the Rome Statute of the International Criminal Court 1998 (last amended 2010).

47 Randle C DeFalco, 'Contextualizing Actus Reus under Article 25(3)(d) of the ICC Statute: Thresholds of Contribution' (2013) 11 Journal of International Criminal Justice 715, 715.

48 ICC *Prosecutor v Mbarushimana, Decision on the Confirmation of Charges* (*ICC-01/04-01/10-465-Red*) 271; ICC *Prosecutor v Ruto et al, Decision on the Confirmation of Charges* (*ICC-01/09-01/11-373*) 351; ICC *Prosecutor v Kenyatta, Decision on the Confirmation of Charges* (*ICC-01/09-02/11-382-Red*) 421.

49 See notably ICTY *Prosecutor v Vidoje Blagojevic and Dragan Jokic, Appeals Chamber Judgment* (*IT-02-60-A*) 134; ICTY *Prosecutor v Mrkšić and Šljivančanin, Appeals Chamber Judgment* (*IT-95-13/1-A*) 200; ICTR *Kalimanzira v Prosecutor, Appeals Chamber Judgment* (*ICTR-05-88-A*) 86; ICTR *Rukundo v Prosecutor, Appeals Chamber Judgment* (*ICTR-2001-70-A*) 52; ICTY *Prosecutor v Lukić and Lukić, Appeals Chamber Judgment* (*IT-98-32/1-T*) 438; SCSL *Prosecutor v Charles Ghankay Taylor, Appeals Chamber Judgment* (*SCSL-03-01-A*) 370; ICTR *Prosecutor v Nyiramasuhuko et al, Appeals Chamber Judgment* (*ICTR-98-42-A*) 3332.

purpose liability can be established when the accused merely makes a significant contribution,[50] which is a lower threshold.[51]

Regarding the *mens rea* element of aiding and abetting, on the one hand the *ad hoc* and hybrid Tribunals require that the accused must have acted with the knowledge that her acts or omissions assisted, encouraged or lent moral support to the perpetrator of the offence. On the other hand, at the ICC the aider and abettor must act with the purpose of facilitating the commission of a crime[52] in addition to the standard *mens rea* requirement in Article 30.[53] Moreover, Article 25(3)(d) of the Rome Statute requires that the contribution of the aider and abettor be intentional, and that it must either: '(i) [b]e made with the *aim of furthering* the criminal activity or criminal purpose of the group […], or (ii) [b]e made in the *knowledge of the intention of the group* to commit the crime'.[54] An individual who finances an entity involved in the perpetration of core crimes cannot be held liable under Article 25(3)(d), unless she either acts with the purpose of furthering the principal's crime or with the knowledge of the intention of the entity to commit core crimes.

Finally, common purpose liability is a residual form of accessorial liability, and it was included in the Rome Statute to grant the ICC the power to prosecute cases where the actions of an accessory go beyond that which is covered by aiding and abetting as defined at the ICC.[55]

3.8 *Planning*

Planning as a mode of liability consists of inchoate and preparatory acts. Although aiding and abetting and planning both involve the conduct of an individual that has a substantial effect on the perpetration of the sanctioned

---

As discussed in Chapter 4, section 4.1.1.1, the precise *actus reus* threshold for aiding and abetting at the ICC remains the subject of debate, and is discussed in more detail below.

50 ICC *Prosecutor v Ongwen, Decision on the Confirmation of Charges* (*ICC-02/04-01/15-422-Red*) 44; ICC *Prosecutor v Al Mahdi, Decision on the Confirmation of Charges* (*ICC-01/12-01/15-84-Red*) 27.

51 Marjolein Cupido, 'Group Acting With a Common Purpose' in de Hemptinne Jérôme, Roth Robert and Van Sliedreat Elies (eds), *Modes of Liability in International Criminal Law* (Cambridge University Press 2019) 316.

52 Article 25(c) of the Rome Statute of the International Criminal Court 1998 (last amended 2010).

53 ibid Article 30. See also ICC *Prosecutor v Bemba et al, Trial Judgment* (*ICC-01/05-01/13-1989-Red*) 97–8.

54 Article 25(3)(d) of the Rome Statute of the International Criminal Court 1998 (last amended 2010). Emphasis added.

55 Manuel J Ventura, 'Aiding and Abetting' in Jérôme de Hemptinne, Robert Roth and Elies von Sliedregt (eds), *Modes of Liability in International Criminal Law* (2019) 183.

offence,[56] they should be differentiated. An individual who finances an entity that is involved in the commission of core crimes renders practical assistance to the main perpetrator, while the planner shares a common plan or design with the principal perpetrator.[57] In fact, the plan or the design of criminal conduct lies at the heart of this mode of liability.[58]

Also, an individual who finances an entity involved in the perpetration of core crimes is an accessory to the crime, as she only plays a facilitating role. Because of this facilitating role the aider and abettor is considered less responsible, whereas the planner is much more involved in her capacity as the mastermind behind the criminal plan.[59] Thus, although the requirement of 'substantial contribution' might *prima facie* appear to be similar, in fact the 'substantial contribution' of the aider and abettor differs significantly from that of the planner.

3.9 *Conspiracy*

Conspiracy, a crime that is only set forth in Article 25(3) of the Rome Statute, is 'an inchoate crime used to punish two or more people who agree to carry out a crime'.[60] Aiding and abetting is a mode of liability. Thus, an individual who finances an entity that is involved in the commission of core crimes can only be held criminally liable if the principal in fact commits the crimes.

There exists additional distinguishing characteristics between the crime of conspiracy and the mode of liability of aiding and abetting. Conspiracy only applies to the crime of genocide,[61] and it does not require the genocide to have taken place for criminal liability to ensue.[62]

---

56 ICTR *Prosecutor v Jean-Paul Akayesu, Trial Chamber Judgment* (ICTR-96-4) 480.

57 J Ohlin, 'Conspiracy' in A Cassese (ed), *The Oxford Companion to International Criminal Justice* (Oxford University Press 2009) 280.

58 ICTR *Prosecutor v Ferdinand Nahimana et al, Appeals Chamber Judgment* (ICTR-99-52-A) 479; ICTY *Prosecutor v Dario Kordic, Mario Cerkez, Appeals Chamber Judgment* (IT-95-14/2-A) 26; ICTY *Prosecutor v Popović et al, Trial Chamber Judgment* (IT-05-88-T) 1006.

59 Ventura, 'Aiding and Abetting' (n 55) 358.

60 Juliet Okoth, *The Crime of Conspiracy in International Criminal Law* (TMC Asser Press 2014) 194.

61 'Fourth Report on Crimes against Humanity, Sean D. Murphy, 18 February 2019, A/CN.4/725' 138 notes that 'Iceland (on behalf of the Nordic countries) and Sierra Leone suggested that the forms of liability should not be interpreted narrowly and should include conspiracy and incitement. The Special Rapporteur notes that the Rome Statute of the International Criminal Court does not refer to either "conspiracy" or "incitement" with respect to crimes against humanity, and hence the Commission elected also not to use such terms'.

62 ICTR *Prosecutor v Nyiramasuhuko et al, Appeals Chamber Judgment* (ICTR-98-42-A) 473; ICTR *Prosecutor v Ferdinand Nahimana et al, Appeals Chamber Judgment* (ICTR-99-52-A)

Aiding and abetting is a mode of liability applicable to every crime and, except at the ICC,[63] requires the completion of the crime for criminal liability to attach.[64] An individual can therefore finance a principal to commit the crime of genocide, but also to commit other core crimes. She is not limited in the types of core crimes that she could finance.

Because genocide does not need to have been perpetrated for the criminal liability of the conspirator of an attempted genocide, the crime of conspiracy does not require the behaviour of the conspirator to have any effect on the crime. By contrast, according to the *ad hoc* and hybrid Tribunals, criminal liability can only be established for aiding and abetting if the acts of the aider and abettor had a substantial effect on, or had contributed to, the commission of the crime.[65] At the ICC the aider and abettor's actions must have had an 'effect' on the crime; a causal link is therefore required.[66] As discussed below, what is meant by 'effect' is a matter of

---

720; ICTR *Prosecutor v Karemera et al, Trial Chamber Judgment* (*ICTR-98-44-T*) 1577; ICTR *Prosecutor v Jean Baptiste Gatete, Appeals Chamber Judgment* (*ICTR-00-61*) 262; ICTY *Prosecutor v Popović et al, Trial Chamber Judgment* (*IT-05-88-T*) 1577; ICTY *Prosecutor v Tolimir, Appeals Chamber Judgment* (*IT-05-88/2-A*) 582, 590.

63 The completion of the crime for the aider and abettor at the ICC is not required for liability to be established. According to Article 25(3)(c) of the Rome Statute, the attempted perpetration of a crime is sufficient.

64 ICTY *Prosecutor v Zlatko Aleksovski, Appeals Chamber Judgment* (*IT-95-14/1-A*) 165; ICTY *Prosecutor v Orić, Trial Chamber Judgment* (*IT-03-68-T*) 282; ICTY *Prosecutor v Popović et al, Trial Chamber Judgment* (*IT-05-88-T*) 1015; ECCC *Prosecutor v Kaing Guek Eav, Trial Chamber Judgment* (*001/18-07-2007-ECCC/TC/E188*) 534.

65 SCSL *Prosecutor v Moinina Fofana and Allieu Kondewa, Appeals Chamber Judgment* (*SCSL-04-14-A-829*) 52, 71, 75, 84; ICTY *Prosecutor v Dusko Tadic, Appeals Chamber Judgment* (*IT-94-1-A*) 229(iii); ICTY *Prosecutor v Vasiljević, Appeals Chamber Judgment* (*IT-98-32-A*) 102(i); ICTY *Prosecutor v Tihomir Blaškić, Appeals Chamber Judgment* (*IT-95-14-A*) 45-6, 48; ICTY *Prosecutor v Kvočka et al, Appeals Chamber Judgment* (*IT-98-30/1*) 89 - 90; ICTY *Prosecutor v Vidoje Blagojevic and Dragan Jokic, Appeals Chamber Judgment* (*IT-02-60-A*) 127, 193, 199; ICTR *Prosecutor v Ferdinand Nahimana et al, Appeals Chamber Judgment* (*ICTR-99-52-A*) 482, 672 934; ICTY *Prosecutor v Zlatko Aleksovski, Appeals Chamber Judgment* (*IT-95-14/1-A*) 164; ICTY *Prosecutor v Mrksic et al, Appeals Chamber Judgment* (*IT-95-13/1*) 81; ECCC *Prosecutor v Kaing Guek Eav, Trial Chamber Judgment* (*001/18-07-2007-ECCC/TC/E188*) 533; ICTY *Prosecutor v Lukić and Lukić, Appeals Chamber Judgment* (*IT-98-32/1-T*) 437; SCSL *Prosecutor v Charles Ghankay Taylor, Appeals Chamber Judgment* (*SCSL-03-01-A*) 362, 368-9, 390, 401, 447, 475, 481–2; ICTY *Prosecutor v Sainovic et al, Appeals Chamber Judgment* (*IT-05-87-A*) 1626, 1649; ICTY *Prosecutor v Popović et al, Appeals Chamber Judgment* (*IT-05-88*) 1732, 1758, 1783, 1812; ICTR *Prosecutor v Nyiramasuhuko et al, Appeals Chamber Judgment* (*ICTR-98-42-A*) 1510, 1512, 1955, 2083, 3332, 3343.

66 ICC *Prosecutor v Bemba et al, Decision on the Confirmation of Charges, Pre-Trial Chamber I* (*ICC-01/05-01/13-749*) 35; ICC *Prosecutor v Bemba et al, Trial Judgment* (*ICC-01/05-01/13-1989-Red*) 90; ICC *Prosecutor v Bemba et al, Appeals Chamber Judgment* (*ICC-01/05-01/*

debate.[67]

Moreover, 'the *actus reus* of the crime of conspiracy to commit genocide is a concerted agreement to act for the purpose of committing genocide' between two or more people.[68] On the other hand, a single individual could aid and abet in the commission of a crime without any agreement. The principal does not even have to know of the actions of the aider and abettor.[69]

Finally, the perpetrators who agree to carry out the crime of conspiracy to commit genocide must share the special intent (*dolus specialis*) to commit genocide,[70] while no such intent is required for an individual who finances the perpetration of core crimes.[71]

3.10 *Incitement*

Although aiding and abetting has been defined by the *ad hoc* Tribunals in some cases as 'facilitating, advising, or instigating the commission of a crime',[72] it is not the same as the inchoate offence of 'incitement'. Incitement only applies to the crime of genocide,[73] whereas aiding and abetting is a mode of liability that

---

08-3636-Red) 1327 ('[w]hether a certain conduct amounts to 'assistance in the commission of the crime' within the meaning of Article 25 [3] [c] of the Statute even without the showing of such an effect can only be determined in light of the facts of each case').

67 See Chapter 4, section 4.1.1.1.

68 ICTR *Prosecutor v Ferdinand Nahimana et al, Appeals Chamber Judgment* (*ICTR-99-52-A*) 894, 896; ICTR *Prosecutor v Jean Baptiste Gatete, Appeals Chamber Judgment* (*ICTR-00-61*) 260; ICTR *Prosecutor v Karemera et al, Appeals Chamber Judgment* (*ICTR-98-44-A*) 643.

69 ICTY *Prosecutor v Radislav Krstic, Appeals Chamber Judgment* (*IT-98-33-A*) 140; SCSL *Prosecutor v Charles Ghankay Taylor, Appeals Chamber Judgment* (*SCSL-03-01-A*) 482–6.

70 ICTY *Prosecutor v Radislav Krstic, Appeals Chamber Judgment* (*IT-98-33-A*) 140; ICTY *Prosecutor v Vidoje Blagojevic and Dragan Jokic, Appeals Chamber Judgment* (*IT-02-60-A*) 127; ICTR *Prosecutor v Nyiramasuhuko et al, Appeals Chamber Judgment* (*ICTR-98-42-A*) 1512.

71 ICTR *Prosecutor v Ferdinand Nahimana et al, Appeals Chamber Judgment* (*ICTR-99-52-A*) 894; ICTY *Prosecutor v Popović et al, Appeals Chamber Judgment* (*IT-05-88*) 529; ICTY *Prosecutor v Tolimir, Appeals Chamber Judgment* (*IT-05-88/2-A*) 586.

72 ICTY *Prosecutor v Semanza, Trial Chamber Judgment* (*ICTR-97-20-T*) 384; ICTY *Prosecutor v Muhimana, Trial Chamber Judgment* (*ICTR- 95-1B-T*) 507; ICTR *Prosecutor v Gacumbitsi, Trial Chamber Judgment* (*ICTR-2001-64-T*) 286.

73 'Fourth Report on Crimes against Humanity, Sean D. Murphy, 18 February 2019, A/CN.4/725' 138 notes that 'Iceland (on behalf of the Nordic countries) and Sierra Leone suggested tha t the forms of liability should not be interpreted narrowly and should include conspiracy and incitement. The Special Rapporteur notes that the Rome Statute of the International Criminal Court does not refer to either "conspiracy" or "incitement" with respect to crimes against humanity, and hence the Commission elected also not to use such terms'.

could apply to any international crime.[74] Hence, an individual who finances an entity that is involved in the perpetration of a core crime can only be held criminally accountable if the principal in fact commits the crime. In addition, the aid provided by the aider and abettor must have a 'substantial effect on the perpetration of the crime'.[75] This is not required for incitement.

The *mens rea* requirement also differs for aiding and abetting and incitement. In the case of incitement the accused must share the specific intent to commit genocide with the main perpetrator. By contrast, an individual who finances an entity involved in the commission of core crimes does not need to share any special intent with the perpetrator of the genocide.[76] According to the *ad hoc* Tribunals, the *mens rea* requirement for the aider and abettor is the knowledge of the principal perpetrator's intent.[77] The intent of the aider and abettor is different under the Rome Statute, and takes the form of 'for the purpose of facilitating the commission' of the crime.[78]

3.11 *Superior / Command Responsibility*

Command responsibility and aiding and abetting share some characteristics. The failure by a superior to prevent or punish the criminal activities of subordinates could, in theory, amount to aiding and abetting (by omission).[79]

However, an essential characteristic of command responsibility is a superior/subordinate relationship in which one person (the superior) must have 'effective control' over others (the subordinates).[80] To establish command responsibility, the superior must have the material ability to prevent or punish

---

74 Article 25(3)(c) of the Rome Statute of the International Criminal Court 1998 (last amended 2010).

75 ICTY *Prosecutor v Tihomir Blaškić, Appeals Chamber Judgment* (*IT-95-14-A*) 48.

76 ICTY *Prosecutor v Anto Furundzija, Trial Chamber Judgment* (*IT-95-17/1-T*) 90; ICTR *Prosecutor v Jean-Paul Akayesu, Trial Chamber Judgment* (*ICTR-96-4*) 545; ICTR *Prosecutor v Ntakirutimana, Appeals Chamber Judgment* (*ICTR-96-10-A & ICTR-96-17-A*) 501.

77 See Chapter 4, section 4.2 for a more detailed discussion of the aider and abetter's *mens rea* requirement.

78 Article 25(3)(c) of the Rome Statute of the International Criminal Court 1998 (last amended 2010).

79 ICTY *Prosecutor v Tihomir Blaškić, Trial Chamber Judgment* (*IT-95-14-T*) 337; SCSL *Prosecutor v Brima et al, Trial Chamber Judgment* (*SCSL-04-16-T*) 777; SCSL *Prosecutor v Brima et al, Appeals Chamber Judgment* (*SCSL-2004-16-A*) 230; ICTY *Prosecutor v Strugar, Trial Chamber Judgment* (*IT-01-42-T*) 355.

80 ICTY *Prosecutor v Zlatko Aleksovski, Appeals Chamber Judgment* (*IT-95-14/1-A*) 76; ICTY *Prosecutor v Mucić et al, Trial Chamber Judgment* (*IT-96-21-T*) 197-8, 256; ICTY *Prosecutor v Tihomir Blaškić, Appeals Chamber Judgment* (*IT-95-14-A*) 375; ICTY *Prosecutor v Hadzihasanovic and Kubura, Appeals Chamber Judgment* (*IT-01-47-A*) 20–1.

the criminal conduct of the subordinates. Such a relationship is not required in aiding and abetting; an individual who finances an entity involved in the commission of core crimes does not possess any form of authority over the principal perpetrator.

Moreover, in the case of command responsibility there must be a failure on the part of the superior to take necessary and reasonable action to prevent or punish violations of international criminal law; thus, the superior must have omitted to act.[81] In the case of an individual who finances an entity involved in the perpetration of core crimes, it is *her* acts (*i.e.* the fact that she provides funding) which result in criminal liability, not any omission on her part.

3.12 *Conclusion*

This section has demonstrated that none of the modes of liability described above apply to the conduct of an individual who finances an entity that uses those funds to perpetrate core crimes. Such an individual cannot be considered to be a principal (in any of the forms in which a principal could act, *to wit* direct commission, indirect commission, co-perpetration, or JCE), because she does not physically carry out all the elements of the offence; nor does she use another person to physically commit the crime; nor does she have joint control over the crime; nor does she act pursuant to a common purpose to embark on a criminal activity that is carried out jointly or by some members of the group. Such an individual is also not an instigator, as she does not prompt the perpetration of the offence; nor does she order the commission of an offence, because she is not a person in a position of authority instructing another person to commit an offence; nor does she contribute to a group acting with a common purpose, because there is no agreement or common plan between her and a group of persons with respect to the perpetration of the crimes; nor does she plan the crime, because she does not share a common plan or design with the principal perpetrator; nor could she be held liable for conspiracy or incitement, because whereas conspiracy and incitement are inchoate crimes, the aider and abettor finances an entity that uses the funds to in fact commit core crimes. Finally, the individual who finances an entity that uses those funds in the perpetration of core crimes cannot be held responsible pursuant to command responsibility, because she does not have 'effective control' over those who commit the crimes. Therefore, the only mode of liability that could apply to her conduct, is aiding and abetting.

---

81 ICTY *Prosecutor v Hadzihasanovic and Kubura, Appeals Chamber Judgment* (IT-01-47-A) 20–21.

4 Definition and Scope of Aiding and Abetting in International Criminal Law

The mode of liability of aiding and abetting is found in the statues of all modern international criminal tribunals, including the ICTY, ICTR, ICC, SCSL and the ECCC.[82] It has been examined and applied by courts in many cases since World War II, and it applies to all international crimes without restriction, including the crime of aggression.[83]

From the analysis of the primary[84] and secondary[85] sources of international criminal law, two preliminary conclusions can be drawn. Firstly, the primary

82 See Article 7(1) of the Statute of the International Criminal Tribunal for the Former Yugoslavia; Article 6(1) of the Statute of the International Criminal Tribunal for Rwanda; Article 25(3)(c) of the Rome Statute of the International Criminal Court 1998 (last amended 2010); Article 6(1) of the Statute of the Special Court for Sierra Leone; article 29 of the Extraordinary Chambers in the Courts of Cambodia Law. See also Article 29 of the Regulation on Panels with Exclusive Jurisdiction over Serious Criminal Offences (East Timor Tribunal); Article 10(2) Statute of the Extraordinary African Chambers; Article 16(1)(2) of the Law on Specialist Chambers and Specialist Prosecutor's Office (Kosovo Tribunal).

83 Article 25(3bis) of the Rome Statute of the International Criminal Court 1998 (last amended 2010).

84 The relevant treaties are: the 1907 Hague Regulations, the London Charter of the International Military Tribunal of 8 August 1945, the 1949 Geneva Conventions and their additional protocols, the Genocide Convention and the Rome Statute. Additionally, the sources of some international courts are included: the United Nations Security Council resolutions 827 (2003) and 955 (2004) setting up respectively the ICTY and ICTR, Security Council resolution 1315 (2000) establishing the Special Court for Sierra Leone, the United Nations Security Council's resolution 1757 (2007) establishing the Statute of the Special Tribunal for Lebanon. These treaty sources are incomplete when it comes to determining the liability of those who finance entities that commit core crimes. Except for the Rome Statute, none of these treaties lays down the exact *actus reus* and *mens rea* requirements of the modes of liability. Article 25 (Individual criminal responsibility) and Article 30 (Mental element) of the Rome Statute describe the elements of the modes of liability, but, as is demonstrated below, this explanation also contains gaps. The definition of the element of complicity according to customary international law rules also contains gaps, as discussed in Chapter 4, section 4.2.3.2. Therefore, reliance on primary sources of international criminal law to determine the content and extent of the complicity rules regarding persons who finance entities involved in the commission of core crimes, is not sufficient. For more detail on the primary sources, see Chapter 2, section 4.1.

85 General principles of international criminal law include principles specific to this branch of law, such as the principle of legality, the principle of specificity, the principle of non-retroactivity, the prohibition of analogy, and the principle of *favor rei*. These principles provide general rules as to the proper interpretation of a norm and how the formation of new international criminal law rules might occur, but they do not provide precise insights

sources do not provide any clarity on whether or not an individual who finances an entity that uses the funds to commit a core crime could be held liable under treaty law and customary international law. Secondly, regarding the supplementary sources, it is necessary to undertake an analysis of applicable international law and a comparative analysis of judicial decisions and the teachings of publicists of the various nations, to establish if general principles of law recognised by the community of States can be derived.

In this section, I analyse the jurisprudence of the ICC and the *ad hoc* and hybrid Tribunals.[86] Aiding and abetting as defined in customary international law is the only mode of liability that allows for the liability of an individual who finances an entity that perpetrates a core crime. However, under the ICC Statue liability for such an individual is precluded.[87]

To determine what the *actus reus* and *mens rea* requirements pertaining to aiders and abettors are, this section examines the rules under the Rome Statute and then those under customary international law. I analyse both the contested and uncontested core elements of aiding and abetting at the ICC and in customary international law. Section 4.1 establishes that an individual who finances an entity that commits core crimes cannot be held liable as an

---

as to the criminal liability of individuals who finance entities involved in the perpetration of core crimes. For more detail on the primary sources, see Chapter 2, section 4.1.

86 ICTY *Prosecutor v Anto Furundzija, Trial Chamber Judgment* (*IT-95-17/1-T*); The most relevant cases are: ICTR *Kalimanzira v Prosecutor, Appeals Chamber Judgment* (*ICTR-05-88-A*); ICTR *Rukundo v Prosecutor, Appeals Chamber Judgment* (*ICTR-2001-70-A*); ICTY *Prosecution v Delalic et al, Appeals Chamber Judgment* (*IT-96-21-A*); ICTY *Prosecutor v Brđanin, Appeals Chamber Judgment* (*IT-99-36*); ICTY *Prosecutor v Gotovina and Markac, Appeals Chamber Judgment* (*IT-06-90-A*); ICTY *Prosecutor v Krnojelac, Appeals Chamber Judgment* (*IT-97-25*); ICTY *Prosecutor v Ntagerura et al, Appeals Chamber Judgment* (*ICTR-99-46*); ICTY *Prosecutor v Orić, Appeals Chamber Judgment* (*IT-03-68*); ICTY *Prosecutor v Simić et al, Appeals Chamber Judgment* (*IT-95-9-A*); ICTR *Karera v Prosecutor, Appeals Chamber Judgment* (*ICTR-01-74-A*); ICTY *Prosecutor v Dusko Tadic, Appeals Chamber Judgment* (*IT-94-1-A*); ICTY *Prosecutor v Kvočka et al, Appeals Chamber Judgment* (*IT-98-30/1*); ICTY *Prosecutor v Radislav Krstic, Appeals Chamber Judgment* (*IT-98-33-A*); ICTY *Prosecutor v Tihomir Blaškić, Appeals Chamber Judgment* (*IT-95-14-A*); ICTY *Prosecutor v Tihomir Blaškić, Trial Chamber Judgment* (*IT-95-14-T*); ICTY *Prosecutor v Vasiljević, Appeals Chamber Judgment* (*IT-98-32-A*); ICTY *Prosecutor v Vidoje Blagojevic and Dragan Jokic, Appeals Chamber Judgment* (*IT-02-60-A*); ICTY *Prosecutor v Zlatko Aleksovski, Appeals Chamber Judgment* (*IT-95-14/1-A*); SCSL *Prosecutor v Charles Ghankay Taylor, Appeals Chamber Judgment* (*SCSL-03-01-A*).

87 Liability is precluded unless she acts with the purpose of her monetary contribution being used for the perpetration of core crimes. This scenario is not discussed in-depth in this work, which examines the grey area of liability of an individual who acted without the purpose that her monetary contribution should be used for the commission of core crimes.

aider or abettor under the Rome Statute, because it requires an aider and abettor to act with purpose when it comes to her contribution.[88] Indeed, the aider and abettor must act with the purpose of facilitating the crime of the principal and with the knowledge of the principal's crime. The interpretation of aiding and abetting under the ICC is not representative of the elements of this mode of liability under customary international law.

Section 4.2 demonstrates that, in the case of the financing of entities, an individual could in principle be held liable as an aider and abettor under the rules of customary international law. In fact, it is the only mode of liability that could apply to an individual who finances an entity that commits a core crime. However, before any conclusions can be dawn concerning her liability, her minimum required levels of knowledge and intent must first be established.

4.1 *Aiding and Abetting at the ICC*

According to Article 25(3)(c) of the Rome Statute:

> [A] person shall be criminally responsible and liable for punishment for a crime [...] if that person, [f]or the purpose of facilitating the commission of such a crime, aids, abets or otherwise assists in its commission or its attempted commission, including providing the means for its commission.

Some analogies can be drawn between aiding and abetting at the *ad hoc* Tribunals and at the ICC. However, the scope of aiding and abetting differs significantly at the *ad hoc* Tribunals and at the ICC. As seen below, a specific behaviour might result in liability for aiding and abetting at the *ad hoc* Tribunals, but not at the ICC.

88 ICC *Prosecutor v Mbarushimana, Judgment on the Appeal of the Prosecutor against the Confirmation of Charges Decision (ICC-01/04-01/10-514)*; ICC *Prosecutor v Lubanga, Appeals Chamber Judgment (ICC-01/04-01/06-3121-Red)*; ICC *Prosecutor v Al Mahdi, Decision on the Confirmation of Charges (ICC-01/12-01/15-84-Red)*; ICC *Prosecutor v Bemba et al, Appeals Chamber Judgment (ICC-01/05-01/08-3636-Red)*; ICC *Prosecutor v Bemba et al, Decision on the Confirmation of Charges, Pre-Trial Chamber I (ICC-01/05-01/13-749)*. The most relevant cases are: ICC *Prosecutor v Katanga, Trial Chamber Judgment (ICC-01/04-01/07-3436-tENG)*; ICC *Prosecutor v Lubanga, Decision on the Confirmation of Charges, Pre-Trial Chamber I (ICC-01/04-01/06-803-tEN)*; ICC *Prosecutor v Lubanga, Trial Chamber Judgment (ICC-01/04-01/06-2842)*; ICC *Prosecutor v Mbarushimana, Decision on the Confirmation of Charges (ICC-01/04-01/10-465-Red)*; ICC *Prosecutor v Ongwen, Decision on the Confirmation of Charges (ICC-02/04-01/15-422-Red)*; ICC *Prosecutor v Ruto et al, Decision on the Confirmation of Charges (ICC-01/09-01/11-373)*.

To be held criminally liable for aiding and abetting at the ICC, the *actus reus* and *mens rea* elements must be fulfilled. The ICC has held that the *actus reus* element consists of 'the provision of practical or material' and 'moral or psychological assistance [...] to the principal perpetrator'.[89] Additionally, the accused's actions must have had an effect on the commission of the crime by the perpetrator (*i.e.* the requirement of a causal link). However, as discussed in section 4.1.1.1 below, the precise threshold for fulfilment of the *actus reus* element is unclear, and it remains the subject of debate.

Regarding the *mens rea* element of aiding and abetting at the ICC, Article 25(3)(c) of the Rome Statute requires the accused to act 'for the purpose of facilitating the commission of [...] a crime'. This purposive standard results in an elevated *mens rea* standard at the ICC, compared to that at the *ad hoc* and hybrid Tribunals. Because of this purposive standard, the actions of an individual who finances an entity involved in the perpetration of core crimes fall outside the scope of liability of an aider and abettor under the Rome Statute.[90] This standard is analysed and discussed in detail in section 4.1.1.2 below.

4.1.1 Contested Elements of *Actus Reus* and *Mens Rea* at the ICC

When discussing the *actus reus* and *mens rea* requirements of aiding and abetting at the ICC, two issues deserve closer scrutiny, namely (i) the question of the precise threshold of the *actus reus* requirement which, to date, remains the subject of debate; and (ii) the elevated purposive *mens rea* standard of the ICC. I am quick to point out that these are not the only disagreements that have arisen in the rules pertaining to aiding and abetting at the ICC. However, I discuss these two issues in greater detail, because they actually influence the determination of the liability of an individual who finances an entity that uses the funds to perpetrate core crimes.[91]

4.1.1.1 *The Actus Reus Threshold at the ICC*

The ICC jurisprudence on *actus reus* element of aiding and abetting – in particular determining the required contribution to, or level of effect on, the

---

89 ICC *Prosecutor v Bemba et al, Trial Judgment* (*ICC-01/05-01/13-1989-Red*) 89 (citing the case law of the *ad hoc* and hybrid Tribunals).

90 For an explanation, see for example footnote 87.

91 For a discussion on issues at the ICC concerning the commission of a crime, a prior agreement and *ex post facto* aiding and abetting, a criminal law duty to act and aiding and abetting, complicity in genocide *versus* aiding and abetting genocide, and encouragement or moral support and the principal perpetrators, see Ventura, 'Aiding and Abetting' (n 55) 190–252.

commission of the crime – has thus far been both lacunose and vague.[92] On the one hand, citing ICTY and ICTR case law, the *Mbarushimana Decision on the Confirmation of Charges* found that for aiding and abetting 'a substantial contribution to the crime may be contemplated'.[93] In discussing the causal link between the accused's actions and the offence, the *Lubanga* Trial Chamber contrasted the effect that the actions of the co-perpetrator and the aider and abettor, respectively, must have on the commission of the crime. It held that, while according to Article 25(3)(c), 'participation of aiders, abettors and accomplices must substantially contribute to the crime, [...] co-perpetration requires an essential contribution'.[94] Thus, the contribution of a principal compared to that of an accomplice is significantly greater.[95] Moreover, the Pre-Trial Chamber II in the *Ruto Confirmation of Charges Decision* also assumed '*arguendo*, that the contribution under subparagraph (c), for the mode of participation of aiding and abetting, should be "substantial" '.[96] Although the liability of a co-perpetrator under Article 25(3)(a) has been recognised when her actions substantially contribute to a crime,[97] this subject nevertheless seems open to debate.[98]

On the other hand, other decisions have neither set a minimum threshold for the contribution that the assistance must provide, nor dismissed the existence of a threshold. In fact, in the *Bemba Confirmation of Charges Decision*, the Pre-Trial Chamber II decided that the elements of the mode of liability of aiding and abetting were met 'insofar as the accessory's contribution has an effect on the commission of the offence and is made with the purpose of facilitating such commission'.[99]

Likewise, the *Blé Goudé Confirmation of Charges Decision* held that:[100]

92 ICC *Prosecutor v Mbarushimana, Decision on the Confirmation of Charges (ICC-01/04-01/10-465-Red)* 279.

93 ibid 279. This could also be the case for ordering, soliciting and inducing.

94 ICC *Prosecutor v Lubanga, Trial Chamber Judgment* (*ICC-01/04-01/06-2842*) 953.

95 ibid 997.

96 ICC *Prosecutor v Ruto et al, Decision on the Confirmation of Charges* (*ICC-01/09-01/11-373*) 354.

97 ICC *Prosecutor v Lubanga, Trial Chamber Judgment* (*ICC-01/04-01/06-2842*) 997.

98 Also open to debate, according to Noto (n 15), is the definition of a 'substantive contribution'. He states that, should the Court confirm a substantial contribution requirement in Article 25(3)(c), 'it is doubtful whether the Court will be able to come up with a satisfactory substantive definition of what a substantial contribution is'.

99 ICC *Prosecutor v Bemba et al, Decision on the Confirmation of Charges, Pre-Trial Chamber I* (*ICC-01/05-01/13-749*) 35.

100 ICC *Prosecutor v Goudé, Decision on the Confirmation of Charges* (*ICC-02/11-02/11-186*) 167.

> [W]hat is required for this form of responsibility is that the person provides assistance to the commission of a crime and that, in engaging in this conduct, he or she intends to facilitate the commission of the crime.

These decisions thus did not set any minimum threshold for the contribution or the effect.

Moreover, in the *Bemba Appeals Judgement* the accused, Mangenda, took issue with the Court's holding regarding the proper *actus reus* threshold, and he argued that the *actus reus* requirement for aiding and abetting mandates a 'substantiality requirement'.[101] The Appeals Chamber ignored the issue by dismissing the accused's argument as moot because his actions had an effect on the crimes. In fact, the Appeals Chamber determined that the text in Article 25(3)(c):[102]

> [O]nly requires that the assistance in the commission (or attempted commission) of the crime be provided for the purposes of facilitating such commission without indicating whether the conduct must have also had an effect on the commission of the offence. The Appeals Chamber considers that the *actus reus* under article 25 (3) (c) of the Statute is certainly fulfilled when the person's assistance in the commission of the crime facilitates or furthers the commission of the crime, as the showing of such an effect indicates that the person indeed assisted in its commission.

It therefore decided not to answer the question of the substantiality threshold because it deemed it unnecessary to find liability in this case. Instead, the Appeals Chamber appeared to address a completely different issue, namely the question of '[w]hether a certain conduct amounts to "assistance in the commission of the crime" within the meaning of Article 25 (3) (c) of the Statute even without the showing of such an effect can only be determined in light of the facts of each case'.[103] It considered that it was in any event, 'unnecessary to dwell into this issue any further in the context of the present case, given that [...] the Trial Chamber found that Mangenda's conduct had an effect on the commission of the offences'.[104] The difficulty with the Appeals Chamber's reasoning is of course that it avoided answering the question raised by the

101 ICC *Prosecutor v Bemba et al, Corrected Version of Appeal Brief* (*ICC-01/05-01/13-2143-Corr-Red*) 320.

102 ICC *Prosecutor v Bemba et al, Appeals Chamber Judgment* (*ICC-01/05-01/08-3636-Red*) 1327.

103 ibid 1327.

104 ibid 1327.

accused, namely what the proper threshold for the *actus reus* requirement actually was. Mangenda never disputed that his actions had an effect on the commission of the crime. Rather, he argued that to be held liable for aiding and abetting his actions needed to have a *substantial* effect on the perpetration of the principal's offence.

By contrast, without analysis or explanation the *Ongwen* and *Al Mahdi Confirmation of Charges Decisions* questioned the very existence of a minimum threshold. The *Ongwen Confirmation of Charges Decision* held that, '[i]t is nowhere required [...] that the assistance be "substantial" or anyhow qualified other than by the required specific intent to facilitate the commission of the crime'.[105] In the *Bemba Trial Judgment*, the Chamber explained that for aiding and abetting, 'the Statute does not require the meeting of any specific threshold. The plain wording of the statutory provision does not suggest the existence of a minimum threshold'.[106] According to the Chamber, support for this interpretative approach could be found by way of analogy to the corresponding text of Article 2(3)(d) of the 1996 *Draft Code of Crimes against the Peace and Security of Mankind* of the ILC.[107] It did not refer to any other judgments. The Chamber also justified such an interpretation based on the fact that Article 25(3)(c) requires the assistance to be purposeful, which is an enhanced *mens rea* standard when compared to that in Article 30.[108] Finally, the Chamber held that although the actions of the aider and abettor need not be *conditio sine qua non* to the commission of the principal crime, those actions must have furthered, advanced or facilitated the commission of the principal offence.[109]

I find the position that a minimum threshold regarding determining the required contribution to/level of effect on the commission of the crime does not exist, to be untenable.[110] The reasoning of the *Mbarushimana Confirmation of Charges Decision* regarding the determination of a threshold seems to be more prudent. In determining the existence of a threshold in Article 25(3)(d), the Pre-Trial Chamber I also referred to the threshold in Article 25(3)(a)-(c). It held that considering the *travaux préparatoires* of the Rome Statute,

105 ICC *Prosecutor v Ongwen, Decision on the Confirmation of Charges* (*ICC-02/04-01/15-422-Red*) 43; ICC *Prosecutor v Al Mahdi, Decision on the Confirmation of Charges* (*ICC-01/12-01/15-84-Red*) 26.

106 ICC *Prosecutor v Bemba et al, Trial Judgment* (*ICC-01/05-01/13-1989-Red*) 93.

107 ibid 93.

108 ibid 94.

109 ibid 95.

110 Ventura, 'Aiding and Abetting' (n 55) 209. Ventura argues that there are good reasons to doubt the conclusion of the *Ongwen* and *Al Mahdi Confirmation of Charges Decisions*.

contributions to offenses need to reach a certain threshold of significance to be within the Court's jurisdiction. It further stated that:[111]

> [A] threshold is necessary to exclude contributions which, because of their level or nature, were clearly not intended by the drafters of the Statute to give rise to individual criminal responsibility. For instance, many members of a community may provide contributions to a criminal organisation in the knowledge of the group's criminality, especially where such criminality is public knowledge. Without some threshold level of assistance, every landlord, every grocer, every utility provider, every secretary, every janitor or even every taxpayer who does anything which contributes to a group committing international crimes could satisfy the elements of 25(3)(d) liability for their infinitesimal contribution to the crimes committed. For these reasons, the Chamber considers that 25(3)(d) liability would become overextended if any contribution were sufficient.

Ultimately the Pre-Trial Chamber I concluded that to be criminally liable under Article 25(3)(d) of the Rome Statute, a person must make a *significant* contribution to the crimes. Other ICC decisions have also supported this view.[112] However, Judge Fernández de Gurmendi rejected the existence of a minimum threshold in her separate opinion in the *Mbarushimana Confirmation of Charges Appeal Decision*, although the majority of the ICC Appeals Chamber did not pronounce itself on this question.[113] There are also other decisions that share Judge Fernández de Gurmendi's interpretation of Article 25(3)(d).[114]

As discussed,[115] there are obvious differences between Article 25(3)(c) and Article 25(3)(d). Nonetheless, the reasoning of the *Mbarushimana Confirmation*

---

111 ICC *Prosecutor v Mbarushimana, Decision on the Confirmation of Charges* (*ICC-01/04-01/10-465-Red*) 277.

112 ICC *Prosecutor v Katanga, Decision Transmitting Additional Legal and Factual Material (Regulation 55(2) and 55(3) of the Regulations of the Court)* (*ICC-01/04-01/07-3371-tENG*) 16, 22; ICC *Prosecutor v Katanga, Trial Chamber Judgment* (*ICC-01/04-01/07-3436-tENG*) 1620, 1632–1636.

113 ICC *Prosecutor v Mbarushimana, Judgment on the Appeal of the Prosecutor against the Confirmation of Charges Decision* (*ICC-01/04-01/10-514*), Separate Opinion of Judge Fernández de Gurmendi, 9–15. Also, on this deicision generally, see DeFalco (n 47) 715.

114 ICC *Prosecutor v Ongwen, Decision on the Confirmation of Charges* (*ICC-02/04-01/15-422-Red*) 71; ICC *Prosecutor v Al Mahdi, Decision on the Confirmation of Charges* (*ICC-01/12-01/15-84-Red*) 27.

115 For a detailed explanation of the differences between the modes of liability of aiding and abetting, on the one hand, and contributing to a group acting with a common purpose, on the other, see Chapter 4, section 3.7.

of Charges Decision regarding Article 25(3)(d)[116] is relevant to Article 25(3)(c) and should also apply thereto. As noted by Ventura, the drafters of the Rome Statute did not intend the mode of liability of aiding and abetting to include every single action that assists the commission of a crime.[117] Instead, the contribution of an aider and abettor should have a substantial effect on the principal's crime, as the jurisprudence of the *ad hoc* Tribunals has correctly established.[118] Otherwise, as noted in *Mbarushimana*, 'every landlord, every grocer, every utility provider, every secretary, every janitor or even every tax-payer' could potentially be held liable.[119]

Moreover, considering any and all contributions to suffice for the *actus reus* requirement of aiding and abetting would be contrary to Article 17(1)(d) of the Rome Statute, which states that 'the Court shall determine that a case is inadmissible where the case is not of sufficient gravity to justify further action by the Court'.[120] The gravity requirement was first introduced in the *1994 draft Code of Crimes against the Peace and Security of Mankind* of the ILC to prevent the Court from being 'swamped by peripheral complaints involving minor offenders, possibly in situations where the major offenders were going free'.[121]

Disregarding the requirement of a 'substantial' contribution could result in the court being overwhelmed by complaints involving minor perpetrators. It is exactly this type of peripheral complaints that the *Ongwen* and *Al Mahdi Confirmation of Charges Decisions* and the *Bemba Trial Judgement* unavoidably would allow.[122]

116 The reasoning of the *Mbarushimana Confirmation of Charges Decision* regarding Article 25(3)(d) was left unaddressed by the *Ongwen* and *Al Mahdi Confirmation of Charges Decisions*, as well as by the *Bemba et al Trial Judgement*.

117 Ventura, 'Aiding and Abetting' (n 55) 210.

118 See Chapter 4, section 4.2.3.1, for more detail on the 'substantial contribution/effect' requirement.

119 ICC *Prosecutor v Mbarushimana, Decision on the Confirmation of Charges* (*ICC-01/04-01/10-465-Red*) 277.

120 Article 17(1)(d) of the Rome Statute of the International Criminal Court 1998 (last amended 2010).

121 'UN General Assembly, Report of the International Law Commission, 4 May 1994, A/CN.4/SR.2330' 9. This contextual interpretation is in accordance with Article 31(3)(c) of the Vienna Convention, which stipulates that '[t]he context for the purpose of the interpretation of a treaty shall comprise, in addition to the text, including its preamble and annexes [... a]ny relevant rules of international law applicable in the relations between the parties'.

122 For more detail on the gravity requirement, see William A Schabas, *The International Criminal Court: A Commentary on the Rome Statute* (2 ed, Oxford University Press 2016) 462–7.

Although at the ICC the exact meaning and scope of the phrase 'gravity' is subject to discussion, the determination of what constitutes a 'substantial' contribution:[123]

> [R]equires a case-by-case assessment, as it is only by examining a person's conduct in proper context that a determination can be made as to whether a given contribution has a larger or smaller effect on the crimes committed.

In any event, '[t]he seriousness of a particular case certainly involves the role and the position played by the suspect in relation to the commission of crimes'.[124]

However, in her separate opinion in the *Mbarushimana Confirmation of Charges Appeal Decision,* Judge Fernández de Gurmendi disagreed with this line of argument and claimed that:[125]

> [T]he threshold of gravity under article 17 (1) (d) of the Statute relates solely to the decision on the admissibility of a case, as a prerequisite for the exercise of the Court's jurisdiction. The Statute clearly distinguishes the definition of the crimes and forms of responsibility from questions relevant to the admissibility of a case. Indeed, if a Chamber considers that a case is not of sufficient gravity, it has the discretion to address the admissibility of the case under the procedural mechanisms established by article 19 of the Statute. Adding limitative criteria to a form of responsibility under the Statute because of the gravity threshold would transfer matters of gravity into the area that determines the individual criminal responsibility of a person, i.e. into the confirmation hearing and trial proceedings.

Although the judge's statement referred to Article 25(3)(d), her reasoning is also relevant to the decisions regarding Article 25(3)(c) by the *Ongwen* and

123 ICC *Prosecutor v Mbarushimana, Decision on the Confirmation of Charges* (*ICC-01/04-01/10-465-Red*) 284.

124 William A Schabas and Mohamed M El Zeidy, 'Article 17: Issues of Admissibility' in Triffterer Otto and Ambos Kai (eds), *The Rome Statute of the International Criminal Court: A Commentary* (3 ed, CH Beck, Hart, Nomos 2016) 814.

125 ICC *Prosecutor v Mbarushimana, Judgment on the Appeal of the Prosecutor against the Confirmation of Charges Decision* (*ICC-01/04-01/10-514*), Separate Opinion of Judge Fernández de Gurmendi, 10.

Al Mahdi Confirmation of Charges Decisions and the *Bemba Trial Judgement*. Judge Fernández de Gurmendi's interpretation of Article 25(3)(d) is problematic because it does not take cognisance of the Rome Statute as a whole. The Rome Statute – like any other treaty – should be read in its entirety, and articles should be interpreted in context and not as isolated provisions.[126]

As mentioned, Article 17(1)(d) requires that a case be considered inadmissible if it is not of sufficient gravity to justify actions by the Court.[127] Thus, allowing a case to proceed when a person's contribution to an offence was *de minimis* would be contrary to the interpretation of the Rome Statute in its entirety.[128]

Moreover, the *Bemba Trial Judgement* was rightly criticized, most notably by Ambos, who pointed out that:[129]

> The lack of an explicit reference to these requirements [*i.e.* a substantial contribution or effect] in the text of the provision [of Article 25(3)(c)] cannot be interpreted as a conscious departure from this standard for Articles 7(1) ICTY and 6(1) ICTR Statute do not contain this reference either.

In fact, the approach to Article 25(3)(a) in the *Bemba Trial Judgement* stands in strong contrast to that of the Court in the *Lubanga Confirmation of Charges Decision*. In *Lubanga*, it was found that the co-perpetrator's contribution must be substantial.[130]

---

126 Article 31(1) of the Vienna Convention on the Law of Treaties, 23 May 1969 states that '[a] treaty shall be interpreted in good faith in accordance with the ordinary meaning to be given to the terms of the treaty in their context and in the light of its object and purpose.'. Furthermore, in ICJ, *Dispute Regarding Navigational and Related Rights (Costa Rica v Nicaragua), Judgment, 13 July 2009*, the Court held that it was 'of the opinion that there is reason to take into account the provisions of the Treaty as a whole [...] in order to draw, if need be, certain necessary implications'.

127 Additionally, article 31(3)(c) Vienna Convention on the Law of Treaties, 23 May 1969, which stipulates that '[t]he context for the purpose of the interpretation of a treaty shall comprise, in addition to the text, including its preamble and annexes [... a]ny relevant rules of international law applicable in the relations between the parties' requires that the Rome Statute be interpreted in a way that is consistent with other international tribunals and courts.

128 This view is also supported by Ventura, 'Aiding and Abetting' (n 55) 211.

129 Kai Ambos, 'Article 25: Individual Criminal Responsibility' in Otto Triffterer and Kai Ambos (eds), *The Rome Statute of the International Criminal Court: A Commentary* (3 ed, Beck/Hart 2016) 1008.

130 ICC *Prosecutor v Lubanga, Decision on the Confirmation of Charges, Pre-Trial Chamber I* (*ICC-01/04-01/06-803-tEN*) 346–8. This approach was upheld in the ICC *Prosecutor v Lubanga, Trial Chamber Judgment* (*ICC-01/04-01/06-2842*) 999–1000; ICC *Prosecutor v*

Except where the text explicitly provides, it is entirely inconsistent to use a certain reasoning for one mode of liability (co-perpetration), and then to state that the same reasoning cannot be applied to another mode of liability (aiding and abetting). There must be consistency in the interpretation of a treaty and in international criminal law more generally. To promote consistency regarding the law of aiding and abetting in all international courts and tribunals, the threshold of 'substantial contribution' as the *actus reus* element must be required. To use one methodology for determining one mode of liability, while using a different approach for another mode of liability, is incompatible with the aim of developing a unified and consistent system of international criminal law. The view that a 'substantial contribution' requirement exists for aiding and abetting is also supported by a large body of scholarly literature on the issue.[131]

Moreover, the jurisprudence on the substantial contribution/effect requirement at the *ad hoc* and hybrid Tribunals is settled. There is no reason to depart from the jurisprudence developed by these Tribunals when it is neither

Lubanga, Appeals Chamber Judgment (*ICC-01/04-01/06-3121-Red*) 469, 473; ICC *Prosecutor v Al Mahdi, Trial Chamber Judgment* (*ICC-01/12-01/15-171*) 19; ICC *Prosecutor v Bemba et al, Trial Judgment* (*ICC-01/05-01/13-1989-Red*) 679, 804. The substantial requirement for co-pertetration stands to this day.

131 Elies van Sliedregt, *Individual Criminal Responsibility in International Law* (Oxford University Press 2012) 128; Kai Ambos, 'Article 25: Individual Criminal Responsibility' (n 129) 1008; Albin Eser, 'Individual Criminal Responsibility' in Antonio Cassese, Paola Gaeta and John RWD Jones (eds), *The Rome Statute of the International Criminal Court: A Commentary* (Oxford University Press 2002) 801; Sarah Finnin, *Elements of Accessorial Modes of Liability: Article 25 (3)(b) and (c) of the Rome Statute of the International Criminal Court* (Brill | Nijhoff 2012) 164; Miles Jackson, *Complicity in International Law* (Oxford University Press 2015) 72; Hector Olasolo Alonso and Enrique Carnero Rojo, 'Forms of Accesorial Liability under Article 25(3)(b) and (c)' in Carsten Stahn (ed), *The Law and the Practice of the International Criminal Court* (Oxford University Press 2015) 587, 590. But see Gerhard Werle and Florian Jessberger, *Principles of International Criminal Law* (3 ed, Oxford University Press 2014) (noting, in passing, that the substantial effect requirement was not found in Article 25[3][c] of the Rome Statute). Furthermore, Flavio Noto, *Secondary Liability in International Criminal Law: A Study on Aiding and Abetting Or Otherwise Assisting the Commission of International Crimes* (Dike 2013)187 argues that 'the Trial Chamber's inclusion [in the Lubanga Trial Chamber Decision] of a substantial effect requirement stretches the wording of Article 25(3)(c), which rather tends towards a qualified mens rea than a restrictive actus reus. The Statue itself does not provide for the latter, and neither do the travaux préparatoires. Most notably, the drafters did not incorporate the rule set out in the 1996 Draft Article 2(3)(d), according to which, the aider must contribute "directly and substantially" to the commission of the crime'; Kai Ambos, *Treatise on International Criminal Law Volume 1: Foundations and General Part* (Oxford University Press 2013) 165.

expressly required by the Rome Statute nor could be deduced from a uniform interpretation of the Rome Statute.[132]

In conclusion, because the *Bemba Appeals Judgement* did not answer the question of whether or not an action must have a substantial effect on the perpetration of the principal's offence to hold a person liable as an aider and abettor, this remains an open question at the ICC. Moreover, the holdings in the *Ongwen* and *Al Mahdi Confirmation of Charges Decisions* and in the *Bemba Trial Judgement* were incorrect in stating that a minimum threshold was not required for the aider and abettor's contribution. Indeed, a person should not be considered an aider and abettor if her contribution is negligible or too small to have a substantial effect on the principal's offence. This would be contrary to the gravity requirement of Article 17(1)(d), contrary to customary international law, and contrary to the aim of advancing consistency within international criminal law.

4.1.1.2 *The Purposive Mens Rea Requirement at the ICC*

Article 25(3)(c) of the Rome Statute requires an aider and abettor to act '[for] the *purpose* of facilitating the commission of [...] a crime'.[133] This purposive mental element imposes an elevated *mens rea* standard compared to the *ad hoc* Tribunals, which have applied a knowledge standard for aiding and abetting.[134] The term 'purpose' also goes beyond the *mens rea* standard in Article 30,[135] which states that: '[u]nless otherwise provided, a person shall be criminally responsible and liable for punishment for a crime [...] only if the material

132 See Article 31(3)(c) Vienna Convention on the Law of Treaties, 23 May 1969, which stipulates that '[t]he context for the purpose of the interpretation of a treaty shall comprise, in addition to the text, including its preamble and annexes [... a]ny relevant rules of international law applicable in the relations between the parties'.

133 Article 25(3)(c) of the Rome Statute of the International Criminal Court 1998 (last amended 2010) emphasis added; STL *Interlocutory Decision on the Applicable Law: Terrorism, Conspiracy, Homicide, Perpetration, Cumulative Charging, Appeals Chamber Judgment* (*STL-11-01/I/AC/R176bis/F0936*) footnote 340; ICC *Prosecutor v Mbarushimana, Decision on the Confirmation of Charges* (*ICC-01/04-01/10-465-Red*) 274, 277; ICC *Prosecutor v Bemba et al, Decision on the Confirmation of Charges, Pre-Trial Chamber I* (*ICC-01/05-01/13-749*) 35; ICC *Prosecutor v Goudé, Decision on the Confirmation of Charges* (*ICC-02/11-02/11-186*) 167, 170; ICC *Prosecutor v Ongwen, Decision on the Confirmation of Charges* (*ICC-02/04-01/15-422-Red*) 43; ICC *Prosecutor v Al Mahdi, Decision on the Confirmation of Charges* (*ICC-01/12-01/15-84-Red*) 26; ICC *Prosecutor v Bemba et al, Trial Judgment* (*ICC-01/05-01/13-1989-Red*) 83.

134 The knowledge standard reflects customary international law. In this regard, see Chapter 4, section 4.2.

135 ICC *Prosecutor v Gombo, Judgment Pursuant to Article 74 of the Statute* (*ICC-01/05-01/13*) 95–98.

elements are committed with intent and knowledge'.[136] The aider and abettor thus 'provides assistance to the commission of a crime and [...] in engaging in this conduct, he or she intends to facilitate the commission of the crime'.[137] As Ventura proposes – correctly in my view – this purposive standard 'should be viewed as a departure from the generally accepted principles of aiding and abetting under customary international law as applicable at the *ad hoc* and hybrid Tribunals'.[138] Therefore, under the Rome Statute the assistance of the aider and abettor is only punishable if a higher standard is satisfied, and the Rome Statute explicitly departs from the jurisprudence developed by the *ad hoc* and hybrid Tribunals.

However, as far as Article 25(3)(c) of the Rome Statute is concerned, there is disagreement in the jurisprudence of the ICC and among scholars about the meaning of the term 'purpose'. 'Purpose', unlike 'intent' and 'knowledge', is not defined in the Rome Statute. Since the Rome Statute was drafted, there have been many attempts to determine what the constitutive elements of the *mens rea* requirement of aiding and abetting are and to define these elements. The first decision to attempt this was the *Mbarushimana Confirmation of Charges Decision*, which held that 'unlike the jurisprudence of the *ad hoc* tribunals [...] knowledge is not enough for responsibility under this article'.[139] In other words, the court established that under the Rome Statute, aiding and abetting requires an elevated *mens rea* standard compared to the knowledge standard of the *ad hoc* Tribunals.

By contrast, the *Bemba Confirmation of Charges Decision* only stated that 'the elements of this mode of liability are met insofar as the accessory's contribution

136 Article 30 of the Rome Statute of the International Criminal Court 1998 (last amended 2010).

137 ICC *Prosecutor v Goudé, Decision on the Confirmation of Charges* (*ICC-02/11-02/11-186*) (n 304) 167.

138 Ventura, 'Aiding and Abetting' (n 55) 222.

139 ICC *Prosecutor v Mbarushimana, Decision on the Confirmation of Charges* (*ICC-01/04-01/10-465-Red*) (n 252) 274. See also paragraphs 281 ('the jurisprudence of the ad hoc tribunals does not require the aider and abettor to share the intent of the perpetrator to commit the crime, whereas under Article 25[3][c] of the Statute the aider and abettor must act with the purpose of facilitating the commission of that crime. There is also scholarly disagreement as to whether the actus reus required should') and 289 ('[d]ifferently from aiding and abetting under Article 25[3][c] of the Statute, for which intent is always required, knowledge is sufficient to incur liability for contributing to a group of persons acting with a common purpose, under Article 25[3][d] of the Statute'), as well as footnote 658 ('Article 25[3][d] allows for the possibility of a person being criminally responsible for acting with a mere knowledge of the group's intent to commit a crime. This is different from article 25[3][c], which sets out a stricter standard of mens rea').

has an effect on the commission of the offence and is made with the purpose of facilitating such commission'.[140] It did not go as far as stating that the *mens rea* requirement for aiding and abetting at the ICC was higher than that at the *ad hoc* Tribunals. Similarly, the *Blé Goudé Confirmation of Charges Decision* found that aiders and abettors were required to have the intent 'to facilitate the commission of the crime'.[141] This Court's statement regarding the elements of Article 25(3)(c) of the Rome Statute was quoted *literatim* and adopted in the *Ongwen* and *Al Mahdi Confirmation of Charges Decisions*.[142] However, neither of these decisions explicitly expressed a view on the relationship between Article 25(3)(c) and Article 30, which states that:

> Unless otherwise provided, a person shall be criminally responsible and liable for punishment for a crime within the jurisdiction of the Court only if the material elements are committed with intent and knowledge.

There is an interpretative void in the jurisprudence of the ICC regarding the role that Article 30 of the Rome Statute (being the default *mens rea* requirement) plays when interpreting the elements of the *mens rea* requirement of aiding and abetting.[143] Scholars have attempted to fill this *lacuna*. Most academics support the *Mbarushimana Confirmation of Charges Decision*. They view the word 'purpose' to entail a stricter *mens rea* requirement than the concept of 'knowledge' as defined by the *ad hoc* Tribunals and Article 30(3) of the Rome Statute.[144] However, there is considerable disagreement about

---

140 ICC *Prosecutor v Bemba et al, Decision on the Confirmation of Charges, Pre-Trial Chamber I* (*ICC-01/05-01/13-749*) 35.

141 ICC *Prosecutor v Goudé, Decision on the Confirmation of Charges* (*ICC-02/11-02/11-186*) 167, 170.

142 ICC *Prosecutor v Ongwen, Decision on the Confirmation of Charges* (*ICC-02/04-01/15-422-Red*) 43; ICC *Prosecutor v Al Mahdi, Decision on the Confirmation of Charges* (*ICC-01/12-01/15-84-Red*) 26. These decisions also cited with approval the formulation contained in the *Bemba et al Confirmation of Charges Decision* in footnotes 43 and 15 respectively.

143 Article 30(2) of the Rome Statute of the International Criminal Court 1998 (last amended 2010) states that 'a person has intent where: (a) In relation to conduct, that person means to engage in the conduct; (b) In relation to a consequence, that person means to cause that consequence or is aware that it will occur in the ordinary course of events'; while Article 30(3) states that: ' "knowledge" means awareness that a circumstance exists or a consequence will occur in the ordinary course of events. "Know" and "knowingly" shall be construed accordingly'.

144 Albin Eser, 'Mental Element - Mistake of Fact and Mistake of Law' in Antonio Cassese, Paola Gaeta and John RWD Jones (eds), *The Rome Statute of the International Criminal Court: A Commentary, Volume 1* (Oxford University Press 2002) 801 ('[purpose] means more than the mere knowledge that the accomplice aids the commission of the offences,

the relationship between Article 25(3)(c) and Article 30. Some suggest that the *mens rea* elements of Article 25(3)(c) and Article 30 apply cumulatively,[145] while others take the position that the application of the *mens rea* element in Article 25(3)(c) displaces that in Article 30.[146]

The *Bemba Trial Judgment* has brought some clarity regarding this issue by interpreting the *mens rea* requirement in Article 25(3)(c) in the light of Article 30 of the Rome Statute:[147]

> Article 30 of the Statute applies to all forms of participation under Article 25 of the Statute, including Article 25(3)(c), 'unless otherwise provided'. Unlike other international instruments, Article 25(3)(c) of the Statute expressly sets forth a specific 'purpose' requirement according to which the assistant must act ('for the purpose of facilitating the commission of such crime'). This wording introduces a higher subjective mental element and means that the accessory must have lent his or her assistance with the aim of facilitating the offence. It is not sufficient that the accessory merely knows that his or her conduct will assist the principal perpetrator in the commission of the offence. Mindful of the twofold intent of the accessory (viz. firstly, the principal offence and, secondly, the accessory's

as would suffice for complicity according to the ICTR and ICTY Statutes'); Van Sliedregt (n 131) 128 ('Article 15[3][c] deviates from the knowledge-based approach to aiding and abetting in the ICTY and ICTR law'); Kai Ambos (n 131) 165–6 ('[purpose] goes beyond the ordinary mens rea requirement within the meaning of Article 30 of the ICC Statute [and] sets aside the […] jurisprudence of the ICTY and the ICTR, since this jurisprudence holds that assistants must only know that their acts will assist the principal in the commission of an offence'); Cryer *et al* (n 23) 374 ('[purpose] is a higher requirement than the "knowledge" required by the ICTY and ICTR'); Jackson (n 131) 50; Ambos, 'Article 25: Individual Criminal Responsibility' (n 129) 1009 ('Article 25[3][c] introduces a subjective threshold which goes beyond the ordinary mens rea requirement within the meaning of article 30' and 'generally implies a specific subjective requirement stricter than mere knowledge'; '[it] therefore, sets aside the […] jurisprudence of the ICTY and ICTR'); Geert-Jan Alexander Knoops, *Mens Rea at the International Criminal Court* (Brill | Nijhoff 2017) 48–9 ('[Article 25[3][c]] differs from the approach taken to aiding and abetting liability at the ad hoc tribunals, where there is only a requirement of knowledge'); Geert-Jan Alexander Knoops, Mens Rea at the International Criminal Court (Brill | Nijhoff 2017) 48, 49 ('Article 25[3][c] […] applies a stricter mens rea requirement than the mens rea requirement for aiding and abetting by the ad hoc tribunals [which recognize knowledge]'; 'it is higher than the general mens rea requirement of article 30').

145 Finnin (n 131) 183, 197; Olasolo Alonso and Carnero Rojo (n 131) 584, 587.

146 Jackson (n 131) 76.

147 ICC *Prosecutor v Bemba et al, Trial Judgment* (*ICC-01/05-01/13-1989-Red*) 97.

> own conduct), the Chamber clarifies that this elevated subjective standard relates to the accessory's facilitation, not the principal offence.

Thus, the Court described the *mens rea* requirement for aiding and abetting according to the Rome Statute to be twofold: firstly, the aider and abettor must have *mens rea* with respect to the principal offence; and secondly, the aider and abettor must have *mens rea* in relation to her own conduct. It also found that the purposive requirement of Article 25(3)(c) for the aider and abettor represents a higher subjective mental element in comparison to that of Article 30. The Trial Chamber continued:[148]

> Additionally, liability for aiding and abetting an offence requires proof that the accessory also had intent with regard to the principal offence pursuant to Article 30 of the Statute, which applies by default. This means that the aider or abettor must at least be aware that the principal perpetrator's offence will occur in the ordinary course of events. Finally, it is not necessary for the accessory to know the precise offence which was intended and which in the specific circumstances was committed, but he or she must be aware of its essential elements.

The Court found that the elevated *mens rea* standard of Article 25(3)(c) only applies to the aider and abettor's own conduct, and not to the consequences of her conduct (the crime perpetrated by the principal, to which the standard of Article 30 applies). Also, according to this decision the aider and abettor must act intentionally, meaning that she must engage in the conduct and be aware that she is carrying out her acts in accordance with Article 30(2)(a) and Article 30(3) and for the purpose of facilitating the crime.

In other words, Article 25(3)(c) adds to the *mens rea* requirement of Article 30 in respect of the aider and abettor's own conduct, whereas the *mens rea* requirement relating to the consequences of the aider and abettor's acts remains that of Article 30. It is therefore sufficient for the aider and abettor to intend to cause the commission of the principal's crime, or to be aware that it could occur in the ordinary course of events.

On appeal the ICC Appeals Chamber mainly addressed the factual errors relating to the Trial Chamber's *mens rea* findings. In fact, the Appeals Chamber did not discuss in any detail the substantive legal requirements of the *mens rea* element of aiding and abetting. It simply stated that an accused did not

148 ibid 98.

have to 'know all the details of the crime in which he or she assists'.[149] The Trial Chamber's Decision is therefore the most current, comprehensive and logical analysis by any ICC Chamber of the meaning of the purposive *mens rea* requirement of Article 25(3)(c).

The *Bemba Trial Judgment Decision* can be contrasted with the ICTY *Popovic Trial Judgement* in which the Court held that:[150]

> Borovčanin knew [...] that a forcible transfer of the civilian population was taking place. In ordering his commanders and units to participate in the operation to move the population, Borovčanin knew that this would assist substantially with the crime of forcible transfer. [...] [T]he Trial Chamber is not satisfied that Borovčanin had any intent to forcibly transfer. Further, the evidence is insufficient to demonstrate that he intended to assist in a forcible transfer. As it is, however, under the jurisprudence of this Tribunal, not only is the accused not required to share the intent of the crime, he or she need not even have the intent to assist with the crime for responsibility through aiding and abetting to attach. It is sufficient for the accused to know that an act will assist the commission of the crime by the principal. The Trial Chamber notes that in the vast majority of cases, the acts of the accused, with the requisite knowledge that it assists a crime, will allow for no other reasonable inference than that the accused intended to assist the commission of an offence. That is, however, not the case in this instance where the participation of Borovčanin's men substantially assisted a crime, but at the same time aided in providing relief to a population facing a humanitarian disaster. The law of the Tribunal however does not allow for a distinction to be drawn on this basis in terms of criminal responsibility.

In *Popovic* the prosecution proved that the accused had allowed his subordinates to transfer civilians, which amounted to the accused's intentional actions. The prosecution was, however, not able to demonstrate that the accused had allowed his troops to forcibly transfer civilians with the purpose of facilitating the crime. However, as correctly noted by the Court, although the accused did not have the intent to assist in the forcible transfer of the population, he was nevertheless responsible for aiding and abetting in the perpetration of the offence because he had the knowledge that his actions assisted the

149 ICC *Prosecutor v Bemba et al, Appeals Chamber Judgment* (*ICC-01/05-01/08-3636-Red*) 1400, 1427–44.

150 ICTY *Prosecutor v Popović et al, Trial Chamber Judgment* (*IT-05-88-T*) 1499–1500.

perpetration of the principals' crime. The Court correctly found that for criminal responsibility to attach, it is not necessary for an aider and abettor to have the intent to assist with the offence. Thus, at the *ad hoc* and hybrid Tribunals the purposive requirement is not necessary; only the knowledge standard is applicable to aiders and abettors (provided that the accused's actions have a substantial effect on the perpetration of the crime).[151]

If the same facts had presented themselves before the ICC, it is far from certain that the accused would have been convicted for aiding and abetting. In fact, the prosecutors at the ICTY proved that Borovčanin had intentionally allowed his subordinates to be used in the forcible transfer of civilians, but not that his act had been committed with the purpose of assisting the principal's crime of forcible transfer. At the ICC the mere awareness on the part of the accused that the crime would occur in the ordinary course is not sufficient to hold the accused responsible for aiding and abetting that crime.

On the one hand, the *Bemba Trial Judgment* reveals that the elevated *mens rea* standard is connected to the aider and abettor's own conduct (*i.e.* mere intentional action is insufficient). On the other hand, it shows that the elevated *mens rea* standard is not applicable to the crime committed by the principal; knowledge of that crime on the part of the aider and abettor is sufficient. This interpretation – that only knowledge is required on the part of the aider and abettor regarding the crime committed by the principal – agrees with the jurisprudence of the *ad hoc* Tribunals and Rome Statute. Additionally, the elevated *mens rea* standard of Article25(3)(c) is applicable to the aider and abettor's intentional acts, which must have been carried out for the purpose of facilitating the principal actor's commission of the crime.

The ITCY in the *Popovic Trial Judgement* noted that if the requisite knowledge on the part of the accused of the crime committed by the principal can be proven, it could lead to an inference that the accused acted for the purpose of facilitating the criminal offence. The Court held that where a positive finding on knowledge can be made, 'in the vast majority of cases [...] it will allow for no other reasonable inference than that the accused intended to assist the commission of an offence'.[152] A similar interpretation can be made from the *Bemba Trial Judgment*, where one of the accused, Babala, advised another, Bemba, to make payments to witnesses to influence their testimony in Court.[153] Babala was convicted for aiding and abetting because of his interference and

151 ibid 1498, 1501.

152 ibid 1500.

153 ICC *Prosecutor v Bemba et al*, *Trial Judgment* (*ICC-01/05-01/13-1989-Red*) 882.

knowledge that 'the payments were illegitimate and aimed at altering and contaminating the witnesses' testimony'.[154]

It should also be noted that the aider and abettor does not have to act with the sole purpose of facilitating the commission of the principal's crime. She might act with multiple purposes, some of them even lawful. For example, in *Popovic* the accused acted with the purpose of facilitating the forcible transfers and for the purpose of providing humanitarian relief.[155] By analogy, the ICC should also take the position that it is permissible for the accused to have had more than one purpose in assisting the principal's offence, as long as one of them was that of facilitating the crime.[156] Such an interpretation of Article 25(3)(c) would be consistent with a plain reading of the text because it does not state that an aider and abettor must act with the sole purpose of facilitating an offence.

In sum, the interpretation of Article 25(3)(c) by the *Bemba Trial Judgment* is the current state of the law applicable at the ICC, because the Appeals Chamber did not avail itself of the opportunity to reject the Trial Judgment's interpretation. The judgment of the Trial Chamber has also gathered academic support and, for all the reasons I have expounded upon, I also accepted it as the correct approach.[157]

In conclusion, this stricter *mens rea* requirement means that an individual who finances an entity that uses the funds to commit core crimes cannot be held liable at the ICC as an aider and abettor, because she lacks the purposive intent to assist the principal in the perpetration of the offence.[158]

4.2 *Aiding and Abetting in Customary International Law*

As with every other mode of liability in international criminal law, aiding and abetting consists of, among other elements, *actus reus* and *mens rea*. Examining the *actus reus* and *mens rea* elements of aiding and abetting in customary

154 ibid 893.

155 ICTY *Prosecutor v Popović et al, Trial Chamber Judgment* (IT-05-88-T) 1500.

156 Finnin (n 131) 202, 203; Ventura, 'Aiding and Abetting' (n 55) 217.

157 Ambos, 'Article 25: Individual Criminal Responsibility' (n 129) 1010 ('it must be noted that the stronger purpose requirement only refers to the act of facilitation, not to the main crime'); Ventura, 'Aiding and Abetting' (n 55) 216; Eser (n 144) 933–34; James G Stewart, 'An Important New Orthodoxy on Complicity in the ICC Statute?' available at <http://jamesgstewart.com/the-important-new-orthodoxy-on-complicity-in-the-icc-statute/> accessed 26 October 2020; Thomas Weigend, 'How to Interpret Complicity in the ICC Statute' available at <jamesgstewart.com/how-to-intepret-complicity-in-the-icc-statute/%0D> accessed 26 October 2020.

158 For an explanation, see for example footnote 87.

international law aids this work by determining under which circumstances an individual could be held liable for financing an entity that is involved in the commission of core crimes. The *ad hoc* and hybrid Tribunals have found that the material element of aiding and abetting requires acts (or omissions) to assist, encourage or lend moral support to crimes.[159] A causal link between the accused's actions and the offence must also reach a required threshold, namely the actions (or omissions) must have had a substantial effect on, or substantially contributed to, the perpetration of the offence.[160] As for the mental element of aiding and abetting, the *ad hoc* and hybrid Tribunals have established that the accused must have acted with the intent and knowledge that her actions (or omissions) assisted the perpetration of the crime.[161] The large body of case law dealing with aiding and abetting has resulted in the crystallisation of core elements that are relatively uncontroversial. However, there are also several disagreements, controversies and points of contention that must be addressed to determine the exact content of the *actus reus* and *mens rea* requirements of aiding and abetting.

This section starts with the uncontroversial elements of aiding and abetting in customary international law. Then, I discuss the contested elements: firstly, the specific direction and the *actus reus* and *mens rea*; secondly, the *actus reus* element of substantial contribution/effect; and thirdly, aiding and abetting's knowledge and intent requirement in customary international law. Addressing the controversial elements aids in clarifying the minimum level of knowledge and intent that an individual who finances an entity involved in the perpetration of core crimes must possess to incur liability.

159 ICTY *Prosecutor v Tihomir Blaškić, Appeals Chamber Judgment* (*IT-95-14-A*) 46; ICTY *Prosecutor v Mrksic et al, Appeals Chamber Judgment* (*IT-95-13/1*) 81; ECCC *Prosecutor v Kaing Guek Eav, Trial Chamber Judgment* (*001/18-07-2007-ECCC/TC/E188*) 533; STL *Interlocutory Decision on the Applicable Law: Terrorism, Conspiracy, Homicide, Perpetration, Cumulative Charging, Appeals Chamber Judgment* (*STL-11-01/I/AC/R176bis/F0936*) 226; SCSL *Prosecutor v Charles Ghankay Taylor, Appeals Chamber Judgment* (*SCSL-03-01-A*) 362, 369, 401, 447, 475, 481–2; ICTY *Prosecutor v Sainovic et al, Appeals Chamber Judgment* (*IT-05-87-A*) 1626, 1649; ICTY *Prosecutor v Popović et al, Appeals Chamber Judgment* (*IT-05-88*) 1732, 1758, 1783, 1812; ICTR *Prosecutor v Nyiramasuhuko et al, Appeals Chamber Judgment* (*ICTR-98-42-A*) 1955, 3332, 3343; MICT *Prosecutor v Vojislav Šešelj, Appeals Chamber Judgment* (*MICT-16-99-A*) 594.

160 For detail on the jurisprudence, see Chapter 4, section 4.2.3.1.

161 For detail on the jurisprudence, see Chapter 4, section 4.2.3.1.

4.2.1 Uncontroversial Elements of *Actus Reus* in Customary International Law

The characteristics of the *actus reus* element of aiding and abetting regarding which there is general agreement at the *ad hoc* and hybrid Tribunals, are as follows:

- The *actus reus* can occur prior to, during or after the perpetration of the crime.[162]
- Liability for aiding and abetting might arise from assisting the principal in the planning, preparation or execution of a plan, policy, programme or strategy.[163]
- The aider and abettor does not need to be physically present during the commission of the crime.[164]

---

162 See notably ICTY *Prosecutor v Tihomir Blaškić, Appeals Chamber Judgment* (*IT-95-14-A*) 48; ICTY *Prosecutor v Ntagerura et al, Appeals Chamber Judgment* (*ICTR-99-46*) 372; ICTY *Prosecutor v Simić et al, Appeals Chamber Judgment* (*IT-95-9-A*) 85; ICTY *Prosecutor v Vidoje Blagojevic and Dragan Jokic, Appeals Chamber Judgment* (*IT-02-60-A*) 127; SCSL *Prosecutor v Brima et al, Trial Chamber Judgment* (*SCSL-04-16-T*) 775; ICTR *Prosecutor v Ferdinand Nahimana et al, Appeals Chamber Judgment* (*ICTR-99-52-A*) 482; SCSL *Prosecutor v Moinina Fofana and Allieu Kondewa, Appeals Chamber Judgment* (*SCSL-04-14-A-829*) 71–2; ICTY *Prosecutor v Mrksic et al, Appeals Chamber Judgment* (*IT-95-13/1*) 81; ICTR *Kalimanzira v Prosecutor, Appeals Chamber Judgment* (*ICTR-05-88-A*) 238; STL *Interlocutory Decision on the Applicable Law: Terrorism, Conspiracy, Homicide, Perpetration, Cumulative Charging, Appeals Chamber Judgment* (*STL-11-01/I/AC/R176bis/F0936*) 226; SCSL *Prosecutor v Charles Ghankay Taylor, Appeals Chamber Judgment* (*SCSL-03-01-A*) 367; ICTR *Prosecutor v Nyiramasuhuko et al, Appeals Chamber Judgment* (*ICTR-98-42-A*) 3332, 3343; ICC *Prosecutor v Bemba et al, Trial Judgment* (*ICC-01/05-01/13-1989-Red*) 96; ICC *Prosecutor v Bemba et al, Appeals Chamber Judgment* (*ICC-01/05-01/08-3636-Red*) 1399.

163 See notably ICTY *Prosecutor v Radislav Krstic, Appeals Chamber Judgment* (*IT-98-33-A*) 137; SCSL *Prosecutor v Charles Ghankay Taylor, Appeals Chamber Judgment* (*SCSL-03-01-A*) 378, 383–385.

164 See notably ICTY *Prosecution v Delalic et al, Appeals Chamber Judgment* (*IT-96-21-A*) 352; ICTY *Prosecutor v Tihomir Blaškić, Appeals Chamber Judgment* (*IT-95-14-A*) 48; ICTY *Prosecutor v Ntagerura et al, Appeals Chamber Judgment* (*ICTR-99-46*) 372; ICTY *Prosecutor v Simić et al, Appeals Chamber Judgment* (*IT-95-9-A*) 85; SCSL *Prosecutor v Moinina Fofana and Allieu Kondewa, Appeals Chamber Judgment* (*SCSL-04-14-A-829*) 71–2; ICTY *Prosecutor v Mrkšić and Šljivančanin, Appeals Chamber Judgment* (*IT-95-13/1-A*) 81; ICTR *Kalimanzira v Prosecutor, Appeals Chamber Judgment* (*ICTR-05-88-A*) 238; SCSL *Prosecutor v Charles Ghankay Taylor, Appeals Chamber Judgment* (*SCSL-03-01-A*) 370; ICTR *Prosecutor v Nyiramasuhuko et al, Appeals Chamber Judgment* (*ICTR-98-42-A*) 3332; ICC *Prosecutor v Bemba et al, Trial Judgment* (*ICC-01/05-01/13-1989-Red*) 96.

- The *actus reus* of the aider and abettor does not need to be specifically directed to assist, encourage or lend moral support to the perpetration of the offence.[165]
- No conviction for aiding and abetting may occur for an inchoate offence; conviction may only follow for fully executed crimes.[166]

A causal link between the actions of the aider and abettor and the crime must also exist. In this regard the requirement of a 'substantial contribution to/effect on' the crime emerges from the jurisprudence of the *ad hoc* and hybrid Tribunals. There is general agreement about the following features of the requirement of a 'substantial contribution to/effect on' the crime:

- The question of whether or not the aider and abettor's actions meet the requirement of a 'substantial contribution/effect on' the crime entails a fact-based inquiry, on a case-by-case basis, based on the evidence as a whole.[167]
- To satisfy the *actus reus* requirement, it is not necessary to prove that every single action individually constituted a substantial contribution to the crime of the principal; it is sufficient to show that all the aider and abettor's acts cumulatively substantially contributed to the offence.[168]

---

165 The issue of the 'specific direction' requirement in the *actus reus* of aiding and abetting was a matter of controversy in international criminal law, but it has since been settled. See notably ICTY *Prosecutor v Perisic, Appeals Chamber Judgment* (*IT-04-81-A*); ICTY *Prosecutor v Perisic, Trial Chamber Judgment* (*IT-04-81-T*); ICTY *Prosecutor v Mrksic et al, Appeals Chamber Judgment* (*IT-95-13/1*) 159; SCSL *Prosecutor v Charles Ghankay Taylor, Appeals Chamber Judgment* (*SCSL-03-01-A*) 466–81; ICTY *Prosecutor v Sainovic et al, Appeals Chamber Judgment* (*IT-05-87-A*) 1617–51; ICTY *Prosecutor v Popović et al, Appeals Chamber Judgment* (*IT-05-88*) 1764.

166 See notably ICTY *Prosecutor v Zlatko Aleksovski, Appeals Chamber Judgment* (*IT-95-14/1-A*) 165; ICTY *Prosecutor v Orić, Trial Chamber Judgment* (*IT-03-68-T*) 281; SCSL *Prosecutor v Brima et al, Trial Chamber Judgment* (*SCSL-04-16-T*) 775; ICTY *Prosecutor v Popović et al, Trial Chamber Judgment* (*IT-05-88-T*) 1015; ECCC *Prosecutor v Kaing Guek Eav, Trial Chamber Judgment* (*001/18-07-2007-ECCC/TC/E188*) 534. Importantly, at the ICC, an aider and abettor may be convicted for an incohate offence according to Article 25(3)(c) of the Rome Statute.

167 See notably ICTY *Prosecutor v Vidoje Blagojevic and Dragan Jokic, Appeals Chamber Judgment* (*IT-02-60-A*) 134; ICTY *Prosecutor v Mrkšić and Šljivančanin, Appeals Chamber Judgment* (*IT-95-13/1-A*) 200; *ICTR Kalimanzira v Prosecutor, Appeals Chamber Judgment* (*ICTR-05-88-A*) 86; ICTR *Rukundo v Prosecutor, Appeals Chamber Judgment* (*ICTR-2001-70-A*) 52; ICTY *Prosecutor v Lukić and Lukić, Appeals Chamber Judgment* (*IT-98-32/1-T*) 438; SCSL *Prosecutor v Charles Ghankay Taylor, Appeals Chamber Judgment* (*SCSL-03-01-A*) 370; ICTR *Prosecutor v Nyiramasuhuko et al, Appeals Chamber Judgment* (*ICTR-98-42-A*) 3332.

168 See notably, ICTY *Prosecutor v Vidoje Blagojevic and Dragan Jokic, Appeals Chamber Judgment* (*IT-02-60-A*) 284; SCSL *Prosecutor v Charles Ghankay Taylor, Appeals Chamber Judgment* (*SCSL-03-01-A*) footnote 1128.

– The contributions of the aider and abettor do not need to be a *conditio sine qua non* for the commission of the crime by the principal; in fact, it is neither necessary to prove that her contribution served as a precondition to the crime nor that the crime would not have been perpetrated without her contribution.[169]

Other characteristics of the requirement of a 'substantial contribution to/effect on' the crime are contested and discussed in detail in section 4.2.3.2.

Regarding the principal perpetrator:

– Evidence of a plan or agreement between the aider and abettor and the principal is not required.[170]
– It is not required for the principal to know of the existence of the aider and abettor or of her contribution.[171]
– The assistance does not need to be given directly to and used by the principal in the commission of the offence; the essential question is whether the aider and abettor's actions substantially contributed to the perpetration of the crime.[172]

---

169 See notably, ICTY *Prosecutor v Zlatko Aleksovski, Appeals Chamber Judgment* (*IT-95-14/1-A*) 164; ICTY *Prosecutor v Tihomir Blaškić, Appeals Chamber Judgment* (*IT-95-14-A*) 48; ICTY *Prosecutor v Simić et al, Appeals Chamber Judgment* (*IT-95-9-A*) 85; ICTY *Prosecutor v Vidoje Blagojevic and Dragan Jokic, Appeals Chamber Judgment* (*IT-02-60-A*) 127, 134; ICTY *Prosecutor v Mrksic et al, Appeals Chamber Judgment* (*IT-95-13/1*) 81; ICTR *Kalimanzira v Prosecutor, Appeals Chamber Judgment* (*ICTR-05-88-A*) 86; ICTR *Rukundo v Prosecutor, Appeals Chamber Judgment* (*ICTR-2001-70-A*) 52; ICTR *Prosecutor v Nyiramasuhuko et al, Appeals Chamber Judgment* (*ICTR-98-42-A*) 2083, 3332, 3343; ICC *Prosecutor v Bemba et al, Trial Judgment* (*ICC-01/05-01/13-1989-Red*) 94.

170 See notably, ICTY *Prosecutor v Dusko Tadic, Appeals Chamber Judgment* (*IT-94-1-A*) 229(ii); ICTY *Prosecutor v Brđanin, Appeals Chamber Judgment* (*IT-99-36*) 263; ECCC *Prosecutor v Kaing Guek Eav, Trial Chamber Judgment* (*001/18-07-2007-ECCC/TC/E188*) 534.

171 There is an exception to this rule, namely that of *ex post facto* aiding and abetting. However, this exception is not relevant to the situation discussed in this work. See notably ICTY *Prosecutor v Dusko Tadic, Appeals Chamber Judgment* (*IT-94-1-A*) 229(ii); ICTY *Prosecutor v Vasiljević, Appeals Chamber Judgment* (*IT-98-32-A*) 102; ICTY *Prosecutor v Brđanin, Appeals Chamber Judgment* (*IT-99-36*) 349; STL *Interlocutory Decision on the Applicable Law: Terrorism, Conspiracy, Homicide, Perpetration, Cumulative Charging, Appeals Chamber Judgment* (*STL-11-01/I/AC/R176bis/F0936*) 227; SCSL *Prosecutor v Charles Ghankay Taylor, Appeals Chamber Judgment* (*SCSL-03-01-A*) 370; ICTR *Prosecutor v Nyiramasuhuko et al, Appeals Chamber Judgment* (*ICTR-98-42-A*) 3332; ICTR *Kalimanzira v Prosecutor, Appeals Chamber Judgment* (*ICTR-05-88-A*) 87.

172 See notably, SCSL *Prosecutor v Charles Ghankay Taylor, Appeals Chamber Judgment* (*SCSL-03-01-A*) 367–68, 401; ICC *Prosecutor v Bemba et al, Appeals Chamber Judgment* (*ICC-01/05-01/08-3636-Red*) 7, 19, 1329.

- The assistance may be provided directly to the principal or to an intermediary.[173]
- Criminal liability may be established by determining the effect the assistance of the aider and abettor had on the commission of the crime by the principal, and not by examining the relationship between the aider and abettor and the principal or the ways in which the assistance was provided.[174]
- It is not necessary for the principal perpetrator to have been identified, tried or convicted for liability to ensue for the aider and abettor; only the crimes with which the aider and abettor has been charged must be established.[175]

In sum, with regard to the material elements of aiding and abetting: (i) an aider and abettor who provides financing used in the perpetration of a core crime does not need to be physically present during the commission of the crime; (ii) her financial assistance need not be specifically directed to assisting the principal's crime; (iii) the total of her financial assistance must be substantial, but does not need to be a *conditio sine qua non* for the commission of the crime by the principal; (iv) her financial assistance can be provided directly to the principal or to an intermediary; (v) the principal must have executed the crime; (vi) the principal and the aider and abettor who provided financing need not have a plan or agreement; (vii) the principal does not need to know that she received financial assistance from the aider and abettor; and (viii) the

173 See notably, ICTY *Prosecutor v Orić, Trial Chamber Judgment* (*IT-03-68-T*) 282, 285; SCSL *Prosecutor v Brima et al, Trial Chamber Judgment* (*SCSL-04-16-T*) 775; ICC *Prosecutor v Bemba et al, Trial Judgment* (*ICC-01/05-01/13-1989-Red*) 96; ICC *Prosecutor v Bemba et al, Appeals Chamber Judgment* (*ICC-01/05-01/08-3636-Red*) 1328–30.

174 See notably, SCSL *Prosecutor v Charles Ghankay Taylor, Appeals Chamber Judgment* (*SCSL-03-01-A*) 366–8, 370–1; ICC *Prosecutor v Bemba et al, Appeals Chamber Judgment* (*ICC-01/05-01/08-3636-Red*) 19, 1329; ICTY *Prosecutor v Dusko Tadic, Appeals Chamber Judgment* (*IT-94-1-A*) 229(ii); ICTY *Prosecutor v Tihomir Blaškić, Appeals Chamber Judgment* (*IT-95-14-A*) 46; ICTY *Prosecutor v Ntagerura et al, Appeals Chamber Judgment* (*ICTR-99-46*) 370; ICTY *Prosecutor v Brđanin, Appeals Chamber Judgment* (*IT-99-36*) 151, 348.

175 See notably ICTY *Prosecutor v Zlatko Aleksovski, Appeals Chamber Judgment* (*IT-95-14/1-A*) 165; ICTY *Prosecutor v Vasiljević, Appeals Chamber Judgment* (*IT-98-32-A*) 143; ICTY *Prosecutor v Radislav Krstic, Appeals Chamber Judgment* (*IT-98-33-A*) 143; ICTY *Prosecutor v Brđanin, Appeals Chamber Judgment* (*IT-99-36*) 355; ICTY *Prosecutor v Popović et al, Trial Chamber Judgment* (*IT-05-88-T*) 1016; ECCC *Prosecutor v Kaing Guek Eav, Trial Chamber Judgment* (*001/18-07-2007-ECCC/TC/E188*) 534; ICTY *Prosecutor v Perisic, Trial Chamber Judgment* (*IT-04-81-T*) 127; SCSL *Prosecutor v Charles Ghankay Taylor, Appeals Chamber Judgment* (*SCSL-03-01-A*) 370; ICC *Prosecutor v Bemba et al, Trial Judgment* (*ICC-01/05-01/13-1989-Red*) 84.

principal does not need to have been identified, tried or convicted for the aider and abettor to be liable.

4.2.2 Uncontroversial Elements of *Mens Rea* in Customary International Law

The general, commonly agreed upon characteristics of the *mens rea* requirement of aiding and abetting at the *ad hoc* and hybrid Tribunals are as follows:

- The individual who financed an organisation that committed a core crime need not know the exact offence that was intended or that was in fact committed by the principal, but she must be aware of its essential elements, including the state of mind of the principal.[176]
- Recklessness is insufficient to establish liability for an aider and abettor; in fact, even her acceptance that her assistance would be a possible consequence of her conduct is insufficient.[177]
- It is not necessary for the aider and abettor to share the intent of the principal.[178]

---

176 See notably ICTY *Prosecutor v Zlatko Aleksovski, Appeals Chamber Judgment* (*IT-95-14/1-A*) 162, 165; ICTY *Prosecutor v Krnojelac, Appeals Chamber Judgment* (*IT-97-25*) 51–2; ICTY *Prosecutor v Tihomir Blaškić, Appeals Chamber Judgment* (*IT-95-14-A*) 50; ICTY *Prosecutor v Simić et al, Appeals Chamber Judgment* (*IT-95-9-A*) 86; ICTY *Prosecutor v Brđanin, Appeals Chamber Judgment* (*IT-99-36*) 484; ICTY *Prosecutor v Vidoje Blagojevic and Dragan Jokic, Appeals Chamber Judgment* (*IT-02-60-A*) 221; ICTR *Prosecutor v Ferdinand Nahimana et al, Appeals Chamber Judgment* (*ICTR-99-52-A*) 482; ICTY *Prosecutor v Orić, Appeals Chamber Judgment* (*IT-03-68*) 43; ICTR *Karera v Prosecutor, Appeals Chamber Judgment* (*ICTR-01-74-A*) 321; ICTY *Prosecutor v Mrkšić and Šljivančanin, Appeals Chamber Judgment* (*IT-95-13/1-A*) 159; ICTY *Prosecutor v Lukić and Lukić, Appeals Chamber Judgment* (*IT-98-32/1-T*) 440; ICTY *Prosecutor v Perisic, Appeals Chamber Judgment* (*IT-04-81-A*) 48; ICTR *Prosecutor v Nyiramasuhuko et al, Appeals Chamber Judgment* (*ICTR-98-42-A*) 2255; ICC *Prosecutor v Bemba et al, Trial Judgment* (*ICC-01/05-01/13-1989-Red*) 98; ICC *Prosecutor v Bemba et al, Appeals Chamber Judgment* (*ICC-01/05-01/08-3636-Red*) 21, 1400.

177 The issue of the minimum threshold of intent is discussed in more detail in Chapter 4, section 4.2.3.2.2. See notably ICTY *Prosecutor v Tihomir Blaškić, Appeals Chamber Judgment* (*IT-95-14-A*) 49; ICTY *Prosecutor v Mrkšić and Šljivančanin, Appeals Chamber Judgment* (*IT-95-13/1-A*) 159; but see also SCSL *Prosecutor v Moinina Fofana and Allieu Kondewa, Appeals Chamber Judgment* (*SCSL-04-14-A-829*) 366; SCSL *Prosecutor v Charles Ghankay Taylor, Appeals Chamber Judgment* (*SCSL-03-01-A*) 414, 438, 533, and footnotes 1284, 1363–4.

178 See notably ICTY *Prosecutor v Zlatko Aleksovski, Appeals Chamber Judgment* (*IT-95-14/1-A*) 162; ICTY *Prosecutor v Radislav Krstic, Appeals Chamber Judgment* (*IT-98-33-A*) 140; ICTY *Prosecutor v Simić et al, Appeals Chamber Judgment* (*IT-95-9-A*) 86; SCSL *Prosecutor v Moinina Fofana and Allieu Kondewa, Appeals Chamber Judgment* (*SCSL-04-14-A-829*) 367; ECCC *Prosecutor v Kaing Guek Eav, Trial Chamber Judgment* (*001/18-07-2007-ECCC/TC/E188*) 535; STL *Interlocutory Decision on the Applicable Law: Terrorism, Conspiracy, Homicide, Perpetration, Cumulative Charging, Appeals Chamber Judgment* (*STL-11-01/I/*

- The accused need not have acted for the purpose of aiding the perpetration of the offence.[179]

In sum, concerning the mental element of aiding and abetting: (i) to be liable an aider and abettor who provides financing to an entity that perpetrates core crimes need not know the exact offence perpetrated by the principal; it is sufficient that she knows that her financial assistance is in furtherance of a certain kind of offence; (ii) recklessly assisting the principal does not lead to liability, nor does the aider and abettor need to share the principal's intent, even when the principal is required to act with special intent (for example for the crime of genocide); and (iii) she does not need to purposefully aid the principal's crime with her financial assistance.

Now that the uncontested elements have been laid down, the following section examines the elements that are still in need of clarification.

4.2.3 Contested Elements of *Actus Reus* and *Mens Rea* in Customary International Law

As seen above,[180] there are many core elements in customary international law upon which the *ad hoc* and hybrid Tribunals and scholars agree regarding the material and mental elements of aiding and abetting. However, there are also issues with regard to which there is (or was) no general agreement. This section discusses the following contested elements that have been resolved: specific direction and the *actus reus* and *mens rea* requirements (section 4.2.3.1), and the *mens rea* element of substantial contribution/effect (section 4.2.3.2).[181]

AC/R176bis/F0936) 225; ICC *Prosecutor v Mbarushimana, Decision on the Confirmation of Charges* (ICC-01/04-01/10-465-Red) 281.

179 See notably ICTY *Prosecutor v Zlatko Aleksovski, Appeals Chamber Judgment* (IT-95-14/1-A) 162; ICTY *Prosecutor v Radislav Krstic, Appeals Chamber Judgment* (IT-98-33-A) 140; ICTY *Prosecutor v Simić et al, Appeals Chamber Judgment* (IT-95-9-A) 86; SCSL *Prosecutor v Moinina Fofana and Allieu Kondewa, Appeals Chamber Judgment* (SCSL-04-14-A-829) 367; ECCC *Prosecutor v Kaing Guek Eav, Trial Chamber Judgment* (001/18-07-2007-ECCC/TC/E188) 535; STL *Interlocutory Decision on the Applicable Law: Terrorism, Conspiracy, Homicide, Perpetration, Cumulative Charging, Appeals Chamber Judgment* (STL-11-01/I/AC/R176bis/F0936) 225; ICC *Prosecutor v Mbarushimana, Decision on the Confirmation of Charges* (ICC-01/04-01/10-465-Red) 281.

180 See Chapter 4, sections 4.2.1 and 4.2.2.

181 There are other contested areas that are not relevant for the purpose of this work, including the following questions: the prior agreement and *ex post facto* aiding and abetting; the criminal law duty to act and aiding and abetting by omission; complicity in genocide *versus* aiding and abetting genocide; and encouragement or moral support and the principal perpetrators. For a discussion on issues concerning a prior agreement and *ex post facto* aiding and abetting, a criminal law duty to act and aiding and abetting, complicity in

It also exposes the lack of clarity regarding the minimum level of knowledge and intent required to hold an aider and abettor liable (section 4.2.3.3).

4.2.3.1 *Specific Direction and the* Actus Reus *and* Mens Rea *Requirements*

In recent times aiding and abetting has been at the centre of a controversy in international criminal law, largely because of the 'specific direction' saga, which originated at the ICTY, then made its way to the SCSL, only to return to the ICTY. The dispute originated in the 1999 *Tadic Appeal Judgment* where the ICTY described aiding and abetting liability as 'acts specifically directed to assist, encourage or lend moral support to the perpetration of a certain specific crime [...] and this support has a substantial effect upon the perpetration of the crime'.[182] This statement was incidental and without any in-depth analysis or reference to sources. In fact, the *Tadic Appeal Judgment* made this statement in the context of trying to draw a distinction between aiding and abetting and JCE as modes of liability.

As time passed several subsequent appeal judgments of the ICTY and ICTR also mentioned this 'specific direction' requirement (either in those explicit terms or by way of alternative formulations, such as 'aimed specifically', 'specifically aimed', or 'directed to').[183] There was, however, also several cases that did refer to the specific direction requirement at all in describing the *actus reus* requirement of aiding and abetting.[184] This divergence in the case law

genocide *versus* aiding and abetting genocide, and encouragement or moral support and the principal perpetrators, see Ventura, 'Aiding and Abetting' (n 55) 190–252.

182 ICTY *Prosecutor v Dusko Tadic, Appeals Chamber Judgment* (*IT-94-1-A*) 229 (iii).

183 ICTY *Prosecutor v Zlatko Aleksovski, Appeals Chamber Judgment* (*IT-95-14/1-A*) 163; ICTY *Prosecutor v Vasiljević, Appeals Chamber Judgment* (*IT-98-32-A*) 102(i), 134–5; ICTY *Prosecutor v Kvočka et al, Appeals Chamber Judgment* (*IT-98-30/1*) 89; ICTY *Prosecutor v Vidoje Blagojevic and Dragan Jokic, Appeals Chamber Judgment* (*IT-02-60-A*) 127; ICTR *Kalimanzira v Prosecutor, Appeals Chamber Judgment* (*ICTR-05-88-A*) 74; For alternative formulations, see ICTY *Prosecutor v Ntagerura et al, Appeals Chamber Judgment* (*ICTR-99-46*) 370 ('specifically aimed'); ICTY *Prosecutor v Simić et al, Appeals Chamber Judgment* (*IT-95-9-A*) 85 ('directed to'); ICTY *Prosecutor v Orić, Appeals Chamber Judgment* (*IT-03-68*) 43 ('directed to'); ICTR *Rukundo v Prosecutor, Appeals Chamber Judgment* (*ICTR-2001-70-A*) 52 ('specifically aimed').

184 ICTY *Prosecution v Delalic et al, Appeals Chamber Judgment* (*IT-96-21-A*) 353 (see also contra paragraph 345); ICTY *Prosecutor v Krnojelac, Appeals Chamber Judgment* (*IT-97-25*) 37 (but see contra paragraph 33); ICTY *Prosecutor v Radislav Krstic, Appeals Chamber Judgment* (*IT-98-33-A*) 137; ICTY *Prosecutor v Tihomir Blaškić, Appeals Chamber Judgment* (*IT-95-14-A*) 46 (but see contra paragraph 45); ICTY *Prosecutor v Brđanin, Appeals Chamber Judgment* (*IT-99-36*) 151; ICTR *Karera v Prosecutor, Appeals Chamber Judgment* (*ICTR-01-74-A*) 321; ICTY *Prosecutor v Gotovina and Markac, Appeals Chamber Judgment* (*IT-06-90-A*) 127; but also see ICTY *Prosecutor v Anto Furundzija, Trial Chamber Judgment* (*IT-95-17/1-T*) 234–5, 249 (in which the elements of aiding and abetting were discussed after an analysis

was only addressed in the *Blagojevic and Jokic Appeal Judgment*. Unfortunately, this holding on specific direction led to even greater confusion. It set out to review previous decisions, notably the *Tadic Appeal Judgement* (which had mentioned the specific direction requirement of aiding and abetting to contrast this mode of liability with JCE), and the *Blaškić Appeal Judgment* (which cited with approval the *Vasiljevi Appeal Judgment* and the *Furundžija Trial Judgment*, although these judgments assumed conflicting positions on specific direction).[185] The *Blagojevic and Jokic Appeal Judgment* observed that:[186]

> [W]hile the Tadic definition has not been explicitly departed from, specific direction has not always been included as an element of the *actus reus* of aiding and abetting. This may be explained by the fact that such a finding will often be implicit in the finding that the accused has provided practical assistance to the principal perpetrator which had a substantial effect on the commission of the crime.

In so finding the Appeals Chamber failed to articulate a clear position on whether specific direction was a requirement of aiding and abetting.[187]

Two years later, in the *Mrkšić and Šljivančanin Appeal Judgment*, the Appeals Chamber stated that 'specific direction' was not 'an essential requirement' of aiding and abetting liability.[188] It relied on *Blagojevic and Jokic*, which was much more ambiguous on the matter than the *Mrkšić and Šljivančanin* Appeals Chamber was willing to concede.

In the *Lukić and Lukić Appeal Judgment* the Appeals Chamber held, with reference to the *Blagojevic and Jokic* and the *Mrkšić and Šljivančanin Appeal Judgments*, that there was no reason to depart from established caselaw. It thus found 'specific direction' was not an 'essential requirement' of aiding and abetting.[189]

This issue came to a head with the 2013 *Perisic Appeal Judgment*.[190] The Appeals Chamber held that 'specific direction' was an essential element of the *actus reus* requirement of aiding and abetting. It began by noting that

---

of customary international law. The articulation of the *actus reus* did not include the specific direction requirement).

185 ICTY *Prosecutor v Vidoje Blagojevic and Dragan Jokic, Appeals Chamber Judgment* (IT-02-60-A) 185–8.

186 ibid 189.

187 ibid 189.

188 ICTY *Prosecutor v Mrkšić and Šljivančanin, Appeals Chamber Judgment* (IT-95-13/1-A) 159.

189 ICTY *Prosecutor v Lukić and Lukić, Appeals Chamber Judgment* (IT-98-32/1-T) 424.

190 ICTY *Prosecutor v Perisic, Appeals Chamber Judgment* (IT-04-81-A).

the 'specific direction' requirement had originated with the *Tadic Appeal Judgement* and that most of the subsequent judgments of the ICTY and ICTR incorporated the *Tadic* definition *verbatim*.[191] Next, it held that *Mrkšić and Šljivančanin* should not be understood to mean that 'specific direction' was not an element at all, but, rather, that this element was often satisfied implicitly through the 'substantial contribution' requirement.[192] In addition, the *Perisic* Appeals Chamber carefully examined *Blagojevic and Jokic* and *Lukić and Lukić*, and concluded that these cases had found no reason to depart from established case law. Thus, 'specific direction' remains an element of aiding and abetting.[193]

Moreover, the Appeals Chamber in *Perisic* mentioned that previous judgments had not fully analysed the specific direction requirement because of 'the fact that prior convictions for aiding and abetting [...] involved relevant acts geographically or otherwise proximate to, and thus not remote from, the crimes of principal perpetrators'.[194] This means that the specific direction requirement could be demonstrated implicitly from the factual context, since the accused was usually present at the crime scene.[195] However, in circumstances where the accused is remote from the crime scene it might be necessary to consider it explicitly to prove specific direction. According to the Appeals Chamber this 'remoteness' consideration would depend on the specific circumstances of each case, but could include geographic distance among other factors.[196]

This decision, however, was not unanimous. Judges Liu and Ramaroson rejected the special direction requirement. Judge Liu noted that 'the jurisprudence of the Tribunal demonstrates that aiding and abetting liability may be established without requiring that the acts of the accused were specifically directed to a crime'.[197] He was not convinced that 'specific direction is an essential element of the *actus reus* of aiding and abetting liability', nor that 'it is necessary to explicitly consider specific direction in cases where the aider and abettor is remote from the relevant crimes'.[198] He commented that, '[g]iven

191 ibid 26–31.
192 ibid 26–31.
193 ibid 35–6.
194 ibid 38.
195 ibid 40.
196 ibid 40.
197 ibid Separate Opinion of Judge Liu, 2 (referring to ICTY *Prosecutor v Mrksic et al, Appeals Chamber Judgment* (IT-95-13/1) 159; and to ICTY *Prosecutor v Lukić and Lukić, Appeals Chamber Judgment* (IT-98-32/1-T) 424).
198 ICTY *Prosecutor v Perisic, Appeals Chamber Judgment* (IT-04-81-A) Separate Opinion of Judge Liu, 2.

that specific direction has not been applied in past cases with any rigor, to insist on such a requirement now effectively raises the threshold for aiding and abetting liability'.[199]

Similarly, Judge Ramaroson found that specific direction was not an explicit requirement of the *actus reus* requirement of aiding and abetting, but that it is implicit in the *mens rea* requirement.[200] Based on the facts of this case the accused's actions did not satisfy the *mens rea* requirement of aiding and abetting.[201] Regarding the remoteness consideration, with reference to *Simić* and *Blaškić*, Judge Ramaroson stated that acts of complicity can be remote from the crime scene without having to be 'specifically directed'.[202] She emphasised that the Appeals Chamber had introduced 'a new distinction in the law of aiding and abetting by declaring that in cases where the accused is remote from the scene of the crime, specific direction must be explicitly analysed'.[203]

In their joint but separate opinions, Judges Meron and Agius held that specific direction could be part of the *mens rea* or the *actus reus* requirements[204] and that:[205]

> [W]ere we setting out the elements of aiding and abetting outside the context of the Tribunal's past jurisprudence, we would consider categorising specific direction as an element of *mens rea*. However, we are satisfied that specific direction can also, as the Appeal Judgement's analysis demonstrates, be reasonably assessed in the context of *actus reus*.

Seven months after the *Perisic* judgment, the SCSL Appeals Chamber rejected the specific direction standard in the *Taylor Appeals Judgment*. The defence framed the specific direction requirement as mainly relating to the element of *mens rea*. The defence also argued that the 'knowledge' *mens rea* requirement applied by the Trial Chamber was erroneous, and that 'purpose' was in fact

199 ibid Separate Opinion of Judge Liu, 3.
200 ibid Separate Opinion of Judge Ramaroson, 8. Unofficial translation by the author.
201 ibid Separate Opinion of Judge Ramaroson, 2–10.
202 ibid Separate Opinion of Judge Ramaroson; 8 (referring to ICTY *Prosecutor v Simić et al, Appeals Chamber Judgment* (IT-95-9-A) 85; and ICTY *Prosecutor v Tihomir Blaškić, Appeals Chamber Judgment* (IT-95-14-A) 48).
203 ICTY *Prosecutor v Perisic, Appeals Chamber Judgment* (IT-04-81-A) Separate Opinion of Judge Ramaroson, 8. This constitutes the author's translation from the French.
204 A similar view was expressed by Judge Afande in the ICTY *Prosecutor v Stanišić and Simatović, Appeals Chamber Judgment* (IT-03-69-A) 30.
205 ICTY *Prosecutor v Perisic, Appeals Chamber Judgment* (IT-04-81-A) Separate opinion of Judges Meron and Agius, 2–4.

the correct *mens rea* standard. The defence argued that the 'purpose' standard corresponded with the concept of 'specific direction' discussed in the ICTY jurisprudence.[206]

However, the SCSL Appeals Chamber found that *Perisic* had followed certain ICTY precedents concerning the specific direction requirement, rather than applying customary international law on aiding and abetting.[207] In considering the *mens rea* argument the SCSL Appeals Chamber analysed in depth the World War II tribunal precedents, the 1996 International Criminal Law *Draft Code of Crimes*, the ICTY jurisprudence, Article 25(3)(c) of the Rome Statute, and the practice of national jurisdictions with regard to aiding and abetting.[208] The Appeals Chamber also found, based on the considerations drawn from an analysis in the *mens rea* context, that specific direction was not an element of the *actus reus* requirement of aiding and abetting.[209] It noted that the ICTY Appeals Chamber in *Perisic* had not found that the specific direction requirement stems from customary international law, and that 'in the absence of any discussion of customary international law, it is presumed that the ICTY Appeals Chamber in *Perisic* was only identifying and applying internally binding precedent'.[210] The SCSL Appeals Chamber also dismissed the remoteness/geographic location requirement of the accused in aiding and abetting cases.[211]

Judge Fisher (joined by Judge Winter) wrote a separate concurring opinion, which addressed the defence's argument that the law on aiding and abetting without the specific direction requirement was too broad and overreaching. The judges opined that the conduct of an accused would only qualify as aiding and abetting if she was aware of the essential elements of the crime that she facilitated. Liability would therefore encompass those actions that had a substantial effect on the offence when carried out with the knowledge that they would assist in the perpetration of the offence.[212]

The dramatically divergent views on the specific direction requirement resulted in an acquittal in one case (*Perisic* at the ICTY) and in a conviction in another (*Taylor* at the SCSL). However, in an extraordinary development in early 2014 a differently constituted Appeals Chamber of the ICTY[213] in the

206 SCSL *Prosecutor v Charles Ghankay Taylor, Appeals Chamber Judgment* (SCSL-03-01-A) 355.
207 ibid 473-5.
208 ibid 417–37 and 446–51.
209 ibid 474–5.
210 ibid 476.
211 ibid 476–80.
212 ibid Concurring opinion of Juge Fisher (joined by Judge Winter), 711–3 and 715–6.
213 In the *Perisic* judgment, the bench was composed of Judge Meron, Judge Agius, Judge Liu, Judge Ramaroson and Judge Vaz. In the *Sainovic* judgment, the bench was composed

Sainovic case concluded that specific direction was not part of customary international law, and consequently that the Appeals Chamber in *Perisic* was 'unequivocally' wrong.[214]

The *Sainovic* Appeals Chamber held that:[215]

> [T]he interpretation given in the Perisic Appeal Judgement would appear to be at odds not only with a plain reading of the Mrkšik and Sljivančanin Appeal Judgement, which states that specific direction is not an 'essential ingredient' of aiding and abetting liability, but also with the Lukik and Lukik Appeal Judgement, which confirmed this holding. [...] It would thus be more appropriate to conclude that the Mrkšik and Sljivančanin Appeal Judgement and the Lukik and Lukik Appeal Judgement, on one hand, and the Perisic Appeal Judgement, on the other hand, diverge on the issue of specific direction.

To determine which position should prevail, the *Sainovic* Appeals Chamber analysed the jurisprudence of the ICTY and the ICTR, and noted that 'the Tadic Appeal Judgement, which focused on JCE liability, does not purport to be a comprehensive statement of aiding and abetting liability', and therefore 'the Perisic Appeal Judgement relied on the flawed premise that the Tadic Appeal Judgement established a precedent with respect to specific direction'.[216]

The *Sainovic* Appeals Chamber also considered the various ICTY and ICTR cases that had recognised the specific direction requirement and those that had not. After an analysis of the *Furundžija Trial Judgement*, the *Delalic et al Appeal Judgment*, the *Blaškić Appeal Judgment* and the *Blagojevic and Jokic Appeal Judgment*, the Appeals Chamber in *Sainovic* concluded that specific direction was not part of customary international law.[217] Additionally, to allay any doubt the *Sainovic* Appeals Chamber also undertook its own in depth analysis of World War II tribunal precedents, the 1996 International Criminal Law *Draft Code of Crimes*, the ICTY jurisprudence, the Rome Statute and domestic law on aiding and abetting (which did not uniformly recognise the specific

of Judge Liu, Judge Güney, Judge Pocar, Judge Ramaroson, and Judge Tuzmukhamedov. Judge Liu and Judge Ramaroson, who had already disagreed with the specific direction requirement in the *Perisic* case, were now to determine the same issue.

214 ICTY *Prosecutor v Sainovic et al, Appeals Chamber Judgment* (IT-05-87-A) 1650

215 ibid 1621.

216 ibid 1623.

217 ibid 1624–6.

direction requirement).[218] This analysis led the *Sainovic* Appeals Chamber to 'unequivocally' reject:[219]

> [T]he approach adopted in the Perisic Appeal Judgement as it is in direct and material conflict with the prevailing jurisprudence on the *actus reus* of aiding and abetting liability and with customary international law in this regard.

Judge Tuzmukhamedov, dissenting, found that according to the facts of the *Sainovic* case, the issue of specific direction did not arise. It was therefore not relevant to the case and should not have been addressed in the judgment, notwithstanding the discretion of the ICTY Appeals Chamber to consider legal questions of general importance. The Judge did not express an opinion on the question of the validity of the specific direction requirement.[220]

The arguments in favour of a specific direction requirement are flawed. Firstly, as Ventura correctly observed:[221]

> There is a problem in legal reasoning that emerges from the specific direction saga and, in particular, the Perišić Appeal Judgment's recognition that this requirement is part of the actus reus of aiding and abetting. A close contextual reading of the Tadić Appeal Judgment (which had originally recognized specific direction as noted by the Perišić Appeal Judgment) reveals that it had only done so in passing in a single sentence; lacked detailed analysis and consideration of the matter; did not have aiding and abetting as a live issue before it (the Tadić Appeal Judgment concerned JCE); and did not explicitly acknowledge any prior precedent because it did not cite any sources to support specific direction. Yet, each of these exact same reasons were employed by the Perišić Appeal Judgment to dismiss the Mrkšić and Šljivančanin Appeal Judgment's rejection of specific direction. Thus, the Perišić Appeal Judgment's approach to the case law was plainly inconsistent. Since the jurisprudence had never analysed the specific direction question in any depth, there was simply no proper legal basis to prefer the Tadić Appeal Judgment (and those cases that had relied on it or, in a footnote trail, led

218 ibid 1627–48.

219 ibid 1650.

220 ibid Dissenting opinion of Judge Tuzmukhamedov, 40–8.

221 Ventura, 'Aiding and Abetting' (n 55) 197.

back to it) over the Mrkšić and Šljivančanin Appeal Judgment (and the Lukić and Lukić Appeal Judgment).

Moreover, empirical research by Professor Stewart demonstrates that prior to *Tadic* specific direction was not mentioned as a requirement for aiding and abetting liability in international criminal law or in national jurisdictions, be it in academic scholarship or in judicial rulings.[222] One notable exception was the *Zyklon B* case, decided by the United States Military Tribunal at Nuremberg. However, this case mentioned specific direction in an obscure footnote dealing with the Trail Chamber's analysis of aiding and abetting which did not consider whether specific direction was a requirement for aiding and abetting.[223] Stewart therefore correctly concludes that in the absence of state practice and *opinio juris*, specific direction was clearly not a customary norm in the law of aiding and abetting.[224] Many commentators also reject the specific direction requirement, concluding that *Tadic* only mentioned 'specific direction' in passing, and that the *Tadic* Appeals Chamber could not have meant to incorporate an arbitrary criterion into the law of aiding and abetting.[225]

222 James G Stewart, 'Aiding and Abetting and Specific Direction in International Criminal Law: A Dataset of Incidents' (2013) available at <https://docs.google.com/spreadsheets/d/1Jb1cirLsSLresUIQaE6V56usj3jvyi6lsbIrKnNKSUY/edit#gid=0> accessed 8 April 2020.

223 ICTY *Prosecutor v Perisic, Appeals Chamber Judgment* (*IT-04-81-A*), footnote 115.

224 Stewart summarises his main nine findings based on this dataset in James G Stewart, '"Specific Direction" Is Unprecedented: Results from Two Empirical Studies' available at <https://www.ejiltalk.org/specific-direction-is-unprecedented-results-from-two-empirical-studies/#more-9258> accessed 21 September 2018 in the following terms: '1. About a third of incidents of aiding and abetting in the case-law of international courts and tribunals mention the words 'specific direction' or 'specifically directed'. 2. To the best of our knowledge, there is only one reference to 'specific direction' prior to the Tadić Judgment. 3. Even when mentioned in the legal section of a judgment, 'specific direction' is almost never applied to the facts of a case. 4. In the vast majority of incidents, 'specific direction' is either not mentioned at all, or only mentioned in a single sentence without elaboration. 5. To the best of our knowledge, there are no acquittals on any incident based on 'specific direction' prior to Perišić before any court, national or international. 6. The law governing aiding and abetting does not apply different standards where defendants assist 'criminal organizations'. 7. To the best of my knowledge, national textbooks on criminal law do not mention 'specific direction' as an element of accomplice liability. 8. All leading treatises on international criminal law, including those dedicated to 'modes of liability' like aiding and abetting, do not mention 'specific direction' in more than a sentence. 9. None of the articles on the theory of complicity address 'specific direction' in more than a sentence.'.

225 Antonio Coco and Tom Gal, 'Losing Direction: The ICTY Appeals Chamber's Controversial Approach to Aiding and Abetting in Perišić' (2014) 12 Journal of International Criminal Justice 345; Manuel Ventura, 'Farewell "Specific Direction": Aiding and Abetting War Crimes and Crimes Against Humanity in Perišić, Taylor, Šainović et Al., and US Alien Tort

However, some scholars defend the specific direction requirement on the basis that it is necessary to address situations where assistance is provided to an organisation that engages in both lawful and unlawful activities.[226] Specific direction is therefore used as a policy argument to permit differentiation between assistance that is used by armed forces to commit crimes, and assistance that is used to engage in lawful acts of war.

In that regard the *Perisic* Appeal Judgment noted that the Bosnian Serb Army (VRS), to which Perisic provided financial assistance, was not a purely criminal organisation as it participated in lawful combat activities.[227] Perisic's financial assistance did not appear incompatible with lawful military operations, and evidence regarding the nature of this assistance could not establish that Perisic

---

Statute Jurisprudence' in Stuart Casey-Maslen (ed), *The War Report: Armed Conflict in 2013* (Oxford University Press 2014); Marko Milanovic, 'The Limits of Aiding and Abetting Liability: The ICTY Appeals Chamber Acquits Momcilo Perisic' available at <https://www.ejiltalk.org/the-limits-of-aiding-and-abetting-liability-the-icty-appeals-chamber-acquits-momcilo-perisic/> accessed 21 September 2018; Alex Fielding, 'Sainovic Appeal Rejects "specific Direction", but Was It Necessary? | Beyond The Hague"' available at <https://beyondthehague.com/2014/01/24/sainovic-appeal-rejects-specific-direction-but-was-it-necessary/#more-662> accessed 21 September 2018; Kevin Jon Heller, 'Two Thoughts on Manuel Ventura's Critique of Specific Direction' available at <http://opiniojuris.org/2014/01/10/two-thoughts-manuel-venturas-critique-specific-direction/> accessed 21 September 2018; Janine Natalya Clark, '"Specific Direction" and the Fragmentation of International Jurisprudence on Aiding and Abetting: Perišić and Beyond' (2015) 15 International Criminal Law Review 411; James G Stewart, 'Judicial Rejection of "Specific Direction" Is Widespread' available at <http://jamesgstewart.com/judicial-rejection-of-specific-direction-is-widespread/> accessed 21 September 2018; Alex Fielding, 'Charles Taylor Appeal: Why Its Rejection of "Specific Direction" Doesn't Matter' available at <https://beyondthehague.com/2013/09/30/charles-taylor-appeal-why-its-rejection-of-specific-direction-doesnt-matter/#more-474> accessed 21 September 2018; Manuel J Ventura, 'Specific Direction à La Perišić, the Taylor Appeal Judgment and What It Could Mean for the ICTY Appeals Chamber in Šainović et Al. – Part I' available at <https://dovjacobs.com/2014/01/09/guest-post-specific-direction-a-la-perisic-the-taylor-appeal-judgment-and-what-it-could-mean-for-the-icty-appeals-chamber-in-sainovic-et-al-part-ii/> accessed 21 September 2018; Marina Aksenova, 'The Specific Direction Requirement for Aiding and Abetting: A Call for Revisiting Comparative Criminal Law' (2015) 4 Cambridge Journal of International and Comparative Law 88.

226 Kai Ambos and Ousman Njikam, 'Charles Taylor's Criminal Responsibility' (2013) 11 Journal of International Criminal Justice 789, 804–8; John RWD Jones, Kevin Heller and Elies van Sliedregt, 'Milestones in International Criminal Justice: Recent Legal Controversies at the UN Yugoslav Tribunal International Law Summary' *Chatham House* 7–8, available at <https://www.chathamhouse.org/sites/default/files/public/Meetings/MeetingTranscripts/161013Yugoslav1.pdf> accessed 9 April 2020.

227 ICTY *Prosecutor v Perisic, Appeals Chamber Judgment* (*IT-04-81-A*) 57.

specifically directed his aid to be used for the criminal activities of the organisation.[228] Thus, while Perisic may have known of crimes by VRS, the Appeals Chamber concluded that Perisic's financial assistance to VRS was meant for the general war effort rather than VRS's crimes; it could not be proven 'beyond reasonable doubt to have facilitated assistance specifically directed towards the VRS Crimes in Sarajevo and Srebrenica'.[229]

This, reasoned the *Perisic* Appeal Judgment, coupled with the fact that Perisic was geographically remote from the crime scene necessitated the consideration of the specific direction requirement. In fact, '[w]here an accused aider and abettor is remote from relevant crimes, [...] consideration of specific direction is required'.[230]

These arguments are unsound. In practice almost no armed force is either wholly criminal or wholly lawful; they are by and large mixed groups. In an armed conflict crimes are unfortunately often committed along with lawful combat activities. Also, it is almost inconceivable that some members of an armed group would continuously carry out criminal activities while others would strictly act lawfully. The mixed nature of most armed groups means that both the group as a whole and its members individually will commit lawful *and* unlawful acts. Therefore, according to the reasoning of the *Perisic* Appeals Chamber specific direction will almost always have to be proven. This raises the concern that insistence on the specific direction requirement would allow a group's legal actions to shield its criminal actions.[231] This would mean that:[232]

> [A]s soon as a group carries out at least some actions – however small in number – that are consistent with IHL, even in a vast and endless sea of criminality, then such a group should fall into the category of the VRS in Perišić; that is, a mixed organization where, according to the Perišić Appeal Judgment, specific direction becomes relevant.

The approach of the *Perisic* Appeals Chamber would mean that if an individual assists a mixed group through financing, she stands to benefit simply because

228 ibid.

229 ibid 69.

230 ibid 39–40 and 42.

231 See generally Alexander Greenwalt, 'Foreign Assistance Complicity' (2016) 54 Columbia Journal of Transnational Law 531, 580–7.

232 Ventura, 'Farewell "Specific Direction": Aiding and Abetting War Crimes and Crimes Against Humanity in Perišić, Taylor, šainović et Al., and US Alien Tort Statute Jurisprudence' (n 225) 14.

of the isolated lawful acts of that group or even those of a few members of that group. Such isolated lawful actions should not shield the individual who financed the group from criminal responsibility.

Moreover, the remoteness consideration is a red herring, because modern technology allows anyone to assist in the perpetration of a crime from almost any geographic location. In the age of global interconnectivity it would be almost impossible to determine when an accused is geographically too remote from the offence not to trigger the specific direction requirement. Thus, an individual who finances a mixed entity from the comfort of her home should not escape criminal liability simply because she is geographically remote from the scene of the crime.

In discussing the specific direction requirement it is also important to touch upon the jurisprudence of the United States of America. The specific direction issue was identified early in a concurring opinion by Judge Katzmann of the United States Court of Appeals for the Second Circuit in the *Khulumani* Alien Tort Statute ('ATS') case.[233] Judge Katzmann stated that, as demonstrated by Article 25(3)(c) of the Rome Statute, for the aider and abettor to assist in the commission of crimes international law required 'purpose' as part of the *mens rea* requirement. He conceded that the ICTY and ICTR have applied 'knowledge' but noted that the term 'specific direction' had been used in ICTY jurisprudence.[234] However, the issue was not raised in other ATS cases until the advent of the 'specific direction' saga at the international criminal tribunals. Noting the disagreement regarding the specific direction requirement at these tribunals, in 2014 the United States Court of Appeals for the Ninth Circuit nevertheless identified the specific direction element in the *actus reus* requirement of aiding and abetting, and sent the case back to the trial court for the matter to be considered.[235] In another case the United States Court of Appeals for the District of Columbia Circuit followed the same approach.[236] In that case the lower court concluded that 'specific direction is not an element of aiding and abetting liability under customary international law'.[237] Interestingly,

233 *Khulumani v Barclay National Bank Ltd, Court of Appeals for the Second Circuit, 504 F3d 254 (2d Cir 2007) 10 December 2007.*

234 ibid Concurring opinion by Judge Katzmann, 278, footnote 15.

235 *Doe I v Nestle USA, Inc, Court of Appeals for the Ninth Circuit, 766 F3d 1013 (9th Cir 2014) 4 September 2014.*

236 *John Doe VIII v Exxon Mobil Corporation, Court of Appeals District of Columbia Circuit (527 FedAppx 7) 26 July 2013.*

237 *John Doe VI v Exxon Mobil Corporation, Court of Appeals District of Columbia Circuit (2015 WL 5042118) 6 July 2015* 11.

with regard to the specific direction requirement at the ICC and in the United States,[238] the *Taylor* Appeals Chamber stated that:[239]

> [A]s customary international law requires that an accused's acts and conduct of assistance, encouragement or moral support have a substantial effect on the commission of the crime, the liability schemes under the United States Model Penal Code and customary international law are fundamentally distinct.

In conclusion, like several legal scholars, I, too, disagree fundamentally with the existence of a specific direction requirement for aiding and abetting in international criminal law. The legal basis for the specific direction requirement is unsound, and its practical application is doctrinally problematic. Fortunately this question seems to have been settled by international criminal tribunals which have not discussed the existence of this requirement in recent cases. Indeed, the 'substantial effect/contribution' requirement is:[240]

> [S]ufficient to ensure distinctions between those who may have had an effect on non-criminal activity and those who had a substantial effect on crimes, when applied to the facts of a given case.

As correctly noted by the *Taylor* Appeals Chamber, the 'substantial effect/contribution' requirement is the standard against which an aider and abettor should be held responsible under international criminal law.[241] This was reiterated by Judge Ramaroson in her separate opinion in the *Perisic* Appeal Judgement[242] and by Judge Fisher and Judge Winter in their concurring opinion in the *Taylor* Appeal Judgment.[243]

---

238 There is currently a split among the various circuits regarding the specific direction requirement at federal level in the United States. It remains to be seen if this issue will be dealt with by the United States Supreme Court.

239 SCSL *Prosecutor v Charles Ghankay Taylor, Appeals Chamber Judgment* (*SCSL-03-01-A*) 447.

240 ibid 392.

241 ibid 392.

242 ICTY *Prosecutor v Perisic, Appeals Chamber Judgment* (*IT-04-81-A*) Separate opinion of Juge Ramaroson, 7.

243 SCSL *Prosecutor v Charles Ghankay Taylor, Appeals Chamber Judgment* (*SCSL-03-01-A*) Concurring opinion of Juge Fisher (joined by Judge Winter), 712–3.

4.2.3.2 *The Actus Reus Element of Substantial Contribution/Effect*

As is evident from the discussion on the specific direction requirement,[244] clarity is needed regarding the definition of the *actus reus* element of a substantial contribution/effect in the context of aiding and abetting. It is necessary to analyse the way in which international criminal tribunals determine what constitutes a substantial contribution/effect. This section firstly examines cases in which courts have attempted to define the substantial contribution/effect requirement; secondly it turns to decisions in which it was found that the accused could not be held liable because her assistance was not substantial; and finally it discusses the implication of a lack of clear definition in practice.

As stated,[245] there are some points of agreement concerning the characteristics of the substantial contribution/effect requirement. However, there is still no clear determination of what exactly constitutes a substantial contribution/effect.[246]

The *Tadic Trial Judgment* was the first to discuss the causal link between the accused's acts and the crime. In its analysis of Article 7(1) of the ICTY Statute about individual criminal responsibility, the Trial Chamber considered the question of 'the amount of assistance that must be shown before one can be held culpable for involvement in a crime'.[247] The Court found it instructive to review post-World War II cases and concluded that these had failed to establish specific criteria.[248] It also analysed the 1996 International Criminal Law *Draft Code of Crimes*, which contained a substantial contribution requirement although it did not contain a definition of this requirement. The *Tadic* Trial Chamber stated that, '[w]hile there is no definition of "substantially", it is clear [...] that the substantial contribution requirement calls for a contribution that in fact has an effect on the commission of the crime', and that 'in virtually every situation, the criminal act most probably would not have occurred in the same way had not someone acted in the role that the accused in fact assumed'.[249]

In another case during the years of the ICTY the *Furundzija* Trial Chamber reviewed the World War II-era jurisprudence to delimitate the *actus reus* requirement of aiding and abetting. In analysing the *Ohlendorf* case, the Trial

244 See Chapter 4, section 4.2.3.1.

245 See Chapter 4, section 4.2.

246 Jackson (n 131) 85; Ventura, 'Aiding and Abetting' (n 55) 201. See also generally Uwe Murmann, 'Problems of Causation with Regard to (Potential) Actions of Multiple Protagonists' (2014) 12 Journal of International Criminal Justice 283; James Stewart, 'Overdetermined Atrocities' (2012) 10 Journal of International Criminal Justice 1189.

247 ICTY *Prosecutor v Dusko Tadic, Trial Chamber Judgment* (IT-94-1-T) 681.

248 ibid 681.

249 ibid 688.

Chamber noted that some of the accused were found not guilty, because they were of such low rank that their failure to protest would have had no impact on the outcome. They also could not have controlled, prevented or modified the perpetration of the crimes.[250] The behaviour of these low-ranking officials was compared to that of others who had been convicted of locating, evaluating and transmitting lists of names of communists, knowing that such transmission would lead directly to the execution of the persons on the lists. Others were also convicted for their failure to protest, knowing that their protests would have made some difference to the course of events.[251] The Trial Chamber in *Furundzija* also noted that in the *Tesch* case an accused had been acquitted, despite knowingly being an integral part of the supply and use of poison gas, because he could not have been in a position to influence the transfer of poison gas to Auschwitz.[252] The Trial Chamber concluded that 'marginal participation' was excluded from the substantial contribution/effect requirement, and that 'it is not necessary for the conduct of the aider and abettor to cause the commission of the crime; it need not be a *conditio sine qua non* of the crime'.[253] This statement was subsequently endorsed in the *Sainovic Appeal Judgment*.[254]

In discussing JCE and detention camp cases the *Kvocka* Trial Chamber held that, regarding participation under aiding and abetting:[255]

> The participation in the enterprise must be significant. By significant, the Trial Chamber means an act or omission that makes an enterprise efficient or effective; e.g., a participation that enables the system to run more smoothly or without disruption. Physical or direct perpetration of a serious crime that advances the goal of the criminal enterprise would constitute a significant contribution. In general, participation would need to be assessed on a case by case basis, especially for low or mid level actors who do not physically perpetrate crimes. It may be that a person with significant authority or influence who knowingly fails to complain or protest automatically provides substantial assistance or support to criminal activity by their approving silence, particularly if present at the

250 ICTY *Prosecutor v Anto Furundzija, Trial Chamber Judgment* (IT-95-17/1-T) 217–21 (referring to the World War II case of *Ohlendorf et al* [Einsatzgruppen case]).

251 ibid 221 (referrencing to the World War II case of *Ohlendorf et al* [Einsatzgruppen case]).

252 ibid 222–3 (referrencing to the World War II case of *Tesch et al* [Zyklon B case]).

253 ibid 231.

254 ICTY *Prosecutor v Sainovic et al, Appeals Chamber Judgment* (IT-05-87-A) 1647.

255 ICTY *Prosecutor v Miroslav Kvocka et al, Trial Chamber Judgment* (IT-98-30/1-T) 309.

> scene of criminal activity. In most situations, the aider or abettor or co-perpetrator would not be someone readily replaceable, such that any "body" could fill his place. He would typically hold a higher position in the hierarchy or have special training, skills, or talents.

Therefore, not all persons who work in detention camps should be held criminally liable. According to the Trial Chamber, to be held criminally liable a person would have to meet a certain minimum threshold:[256]

> [T]he threshold required to impute criminal responsibility to a mid or low level participant in a joint criminal enterprise as an aider and abettor or co-perpetrator of such an enterprise normally requires a more substantial level of participation than simply following orders to perform some low level function in the criminal endeavor on a single occasion. The level of participation attributed to the accused and whether that participation is deemed significant will depend on a variety of factors, including the size of the criminal enterprise, the functions performed, the position of the accused, the amount of time spent participating after acquiring knowledge of the criminality of the system, efforts made to prevent criminal activity or to impede the efficient functioning of the system, the seriousness and scope of the crimes committed and the efficiency, zealousness or gratuitous cruelty exhibited in performing the actor's function. It would also be important to examine any direct evidence of a shared intent or agreement with the criminal endeavor, such as repeated, continuous, or extensive participation in the system, verbal expressions, or physical perpetration of a crime. Perhaps the most important factor to examine is the role the accused played vis-à-vis the seriousness and scope of the crimes committed.

The Trial Chamber concluded by stating that '[t]he aider or abettor or co-perpetrator of a joint criminal enterprise contributes to the commission of the crimes by playing a role that allows the system or enterprise to continue its functioning'.[257] However, for purposes of this work the relevance of this analysis is undermined by the fact that the *Kvočka Trial Chamber* interwove JCE and aiding and abetting, despite the fact that they constitute two different modes of liability. The *Kvočka* Appeals Chamber correctly stated that it would

256 ibid 311.
257 ibid 312.

be inaccurate to speak of complicity in a joint criminal enterprise, and that a distinction between these two forms of participation is important.[258]

Nevertheless, the holding of the *Kvočka* Trial Judgment was reflected in the *Orić* Trial Judgment, which stated that the accused's actions must be 'substantial and efficient enough to make the performance of the crime possible or at least easier'.[259]

In the context of aiding and abetting by omission the *Mrkšić and Šljivančanin* Appeals Chamber determined that the accused was mistaken in arguing that aiding and abetting by omission required the substantial contribution requirement to be conflated with the notion of an elevated degree of influence.[260]

In 2013 the substantial contribution/effect requirement was explored in more detail by the Appeals Chamber in the *Taylor* case. The court reiterated that it had:[261]

> [C]onsistently required, when considering a variety of fact patterns, that an accused's acts and conduct had a substantial effect on the commission of the crimes for which he is to be held individually criminally liable.

It rejected the accused's argument that 'the aider and abettor must provide assistance to the physical actor and that this assistance must be used in the commission of the crime'.[262] The Appeals Chamber reviewed World War II-era and more recent cases, as well as the factual scenarios of these cases regarding the provision of assistance that had a substantial effect on the commission of a crime.[263] It observed that a person substantially contributed to a crime if she:
- 'supported and sustained the organised commission of crimes';[264]
- 'made [...] civilians more vulnerable and less able to defend themselves from attacks [...] and also provided a pretext for attacks';[265]
- 'supported and sustained the functioning of the organised commission of crimes';[266]

258 ICTY *Prosecutor v Kvočka et al, Appeals Chamber Judgment* (IT-98-30/1) 91–2.
259 ICTY *Prosecutor v Orić, Trial Chamber Judgment* (IT-03-68-T) 282.
260 ICTY *Prosecutor v Mrksic et al, Appeals Chamber Judgment* (IT-95-13/1) 156.
261 SCSL *Prosecutor v Charles Ghankay Taylor, Appeals Chamber Judgment* (SCSL-03-01-A) 371.
262 ibid 370.
263 ibid 371–8.
264 ibid 372 (referring to the ICTY *Brima* case).
265 ibid 373 (referring to the ICTY *Brđanin* case).
266 ibid 374 (referring to the ICTY *Brđanin* case).

- 'supported and enhanced the capacity of the [principal] to carry out its plan to commit crimes';[267]
- 'supported and sustained the [unlawful] system of arrests and detention';[268]
- 'contribut[ed] to and ma[de] possible [the victims'] deportation to Germany';[269] and
- 'permitted the continued existence and further development of th[e] inhuman situation'.[270]

The *Taylor* Appeals Chamber also held that a person provided a substantial contribution if 'the personnel attributable to him participated in guarding and detaining the eventual victims'.[271] It concluded its review of the cases by recognising that:[272]

> [T]he essential question when determining whether an accused culpably assisted the commission of the crimes is the effect of the accused's assistance on the commission of the crimes, not the manner in which such assistance was provided.

Next, the *Taylor* Appeals Chamber analysed cases in which courts had found that the accused's assistance had for various reasons not had a substantial effect on the crime. For example, the participation of the accused 'in the distribution of orders, [... the] propos[al of] laws discriminating against Jews and Poles and [the] sign[ing of] decrees forcing certain groups of Poles to accept German citizenship' were not sufficient evidence to connect the accused to the crimes;[273] neither was the fact that the accused 'was not in a position where his lack of objection in any way contributed to the success of any executive operation'.[274] Also, the fact that the accused 'was responsible for conducting interrogations of some detainees' did not lead the court to find that these acts 'gave substantial assistance to the commission of acts of unlawful arrest, detention and confinement of non-Serbs'.[275]

---

267 ibid 375 (referring to the ICTY *Blagojević and Jokić* case).
268 ibid 376 (referring to the ICTY *Simić* case).
269 ibid footnote 1194 (referring to the World War II *Becker et al* case).
270 ibid 378 (referring to the World War II *Roechling* case).
271 ibid 375 (referring to the ICTY *Blagojević and Jokić* case).
272 ibid 380.
273 ibid footnote 1231 (referring to the World War II *Ministries, Pohl, and Farben* cases).
274 ibid footnote 1231 (referring to the World War II *Einsatzgruppen* case).
275 ibid footnote 1231 (referring to the ICTY *Simić* case).

The *Taylor* Appeals Chamber also held that the mere provision of the means to perpetrate a crime is not necessarily sufficient for criminal liability as an aider and abettor, particularly in cases where:[276]

> [T]he very fungibility of the means may establish that the accused is not sufficiently connected to the commission of the crime. Similarly, on the facts of a case, an accused's contribution to the causal stream leading to the commission of the crime may be insignificant or insubstantial, precluding a finding that his acts and conduct had a substantial effect on the crimes.

Several cases in which the accused was found not to have met the substantial threshold for aiding and abetting can provide guidance in determining what constitutes a substantial contribution. The *Sainovic Appeal Judgment* found that despite the accused having had some effect on the crime the 'failure to take investigative and punitive measures against the commission of forcible displacement' was insufficient to show a substantial contribution.[277] The Appeals Chamber concluded that there was not enough evidence to prove that the accused's failure to take adequate measures would have substantially contributed to the perpetration of crimes.[278] Similarly, in the *Delalic Appeal Judgment* the accused had 'signed orders […] for the classification of detainees and their release', but he 'had no independent authority to do so'.[279] His involvement in the continuing detention or release of detainees was thus not sufficient to constitute a substantial effect on the crime.[280] In the *Kupreškic Appeal Judgment*, the Court stated that the accused did not substantially contribute to the commission of persecutory acts by providing weapons because there was no evidence that the weapons he provided had been used for attacking the local Muslim population. Moreover, about six months had passed between the accused providing the weapons and the attack.[281] Likewise, in the *Strugar* case the accused did not initiate, or ensure that his subordinates initiated, an effective investigation and he did not take steps to punish and discipline the offenders.[282] The ICTY Trial Chamber was not satisfied that the accused's lack

276 ibid 391.
277 ICTY *Prosecutor v Sainovic et al, Appeals Chamber Judgment* (IT-05-87-A) 1682.
278 ibid 1683.
279 ICTY *Prosecution v Delalic et al, Appeals Chamber Judgment* (IT-96-21-A) 357.
280 ibid 358.
281 ICTY *Prosecutor v Kupreskic et al, Appeals Chamber Judgment* (IT-95-16-A) 277.
282 ICTY *Prosecutor v Strugar, Trial Chamber Judgment* (IT-01-42-T) 444.

of actions, 'well after the offences were committed', could have had a direct and substantial effect on the perpetration of the crimes.[283] Perplexingly, in *Fofana and Kondewa* the SCSL Appeals Chamber found that, notwithstanding the fact that the accused had 'provided commanders with arms, ammunition and a vehicle prior to their attack', his 'provision of logistics [was] not sufficient to establish beyond reasonable doubt that he contributed as an aider and abettor to the commission of specific criminal acts'.[284]

In other cases, the lack of a substantial contribution/effect was discussed in the context of circumstantial evidence. The courts found that the substantial contribution/effect requirement had not been met because the conclusions drawn at trial were not the only reasonable conclusions based on the evidence. Thus, in the *Nyiramasuhuko Appeal Judgement* the conviction of the accused as an aider and abetter was set aside, not because of insufficient evidence *per se*, but because the Trial Chamber had not explained how the conclusions drawn at trial were the only reasonable ones based on the circumstantial evidence on the record.[285] The Appeals Chamber stated that the narrow timeframes between the accused's threat to the victims and their murders and the fact that the accused was seen driving the victims' vehicle were insufficient to show that the only reasonable conclusion was that the accused's actions had had a substantial effect. In fact, no evidence had been led regarding the circumstances of the murders or how the accused had obtained the vehicle.[286] The Appeals Chamber also held that the Trial Chamber was not justified in relying on the accused's prior conduct to support the finding that his presence at the crime scene, alongside that of the principal perpetrators, substantially contributed to the commission of the crime, because the principal perpetrators had no knowledge of the accused's prior criminal behaviour.[287]

In sum, the substantial contribution/effect requirement has been part of the *actus reus* element of aiding and abetting since the post-World War II tribunals. This requirement, which establishes a causal link between the aider and abettor and the offence, has also been affirmed and further developed by the *ad hoc* Tribunals and the SCSL. As discussed, there are numerous cases that could serve as guidance on the interpretation of the substantial contribution/effect requirement. However, for the most part the jurisprudence of the international

283 ibid 355.

284 SCSL *Prosecutor v Moinina Fofana and Allieu Kondewa, Appeals Chamber Judgment* (*SCSL-04-14-A-829*) 102.

285 ICTR *Prosecutor v Nyiramasuhuko et al, Appeals Chamber Judgment* (*ICTR-98-42-A*) 1510.

286 ibid 1510–2.

287 ibid 2086–8.

tribunals simply points to the evidence and/or factual findings of earlier cases and then determines whether the substantial contribution/effect requirement has been met or not. The jurisprudence of the international tribunals generally tends to refrain from clearly defining the substantial contribution/effect requirement, and it also does not provide detailed explanations of the reasons why an accused's actions did or did not amount to a substantial contribution to the crimes. As noted by Ambos, '[t]he substantiality requirement is far from precise, and the case law has not contributed to its clarification, instead leaving the decision to each individual case'.[288] The *Taylor* Appeals Chamber therefore rightly observed that:[289]

> [T]he causal link between the accused's acts and conduct and the commission of the crime is to be assessed on a case-by-case basis: this case-by-case assessment ensures both that the culpable are properly held responsible for their acts and that the innocent are not unjustly held liable for the acts of others.

Thus, judges interpret this objective standard according to the circumstances of each case. In practice this means that judges have some discretion in determining whether an accused's actions meet the substantial contribution/effect requirement. This judicial discretion could make the difference between a conviction or an acquittal. Of course, as had occurred in the *Fofana and Kondewa* case,[290] it might be that judicial discretion in making the substantial contribution determination results in an acquittal which, in my opinion, is not justified. This is not to say that the latitude afforded judges in determining the existence of substantial contribution/effect or the lack thereof, is unnecessary. Ventura notes that giving judges some discretion is:[291]

> [N]ot necessarily unusual in a criminal law context and may be understandable when one considers that in mass atrocity cases there are a myriad of factors and variables at play that can affect the outcome of the substantial contribution question.

---

288 Kai Ambos (n 131)164–5.

289 SCSL *Prosecutor v Charles Ghankay Taylor, Appeals Chamber Judgment* (*SCSL-03-01-A*) 391.

290 SCSL *Prosecutor v Moinina Fofana and Allieu Kondewa, Appeals Chamber Judgment* (*SCSL-04-14-A-829*) 102.

291 Ventura, 'Aiding and Abetting' (n 55) 206.

In fact, the jurisprudence makes clear that in some cases it can definitively be determined whether or not the accused's contribution was substantial. In other cases a multitude of circumstances must be taken into consideration to reach a conclusion. For example, the question of authority and influence; the magnitude of the assistance provided; the fact that the offence would have been substantially less likely to have been committed without the aider and abettor's assistance; and the fact that the cumulative effect of the accused's assistance in all cases amounted to a substantial contribution to the principal's crime, are all circumstances that play a role in the decision-making process.

Moreover, in describing the substantial contribution/effect requirement one should bear in mind that this requirement is not unique to the mode of liability of aiding and abetting, but that it is also found in planning, ordering and instigating.[292] The *Fofana and Kondewa* Appeals Chamber noted that:[293]

> A finding that an accused's conduct had a 'substantial effect' for the purpose of aiding and abetting will therefore normally also satisfy the 'substantial effect' requirement for the purpose of instigating.

Hence, the descriptions and analyses of the substantial contribution/effect requirement in aiding and abetting should apply with equal force to the standard under these other modes of liability and *vice versa*.

Lastly, it is important to consider that thresholds are in general 'notoriously difficult to define'.[294] The *substantial* contribution requirement is part of the *actus reus* requirement of aiding and abetting, the *significant* contribution requirement is part of the *actus reus* requirement of a JCE, and the *essential* contribution requirement is part of the objective elements of co-perpetration at the ICC. At first blush these various standards might seem to be the same, but each represents a different threshold for liability. The 'substantial' threshold is higher than the 'significant' threshold, but lower than the 'essential' threshold. Nevertheless, it is difficult to provide a clear-cut definition of each of these standards because:[295]

292 See SCSL *Prosecutor v Charles Ghankay Taylor, Appeals Chamber Judgment* (SCSL-03-01-A) 368; as well as SCSL *Prosecutor v Moinina Fofana and Allieu Kondewa, Appeals Chamber Judgment* (SCSL-04-14-A-829) 84.

293 SCSL *Prosecutor v Moinina Fofana and Allieu Kondewa, Appeals Chamber Judgment* (SCSL-04-14-A-829) 84.

294 Ventura, 'Aiding and Abetting' (n 55) 207.

295 Manuel Ventura, 'The "Reasonable Basis to Proceed" Threshold in the Kenya and Côte d'Ivoire Proprio Motu Investigation Decisions: The International Criminal Court's Lowest

> [L]anguage eventually reaches a certain vanishing point [...] where it is simply unable to adequately articulate fine distinctions between evidentiary thresholds with a sufficient level of precision, a precision that only numbers can really provide.

Because of the inherent imprecision of words, to better understand and define a particular threshold it can be useful to recognise this limitation and to distinguish it from the others.

4.2.3.3 *Knowledge and Intent Requirement of Aiding and Abetting in Customary International Law*

The *mens rea* elements of aiding and abetting need clarification in international criminal law. According to the *ad hoc* and hybrid Tribunals an aider and abettor must have acted with the knowledge and intent that her actions assisted the perpetration of the crime.[296] In customary international law some significant uncertainties remain. The degree of knowledge and intent that the aider and abettor must display have been at the centre of disagreement at the *ad hoc* and hybrid Tribunals.[297] Specifically, it is questionable whether the

---

Evidentiary Standard?' (2012) 12 The Law and Practice of International Courts and Tribunals 49, 79.

296 ICTR *Karera v Prosecutor, Appeals Chamber Judgment* (ICTR-01-74-A) 321; ICTY *Prosecutor v Dusko Tadic, Appeals Chamber Judgment* (IT-94-1-A) 229(iv); ICTY *Prosecutor v Krnojelac, Appeals Chamber Judgment* (IT-97-25) 33; ICTY *Prosecutor v Vasiljević, Appeals Chamber Judgment* (IT-98-32-A) 102(ii); ICTY *Prosecutor v Tihomir Blaškić, Appeals Chamber Judgment* (IT-95-14-A) 46, 49; ICTY *Prosecutor v Kvočka et al, Appeals Chamber Judgment* (IT-98-30/1) 89–90; ICTY *Prosecutor v Ntagerura et al, Appeals Chamber Judgment* (ICTR-99-46) 370; ICTY *Prosecutor v Simić et al, Appeals Chamber Judgment* (IT-95-9-A) 86; ICTY *Prosecutor v Vidoje Blagojevic and Dragan Jokic, Appeals Chamber Judgment* (IT-02-60-A) 127; ICTR *Prosecutor v Ferdinand Nahimana et al, Appeals Chamber Judgment* (ICTR-99-52-A) 482; ICTY *Prosecutor v Orić, Appeals Chamber Judgment* (IT-03-68) 43; ICTY *Prosecutor v Zlatko Aleksovski, Appeals Chamber Judgment* (IT-95-14/1-A) 162–3; ICTY *Prosecutor v Mrkšić and Šljivančanin, Appeals Chamber Judgment* (IT-95-13/1-A) 159; ICTY *Prosecutor v Haradinaj et al, Appeals Chamber Judgment* (IT-04-84) 58; ICTR *Kalimanzira v Prosecutor, Appeals Chamber Judgment* (ICTR-05-88-A) 86; ICTR *Rukundo v Prosecutor, Appeals Chamber Judgment* (ICTR-2001-70-A) 53; ICTR *Prosecutor v Ntawukuriryayo, Appeals Chamber Judgment* (ICTR-05-82) 222; ICTY *Prosecutor v Lukić and Lukić, Appeals Chamber Judgment* (IT-98-32/1-T) 440; ICTY *Prosecutor v Perisic, Appeals Chamber Judgment* (IT-04-81-A) 48; SCSL *Prosecutor v Charles Ghankay Taylor, Appeals Chamber Judgment* (SCSL-03-01-A) 384; ICTY *Prosecutor v Sainovic et al, Appeals Chamber Judgment* (IT-05-87-A) 1649; ICTY *Prosecutor v Popović et al, Appeals Chamber Judgment* (IT-05-88) 1758; ICTR *Prosecutor v Nyiramasuhuko et al, Appeals Chamber Judgment* (ICTR-98-42-A) 1955, 2255.

297 Christopher Gosnell, 'Damned If You Don't: Liability for Omissions in International Criminal Law' in Yvonne McDermott, William A Schabas and Niamh Hayes (eds),

doctrine of wilful blindness (defined in section 4.2.3.3.1.2) would be sufficient. Also, regarding intent, it is uncertain whether *dolus eventualis* or *dolus indirectus* should be the minimum standard for aiding and abetting.[298]

In this section I define the different knowledge standards (active knowledge, wilful blindness, negligence and 'had reason to know') and intent standards (*dolus directus, dolus indirectus, dolus eventualis*, and recklessness), and provide an overview of their application at international courts, tribunals and in international instruments. These general definitions help to address a lack of clarity that surrounds these terms in international criminal law. However, these definitions only clarify that different levels of knowledge and intent exist and they explain the content of each. These definitions and overview of the use of the different standards of knowledge and intent are not sufficient to establish the minimum standard of knowledge and intent to hold an aiding and abettor liable under customary international law. To provide clarity about the minimum standards of knowledge and intent I engage in the comparative analysis in Chapter v.

4.2.3.3.1 Standards of Knowledge

There are three degrees of knowledge: (i) active knowledge; (ii) wilful blindness (also referred to as wilful ignorance or deliberate ignorance); and (iii) 'had reason to know'. There is also a further standard, namely negligence. The different standards of knowledge might implicate the liability of the individual who finances an entity involved in the perpetration of core crimes if the other material and mental elements are fulfilled. However, negligence is not considered sufficient to trigger liability for aiders and abettors. The English case of *Roper v Taylor's Central Garages* efficiently differentiates between active knowledge (referred to as actual knowledge), 'had reason to know' (referred to as 'ought to have known'), wilful blindness, and negligence:[299]

> The first is actual knowledge, which the justices may find because they infer it from the nature of the act done, for no man can prove the state of another man's mind; and they may find it even if the defendant gives evidence to the contrary. They may say, 'We do not believe him; we think that that was his state of mind'. They may feel that the evidence falls short

The Ashgate Research Companion to International Criminal Law: Critical Perspectives (Routledge 2013) 113.

298 '*Dolus eventualis*' is defined in Chapter 4, section 4.2.3.2.2.3, and 'intent in the second degree' is defined in Chapter 4, section 4.2.3.2.2.2.

299 *Roper v Taylor's Central Garages* [1951] 2 TLR 284 (KBD).

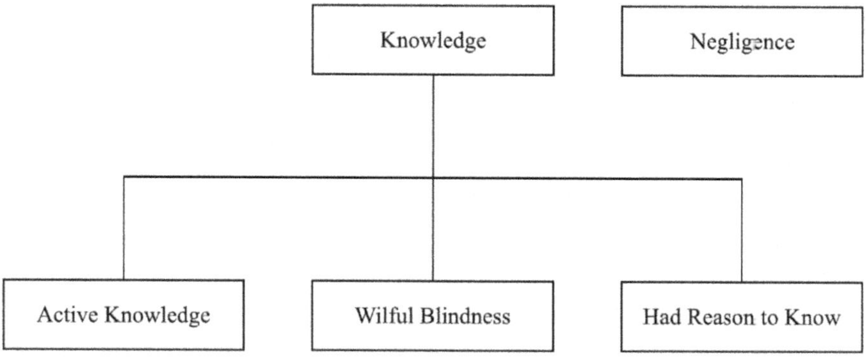

FIGURE 1 Standards of knowledge in international criminal law

> of that, and if they do they have then to consider what might be described as knowledge of the second degree; whether the defendant was, as it has been called, shutting his eyes to an obvious means of knowledge [wilful blindness ...] The third kind of knowledge is what is generally known in the law as constructive knowledge: it is what is compassed by the words 'ought to have known' in the phrase 'knew or ought to have known'. It does not mean actual knowledge at all; it means that the defendant had in effect the means of knowledge [...] The case of shutting the eyes is actual knowledge in the eyes of the law; the case of merely neglecting to make inquiries is not knowledge at all - it comes within the legal conception of constructive knowledge, a conception which, generally speaking, has no place in the criminal law.

4.2.3.3.1.1 *Active Knowledge*

The question of the specificity of knowledge has arisen in international criminal law. The ICTY and ICTR have developed an 'essential matters' test, as well as a test that requires only that the accomplice must have considered that one of several crimes would be perpetrated, including the actual crime, even if she did not know exactly which one. In *Haradinaj*, the Appeals Chamber considered that it was:[300]

300 ICTY *Prosecutor v Haradinaj et al, Appeals Chamber Judgment* (*IT-04-84*) 58; (referring to ICTY *Prosecutor v Zlatko Aleksovski, Appeals Chamber Judgment* (*IT-95-14/1-A*) 163; ICTY *Prosecutor v Orić, Appeals Chamber Judgment* (*IT-03-68*) 43). See also ICTY *Prosecutor v Mrksic et al, Appeals Chamber Judgment* (*IT-95-13/1*) 159; ICTY *Prosecutor v Simić et al, Appeals Chamber Judgment* (*IT-95-9-A*) 86; ICTR *Prosecutor v Ferdinand Nahimana et al, Appeals Chamber Judgment* (*ICTR-99-52-A*) 482.

> [F]irmly established that, to satisfy the *mens rea* requirement for aiding and abetting, '[it] must be shown that the aider and abettor knew that his own acts assisted the commission of that specific crime by the principal' (for example, murder, extermination, rape, torture) and that the aider and abettor was 'aware of the essential elements of the crime which was ultimately committed by the principal'. Where the *mens rea* of the principal perpetrator is an element of the principal crime, the aider and abettor need not share the intent of the principal perpetrator, but he or she must be aware of the intent of the principal perpetrator.

It should be noted that knowledge as awareness of circumstances only means knowledge of the factual circumstances envisaged in a particular international rule; it does not mean awareness of the legal appraisal of those circumstances.[301]

4.2.3.3.1.2 *Wilful Blindness, Negligence and 'Had Reason to Know'*

In the words of Glanville Williams:[302]

> A court can properly find wilful blindness only where it can almost be said that the defendant actually knew. He suspected the fact; he realised its probability; but he refrained from obtaining the final confirmation because he wanted in the event to be able to deny knowledge. This, and this alone, is wilful blindness.

Wilful blindness means that the accused deliberately avoids turning her suspicion into certain knowledge by refraining from making simple inquires, because she wishes to escape criminal liability. This definition of wilful blindness excludes the negligent actions of an accomplice. Acting negligently with respect to a material element of an offense implies that a person:[303]

> [S]hould be aware of a substantial and unjustifiable risk that the material element exists or will result from his conduct. The risk must be of such a nature and degree that the actor's failure to perceive it [...] involves a gross deviation from the standard of care that a reasonable person would observe in the actor's situation.

301 Antonio Cassese and Paola Gaeta, *Cassese's International Criminal Law* (Oxford University Press 2013) 52.

302 Glanville Williams, *Criminal Law: The General Part* (2 ed, Stevens & Sons 1961) 159.

303 USA, the Model Penal Code, section 2.02.

As noted by the Ontario Court of Appeal in *R v F W Woolworth Co Ltd*:[304]

> The fact that a person ought to have known that certain facts existed [...] does not constitute knowledge for the purpose of criminal liability, and does not by itself form a basis for the application of the doctrine of wilful blindness.

In *Regina v Finta*, Cory J, writing for the majority of Supreme Court of Canada, held that 'the *mens rea* requirement of both crimes against humanity and war crimes would be met if it were established that the accused was wilfully blind to the facts or circumstances that would bring his or her actions within the provisions of these offences'.[305] The ICTY echoed this view in the *Tadic Trial Judgment*.[306] In discussing the knowledge requirement in Article 30 of the Rome Statute, Piragoff and Robinson argue that 'it may also be open to the Court to interpret "awareness" to include wilful blindness in some situations'.[307]

Additionally, in cases concerning command responsibility the ITCY and ICTR have recognised a 'had reason to know' standard.[308] Similarly, Article 28(a)(i) of the Rome Statute stipulates that if a 'military commander or person either knew or, owing to the circumstances at the time, should have known that the forces were committing or about to commit such crimes', she will be liable. Article 86(2) of the Additional Protocol ('AP') also allows for the liability of superiors who 'knew [...] or had information which should have enabled them to conclude in the circumstances at the time' that a crime was being committed.

In sum, an individual who finances an entity that commits core crimes can neither be held liable for acting negligently, as negligence excludes the criminal liability of the aider and abettor in international criminal law, nor under the 'had reason to know' standard, as this standard is reserved for

---

304 *R v FW Woolworth co (1974) 18 CCC (2nd) 23 (Ont CA)* 32.

305 *R v Finta [1994] 1 SCR 701* 819.

306 ICTY *Prosecutor v Dusko Tadic, Trial Chamber Judgment (IT-94-1-T)* 657.

307 Donald Piragoff and Darryl Robinson, 'Mental Element' in Otto Triffterer (ed) *Commentary on the Rome Statute of the International Criminal Court Observers' Notes, Article by Article* (2 ed, Hart Publishing 2008) 861.

308 ICTY *Prosecutor v Pavle Strugar, Appeals Chamber Judgment (IT-01-42-A)* 303; ICTR *Prosecutor v Ferdinand Nahimana et al, Appeals Chamber Judgment (ICTR-99-52-A)* 791, 840; ICTR *The Prosecutor v Ignace Bagilishema, Appeal Judgment: Reasons (ICTR-95-1A-A)* 28, 33–7, 42; ICTY *Prosecutor v Tihomir Blaškić, Appeals Chamber Judgment (IT-95-14-A)* 62; ICTY *Prosecution v Delalic et al, Appeals Chamber Judgment (IT-96-21-A)* 238-9; ICTY *Prosecutor v Krnojelac, Appeals Chamber Judgment (IT-97-25)* 154–6; ICTY *Prosecutor*

commanders. However, it is uncertain whether active knowledge or wilful blindness is the minimum standard for criminal liability of an individual who finances an entity that commits core crimes. As discussed in Chapter VI, section 2, at the international level a blanket disregard of the doctrine of wilful blindness would be a mistake, as this doctrine could, at least in some cases, be 'tantamount to knowledge'.[309]

4.2.3.3.2 Standards of Intent

When referring to intent judges have employed terms such as 'general intent', 'specific intent', 'recklessness', '*dolus directus*', '*dolus indirectus*', '*dolus eventualis*', 'intent in the first degree', 'intent in the second degree', 'oblique intent', and 'negligence'. These terms are defined and classified according to their degree of gravity. In international criminal law the culpable mental states are intent in the first degree (also referred to as specific intent or *dolus directus*), requiring the highest threshold; then intent in the second degree (also referred to as general intent, *dolus indirectus*, or oblique intent); then *dolus eventualis*; and lastly recklessness. These forms of *dolus* depend on the strength of the volitional element vis-à-vis the cognitive element.[310] The most controversial form of intent is *dolus eventualis*.

4.2.3.3.2.1 *Intent in the First Degree*

Intent in the first degree is the gravest form of culpability in which the volitional element dominates.[311] An aider and abettor acts with intent in the first degree if she desires to bring about the result. Therefore, she has the will to assist the principal in bringing about the offence.[312] In the *Enigster* case the District Court of Tel Aviv noted that when determining whether the accused had acted with intent, '[i]t is a well-known rule that any person in his right mind is held to intend the natural consequences of his actions'.[313] Intent in the first degree is also defined as a 'purpose-bound will'.[314]

---

v Hadzihasanovic and Kubura, Appeals Chamber Judgment (*IT-01-47-A*) 30–1; ICTR *Prosecutor v Karemera et al, Appeals Chamber Judgment* (*ICTR-98-44-A*) 307.

309 Piragoff and Robinson (n 307) 861.

310 ICC *Prosecutor v Bemba et al, Decision on the Confirmation of Charges, Pre-Trial Chamber I* (*ICC-01/05-01/13-749*) 357.

311 George P Fletcher, *Rethinking Criminal Law* (Oxford University Press 2000) 444.

312 Cassese and Gaeta (n 301) 43.

313 ibid 44 citing the District Court of Tel Aviv in the *Enigster* case, 14.

314 Volker Krey, *Deutsches Strafrecht, Allgemeiner Teil, Lehrbuch in Deutsch Und Englisch: Teil II* (Kohlhammer ed, 2003) 109.

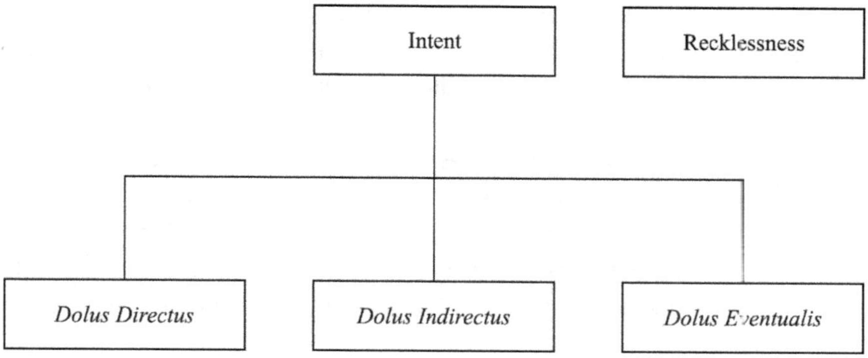

FIGURE 2 Standards of intent in international criminal law

Section 2.02 of the Model Penal Code provides a definition of purpose, which this work follows, because it is representative of the understanding by the *ad hoc* Tribunals of what intent in the first degree means:

> A person acts purposely with respect to a material element of an offense when:
> (i) if the element involves the nature of his conduct or a result thereof, it is his conscious object to engage in conduct of that nature or to cause such a result; and
> (ii) if the element involves the attendant circumstances, he is aware of the existence of such circumstances or he believes or hopes that they exist.

It does not matter whether the intended result is the accused's ultimate goal or merely an intermediate one necessary to achieve an ultimate goal.[315]

4.2.3.3.2.2 *Intent in the Second Degree*

Intent in the second degree, also referred to as *dolus indirectus* and oblique intent, is the foreseeability of a consequence as certain. The aider and abettor's primary purpose therefore is not the secondary consequence of her actions. In the words of Ashworth and Horder, the accused 'should be classified as having intended the result rather than as having been merely reckless towards it'.[316]

315 ibid.

316 Andrew Ashworth and Jeremy Horder, *Ashworth's Principles of Criminal Law* (9 ed, Oxford University Press 2019) 192.

The consequences of her actions may be undesired lateral consequences of her actions; she may also be indifferent or even regret their occurrence. Regarding oblique intent the Supreme Court of the United Kingdom has stated that:[317]

> Intention is not to be restricted to consequences that are wanted or desired, but includes consequences which a defendant might not want to ensue, but which the jury find (a) are the virtually certain result of the defendant's actions (barring some unforeseen intervention); and (b) are consequences which the defendant appreciated were virtually certain to occur.

With *dolus indirectus* the knowledge requirement (cognitive element) dominates, whereas the intent requirement (volitional element) is weaker.[318] It is sufficient that the aider and abettor had the knowledge that her actions would bring about the undesired lateral consequences; she does not need to have desired their occurrence.[319] In sum, intent in the second degree differs from intent in the first degree in the lack of desire to achieve the objective elements of the offence.[320]

4.2.3.3.2.3 *Dolus Eventualis*

Dolus eventualis has been defined differently in different jurisdictions.[321] According to the strict defintion of *dolus eventualis* there must be a considerable chance that a consequence occurs. This is the approch adopted in the Netherlands, and it is also the one that I have adopted.[322] By contrast,

---

317 *Regina v Armel Gnango* [2011] UKSC 59; [2012] 1 AC 827 125.

318 Mohamed Elewa Badar, *The Concept of Mens Rea in International Criminal Law The Case for a Unified Approach* (Hart Publishing 2013) 424.

319 Krey (n 314) 113.

320 Badar (n 318) 424.

321 Thomas Weigend, 'Intent, Mistake of Law, and Co-Perpetration in the Lubanga Decision on Confirmation of Charges' (2008) 6 Journal of International Criminal Justice 471, 483 when referring to *dolus eventualis,* states that 'it is thus far from clear that speakers from different backgrounds mean the same thing when the use the same Latin expression'; Piragoff and Robinson (n 307) 860, footnote 67 '[t]he concept "dolus eventualis" does not have a monolithic or uniform meaning within all civil law systems. Nevertheless, in all civil law systems, it appears to include the concept connoted by the phrase "will occur in the ordinary course of events"; i.e., an awareness of a substantial or high degree of probability that the consequence will occur.'

322 Jeroen Blomsma, *Mens Rea and Defences in European Criminal Law Book* (Intersentia 2012) 105 citing J. de Hullu, Materieel strafrecht over algemene leerstukken van strafrechtelijke aansprakelijkheid naar Nederlands recht, Kluwer, 2006, 222; W Van Kouwen,

the German Supreme Court has consistently held that any possibility that is not entirely unlikely is sufficient to prove *dolus eventualis*.[323] I disagree with the German perspective, because it is overinclusive. *Dolus eventualis* is an extended form of *dolus* which equates to foreseen consequences with intended results.[324] It requires the accused to have been aware of the possible consequences of her acts and that she had consciously chosen to act nonetheless, accepting these consequences.[325]

Dolus eventualis is a civil law concept that some common law jurisdictions have adopted, while in other common law jurisdictions this standard is unknown.[326] Thus, it needs to be distinguished from recklessness (also referred to as 'negligence' by certain courts and authors). In jurisdictions that only recognise intent and recklessness an accused's reckless conduct will generally be regarded as less reprehensible than the same conduct or result brought about intentionally.[327] A crime committed recklessly also generally brings about a lower sentencing range than an intentional crime. Recklessness is not sufficient to hold an aider and abettor accountable in international criminal law. Thus, *dolus eventualis* must be distinguished from the common law form of recklessness/negligence, which requires a positive aversion to the harmful consequence.[328] By contrast, *dolus eventualis* implies not only that the accused is aware of a risk, but also that she accepts the possibility of its realisation (volitional element). She therefore reconciles herself with the 'inducing effect' of

K Bruinberg, Supreme Court of the Netherlands, Criminal Division (Hoge Raad der Nederlanden Strafkamer) – HIV Transmission: 70(6) Criminalisation, Journal of Criminal Law 485 (2006) 485 which translate 'aanmerkelijk' as 'considerable'.

323 *7 July 1999 BGH NStZ 1999* 507; *12 August 2009 BGH BeckRS 2009* 25029; *30 August 2006 BGH 2 StR 198/06* 16 stating that 'wenn er den Erfolgseintritt als (nur) möglich und nicht ganz fernliegend erkennt' which translate to 'if he recognizes the occurrence of success as (only) possible and not entirely remote'. Unofficial translation by the author.

324 Blomsma (n 322) 99.

325 ibid.

326 See Chapter V.

327 Blomsma (n 322) 102.

328 Fletcher, *Rethinking Criminal Law* (n 311) 446. Also, this approach is similar to the one adopted by section 2.02 of the Model Penal Code, which provides the following definition of recklessness: 'A person acts recklessly with respect to a material element of an offense when he consciously disregards a substantial and unjustifiable risk that the material element exists or will result from his conduct. The risk must be of such a nature and degree that, considering the nature and purpose of the actor's conduct and the circumstances known to him, its disregard involves a gross deviation from the standard of conduct that a law-abiding person would observe in the actor's situation.'

her conduct.[329] The *Oric* Trial Chamber stated that intention does not include recklessness.[330] Fletcher suggests that *dolus eventualis* means:[331]

> [A] particular subjective posture toward the result. The tests [...] vary; the possibilities include everything from being indifferent to the result, to 'being reconciled' with the result as a possible cost to attaining one's goal.

This view is problematic because it blurs the line between recklessness and *dolus eventualis*. It allows *dolus eventualis* to encompass blunt indifference.[332] It is my argument that *dolus eventualis* should only be interpreted as foresight of the likelihood of the occurrence of the consequences and the acceptance of those consequences. In my opinion indifference towards the occurrence of the consequences is not sufficient. In sum, *dolus eventualis* entails a higher volitional threshold than recklessness.[333]

Dolus eventualis has been endorsed in the jurisprudence of the *ad hoc* tribunals.[334] The *Stakić* Trial Chamber provided the following technical definition: '[I]f the actor engages in life-endangering behaviour, his killing becomes intentional if he "reconciles himself" or "makes peace" – with the likelihood of death'.[335] With regard to the mental element of an accused acting as part of a JCE the *Tadic* Appeals Chamber stated:[336]

> In order for responsibility for the deaths to be imputable to the others, however, everyone in the group must have been able to predict this result. It should be noted that more than negligence is required. What is required is a state of mind in which a person, although he did not intend to bring about a certain result, was aware that the actions of the group were most likely to lead to that result but nevertheless willingly took that risk. In other words, the so-called *dolus eventualis* is required.

---

329 ICTY *Prosecutor v Orić, Trial Chamber Judgment* (IT-03-68-T) footnote 773.

330 ibid footnote 1020.

331 Fletcher, *Rethinking Criminal Law* (n 311) 445–6.

332 This position has been adopted in South African law, as discussed in Chapter 5, section 2.4 below.

333 Kai Ambos (n 131) 277.

334 ICTY *Prosecutor v Dusko Tadic, Appeals Chamber Judgment* (IT-94-1-A) 219–20; ICTY *Prosecutor v Milomir Stakic, Trial Chamber Judgment* (IT-97-24-T) 587; ICTY *Prosecutor v Mucić et al, Trial Chamber Judgment* (IT-96-21-T) 437.

335 ICTY *Prosecutor v Milomir Stakic, Trial Chamber Judgment* (IT-97-24-T) 587.

336 ICTY *Prosecutor v Dusko Tadic, Appeals Chamber Judgment* (IT-94-1-A) 220.

The question of a *dolus eventualis* standard for aiding and abetting has been discussed in the jurisprudence of the ICC. For some time it was a point of controversy whether Article 30 of the Rome Statute, notwithstanding the 'unless otherwise provided' formulation, allowed for *dolus eventualis*.[337] Article 30(2) states that: '[A] person has intent where: (a) In relation to conduct, that person means to engage in the conduct; (b) In relation to a consequence, that person means to cause that consequence or is aware that it will occur in the ordinary course of events'. In the context of establishing the elements of co-perpetration based on joint control over the crime, the Pre-Trial Chamber of the ICC in the *Lubanga Confirmation of Charges Decision* held that an accused's *mens rea* could be assumed if the accused:[338]

> [I]s aware of the risk that the objective elements of the crime may result from his or her actions or omissions, and [...] accepts such an outcome by reconciling himself or herself with it or consenting to it (also known as *dolus eventualis*).

The Court then distinguished between two scenarios, each of which reaches the required threshold:[339]

> Firstly, if the risk of bringing about the objective elements of the crime is substantial (that is, there is a likelihood that it 'will occur in the ordinary course of events'), the fact that the suspect accepts the idea of bringing about the objective elements of the crime can be inferred from: i. the awareness by the suspect of the substantial likelihood that his or her actions or omissions would result in the realisation of the objective elements of the crime; and ii. the decision by the suspect to carry out his or her actions or omissions despite such awareness. Secondly, if the risk of bringing about the objective elements of the crime is low, the suspect must have clearly or expressly accepted the idea that such objective elements may result from his or her actions or omissions.

In its analysis the Pre-Trial Chamber did not articulate any reasons for this interpretation, except for referring to the *ad hoc* Tribunals' recourse to *dolus*

337 Kai Ambos (n 131) 276.

338 ICC *Prosecutor v Lubanga, Decision on the Confirmation of Charges, Pre-Trial Chamber I* (*ICC-01/04-01/06-803-tEN*) 352.

339 ibid 353–4.

eventualis.[340] By contrast, the Pre-Trial Chamber II in the *Bemba Confirmation of Charges Decision* stated that Article 30 embraced only direct intent and indirect intent.[341] It found that *dolus eventualis* was not included in Article 30 of the Rome Statute because 'the express language of the phrase "will occur in the ordinary course of events" [...] does not accommodate a lower standard than the one required by *dolus directus* in the second degree (oblique intention)'.[342] It also stated that the standard set forth by Article 30:[343]

> [I]s undoubtedly higher than the principal standard commonly agreed upon for *dolus eventualis*. [...] Hence, had the drafters of the Statute intended to include *dolus eventualis* in the text of article 30, they could have used the words 'may occur' or 'might occur in the ordinary course of events' to convey mere eventuality or possibility, rather than near inevitability or virtual certainty.

The Pre-Trial Chamber II in *Bemba* also referred to the *travaux préparatoires*, which show that 'the idea of including *dolus eventualis* was abandoned at an early stage of the negotiations'.[344] In 2012 the *Lubanga* Trial Chamber, in arguing that Article 30(2)(b) excluded the concept of *dolus eventualis*, concurred with the view put forth in *Bemba*. It is also the perspective that I adopt in this work.[345]

Yet, *dolus eventualis* has also been recognised as a viable *mens rea* standard by the ECCC in the *Chea Nuon and Samphan Khieu* judgment (Case 002/01).[346] The court found that *dolus eventualis* was sufficient to hold an accused liable for the crime of extermination:[347]

> While the *mens rea* for the crime of extermination has not been consistently defined in the jurisprudence of the ICTY and ICTR, appeal jurisprudence from these tribunals has seemingly evolved to exclude *dolus eventualis* from the definition of the *mens rea* for extermination. The Chamber considers that there was no reasoned basis for a departure

340 ibid 352.

341 ICC *Prosecutor v Bemba et al, Decision on the Confirmation of Charges, Pre-Trial Chamber I* (ICC-01/05-01/13-749) 357-9.

342 ibid 360.

343 ibid 363.

344 ibid 366.

345 ICC *Prosecutor v Lubanga, Trial Chamber Judgment* (ICC-01/04-01/06-2842) 1011–2.

346 ECCC *Prosecutor v Chea Nuon and Samphan Khieu, Trial Chamber Judgment* (Case No 002/19-09-2007/ECCC/TC).

347 ibid.

from the original approach taken in the Krstić Trial Judgement, which encompassed *dolus eventualis* and was based on a review of pre-1975 jurisprudence.

International UN-mandated inquires, notably those on the Sri-Lanka and Gaza conflicts, have also held that murder could be committed with *dolus eventualis* or recklessness.[348]

5 Assessment

Aiding and abetting liability has been developed and interpreted since the World War II tribunals and it has crystallised into a norm of customary international law.[349] Although clear core requirements can be identified for this mode of liability, the jurisprudence reveals numerous unresolved tangential issues. Regarding aiding and abetting at the ICC, the minimum threshold of contribution has sparked debate at the ICC and among scholars. I argue that to be held liable the accused must, through her financial assistance, substantially contribute to the crime, which 'substantial contribution' needs to be established on a case-by-case basis. This approach accords with the jurisprudence of the *ad hoc* and hybrid Tribunals. Also, the ICC's purposive *mens rea* requirement has sparked controversy. This requirement presents an elevated *mens rea* standard compared to that of the *ad hoc* and hybrid Tribunals. This stricter *mens rea* requirement means that an individual who finances an entity that commits core crimes cannot be held liable as an aider and abettor at the ICC because she lacks the purpose to assist the principal in the perpetration of the offence.[350]

348 Sarah Knuckey, 'Murder in Common Article 3' in Andrew Clapham, Paola Gaeta and Marco Sassoli (eds), *The 1949 Geneva Convention : A Commentary* (Oxford University Press 2015) 459 citing the report of the Secretary-General's Panel of Experts on Accountability in Sri Lanka, 31 March 2011, paragraph 205, 251, stating that the *mens rea* 'encompasses reckless disregard for life' and reporting credible allegations of attacks on hospitals and humanitarian objects as possible murder, whether the targeting was 'direct, or reckless' and the report of the United Nations Fact-Finding Mission on the Gaza Conflict, A/HRC/12/48, 25 September 2004, paragraph 1433, referring to an incident as indicating 'an intention, or at least recklessness, to cause harm to civilians, which may amount to wilful killings'.

349 ICTY *Prosecutor v Dusko Tadic, Trial Chamber Judgment* (IT-94-1-T) 663–9; ICTY *Prosecutor v Anto Furundzija, Trial Chamber Judgment* (IT-95-17/1-T) 191–249; ECCC *Prosecutor v Kaing Guek Eav, Trial Chamber Judgment* (001/18-07-2007-ECCC/TC/E188) 475. See generally Czaplinski (n 8).

350 For an explanation, see, for example, footnote 87.

Regarding aiding and abetting at the *ad hoc* and hybrid Tribunals, a prominent point of contention has been whether a specific direction requirement is contained in the *actus reus* and *mens rea* elements of the mode of liability of aiding and abetting. This requirement has now been overwhelmingly rejected by both jurisprudence and academic opinion. However, the result has been an increased focus on the substantial contribution/effect requirement. At present substantial contribution/effect can be inferred from various *indicia* and must be established on a case by case basis.

There are two further issues that require attention and harmonisation in determining the *mens rea* elements of aiding and abetting in customary international law, *i.e.* determining the minimum standards of knowledge and intent that an aider and abettor must possess. There are competing positions on the *mens rea* thresholds in the international arena. Porro notes that in international criminal law there remains divergences regarding 'whether and to what extent the sphere of criminal responsibility may be linked to mental attitudes which do not attain the threshold of foresight of the unlawful outcome in terms of practical certainty'.[351] The discrepancies seem to stem from the fact that international courts and tribunals have not clearly determined what the minimum levels of knowledge and intent of the aider and abettor should be. Moreover, courts and tribunals have proposed divergent definitions of the concepts of intent and knowledge. In fact, the *ad hoc* Tribunals have used a variety of terms to determine and define the *mens rea* elements, which have contributed to the confusion about the mental elements of an aider and abettor. Defining these terms can only bring a degree of clarity regarding the different levels of knowledge and intent that exist. However, it does not establish the minimum standards of knowledge and intent required to hold an aider and abettor liable under customary international law. Accordingly, Chapter V turns to national jurisdictions and engages in a comprehensive comparative analysis of the applicable law in the community of States. The aim of this analysis is to determine whether commonly shared values exist across these jurisdictions regarding the minimum standards of knowledge and intent required to hold an aider and abettor liable.[352]

351 Sara Porro, *Risk and Mental Element: An Analysis of National and International Law on Core Crimes* (Stämpfli 2014) 235.

352 There are other contested areas that are not relevant for the purpose of this work. These include the following: the prior agreement and *ex post facto* aiding and abetting; the criminal law duty to act and aiding and abetting by omission; complicity in genocide *versus* aiding and abetting genocide; and encouragement or moral support to the principal perpetrators.

CHAPTER 5

Comparative Analysis of Aiding and Abetting in National Jurisdictions

1 Introduction

Most of the *acuts reus* and *mens rea* elements of aiding and abetting in customary international law are settled. However, important uncertainties remain surrounding the minimum degree of knowledge and intent that the aider and abettor must possess. It is questionable whether the doctrine of wilful blindness would constitute a sufficient degree of knowledge. It is also not clear whether *dolus eventualis* could suffice as the minimum standard of intent.

To answer these questions this Chapter turns to national jurisdictions and a comprehensive comparative analysis of the of applicable law in Africa (section 2), Asia (section 3), Europe (section 4), Latin America (section 5), North America (section 6) and Oceania (section7). In this comparative analysis, the national laws concerning the minimum level of knowledge and intent of an aider and abettor in the following countries are analysed: Argentina, Australia, Brazil, Cameroon, Canada, China, Egypt, England and Wales, France, Germany, India, Israel, Italy, Malawi, Malaysia, Mexico, Russia, South Africa, Turkey and the United States of America. As stated at the outset, these countries represent Western and non-Western legal traditions, economically developed and economically developing countries, civil law and common law jurisdictions, as well as jurisdictions with a variety of religious traditions – Christian, Hindu, Jewish, Muslim, and secular.[1]

It should be noted that while this work is concerned with the financing of entities that commit core crimes, this comparative analysis examines the *mens rea* elements of common crimes generally, and not only with respect to the financing of core crimes. This is because it is the definition of the *mens rea* elements of aiding and abetting in national criminal law that informs the

1 As noted in Chapter 1, section 6, material available in numerous languages such as Arabic, English, French, German, Portuguese, Russian, Spanish, and Turkish is also taken into consideration. Finally, I also chose counties where the main religions were represented, such as Christianity, Islam, Judaism, and Hinduism, as well as secular States. The purpose of this diversity is to emphasise the representativity of States, which in turn guarantees the quality of the comparative analysis.

 | DOI:10.1163/9789004470934_006

definition of aiding and abetting in international criminal law where core crimes are dealt with.

The general trend seems to be that national courts and tribunals tend to require active knowledge or wilful blindness and *dolus indirectus* or *dolus eventualis*, even though these exact terms might not be used. As noted by Cassese, '[i]n spite of broad differences in terminology, most legal systems tend to take the same basic approach to the specific regulation of each aspect of *mens rea* and its implications'.[2]

The purpose of this comparative analysis, combined with the analysis of the applicable international law (Chapter 4, section 4.2.3.3) is to determine whether general principles of law recognised by the community of States could be derived regarding the minimum standard of knowledge and intent that an aider and abettor must possess.

2 Africa

In Africa this work analyses the aider and abettors' knowledge and intent requirements in Cameroon, Egypt, Malawi and South Africa.[3] Cameroon and South Africa are mixed jurisdictions, Egypt is a civil law state, and Malawi is a common law jurisdiction. The main languages spoken in these countries are French, English and Arabic. These countries also represent a mix of economically developed and developing states and both Christian, and Muslim traditions.

2.1 *Cameroon*

Cameroon is a mixed jurisdiction and its criminal law is based on French criminal law.[4] Liability for aiders and abettors is set forth in Articles 97 to 99 of the

---

2 Antonio Cassese and Paola Gaeta, *Cassese's International Criminal Law* (Oxford University Press 2013) 41.

3 The knowledge and intent requirements of aider and abettors is analysed in Cameroon, Egypt, Malawi and South Africa, because these are the countries where I was able to find the online and print academic texts and judicial decisions necessary for the comparative analysis and where I was able to understand the languages in which the academic texts and judicial decisions were written.

4 Philippe Keubou Dschang, 'Cameroon' in Ulrich Sieber, Hans-Georg Koch and Jan-Michael Simon (eds), *Participation in Crime: Criminal Liability of Leaders of Criminal Groups and Networks* (Duncker & Humblot Publishers 2020) 66, 70: for example, in the absence of Cameroonian textbooks, French textbooks are used in Cameroon in a didactic manner. Furthermore, in the absence of Cameroonian jurisprudence, reference can be made to French jurisprudence.

Cameroonian Penal Code. Article 97 states that 'an accessory shall mean a person who abets the commission of a felony or misdemeanour, that is who aids or facilitates the preparation or the commission of such an offence'.[5]

Regarding the knowledge requirement, the aider and abettor must possess the awareness of associating herself with the criminal offence.[6] She must know the kind of offence, but not necessarily the exact offence, that the principal will commit.[7] Neither the jurisprudence of Cameroonian courts nor the works of scholars discuss the doctrine of wilful blindness.

Concerning the intent element of aiding and abetting, the accomplice must act with the willingness to assist in the commission of the offence.[8] In Cameroonian criminal law an important question is whether the aider and abettor remains punishable when the offence committed by the principal does not correspond exactly to what the aider and abettor had envisaged. This is the case when the crime perpetrated by the principal goes beyond the aider and abettor's expectations. Article 99 of the Cameroonian Penal Code takes account of foreseeable consequences:

> [A]ccessory to the commission or attempted commission of a felony or misdemeanor shall also be responsible in respect of any other offence committed or attempted as a foreseeable consequence of the agreement or abetment.

In other words, this Article pertains to a situation in which the actual offence committed by the principal differs from the one that the accomplice intended to aid. To address this concern the following distinction is made: If the difference between the foreseen and the actual offences relates to their constituent elements, complicity is not punishable if the object of the crime (for example, the victims) are different.[9] An aider and abettor is also not criminally liable if the principal voluntarily changes targets. However, if the offence foreseen by the aider and abettor and the offence that the principal in fact committed differ only in their circumstances, and the actual offence involves an aggravating

---

5 ibid 65. Unofficial translation by the author. Aiders and abettors are subject to the same penalties as the principal perpetrator. The distinction between principal and accomplice is purely theoretical, because in principle the distinction has no bearing on the sentencing. However, judges may use their powers to punish the accomplice less severely.

6 ibid 68.

7 Carlson Anyangwe, *Criminal Law: The General Part* (Langaa RPCIG 2015) 339.

8 Dschang (n 4) 68.

9 ibid.

circumstance not contemplated by the aider and abettor, then she would be liable as an aider and abettor.[10] In sum, not only the material elements of the offence but also the intent of the principal must have been foreseeable for an aider and abettor to be held criminally liable.[11]

Keubou emphasises the fact that where two offences differ only in their circumstances, and the offence committed involves an aggravating circumstance, the aider and abettor would be criminally liable. He states that the aider and abettor would be liable in the situation where the principal uses violence, for example, turning a simple robbery into an aggravated robbery.[12] However, she will not be liable in the scenario where the principal commits a rape during a robbery because the rape is not an aggravating circumstance of the robbery, and was not committed to facilitate the commission of the intended offence. Moreover, rape is not a foreseeable consequence of the offence of robbery. The protected values are also not the same.[13] Anyangwe states that:[14]

> It is immaterial whether the [aider and abettor] desired the other offence or not. The test of foreseeability here is a subjective rather than an objective one. It is not whether a reasonable person would have foreseen the commission of the other offence as a consequence of the agreement or abetment, it is whether the particular defendant could have foreseen it.

This conception of intent is similar to *dolus indirectus* as contemplated in this work.

In sum, under Cameroonian criminal law an aider and abettor must act with at least active knowledge and *dolus indirectus*.

2.2 *Egypt*

Egypt is a civil law jurisdiction. The Egyptian Penal Code contains several articles addressing accomplice liability.[15] Article 40 provides for three kinds of

---

10 ibid 69; Anyangwe (n 7) 351.

11 Ahmadou Oumarou, *Code de Lois Pénales* (2 ed, Presses Universitaires d'Afrique 2006) 82.

12 Dschang (n 4) 85.

13 ibid.

14 Anyangwe (n 7) 352.

15 Mahmoud M Mostafa, *Principes de Droit Pénal Des Pays Arabes* (Librairie Générale de Droit et de Jurispurdence 1972)16 notes that the current Egyptian Penal Code is that of 1937. Before that, it was the Indigenous Penal Code of 1883 which had been inspired by the French Penal Code, but which was completely overhauled in 1904. It was not inspired by the French Code, because the legislative authorities at that time were British. They therefore had recourse to the legislations of India, Sudan, Belgium and Italy. This background is relevant to understand the controversies surrounding the intent requirement.

accomplices: (i) the instigator; (ii) the one who agrees with another to commit a crime; and (iii) the one who knowingly gives the principal a tool or other object to commit the offence or who assists the principal in any way in preparing for, perpetrating or completing the crime. This last form of accomplice liability is what I refer to in this work as aider and abettor liability.

Regarding the knowledge requirement, an aider and abettor must act with the knowledge that she is assisting the principal and that her acts will assist the perpetration of an offence by the principal.[16] Neither judicial decisions nor authors on Egyptian criminal law discuss the doctrine of wilful blindness.

The interesting position in Egyptian criminal law concerns the intent requirement.[17] The Egyptian Penal Code – which was heavily influenced by the French Penal Code,[18] but which has also drawn inspiration from other jurisdictions regarding accomplice liability[19] – sets forth general principles concerning *dolus eventualis* (referred to as *alqasd ehtemali*) and the liability of aiders and abettors.[20] Article 43 (unintended crimes) states that:[21]

> A person who participates in a crime shall bear its penalty, even though the resulting crime is not the one he has initially intended, so long the crime that actually took place is a probable result for his [...] assistance.

Also, from a jurisprudential perspective, before the adoption of the current Egyptian Penal Code the Court of Cassation stated in 1930 that aiders and abettors could be held liable for all crimes they should have reasonably anticipated because of their assistance, and decided that:[22]

> [*D*]*olus eventualis* substitutes intent, in the strict sense of the word, in establishing the element of intentionality. It can only be defined as a

16 Martin Forstner, *Der Allgemeine Teil Des Ägyptischen Strafrechts* (Nomos 1986) 118–20.

17 ibid 165–6.

18 Mohamed Elewa Badar, *The Concept of Mens Rea in International Criminal Law The Case for a Unified Approach* (Hart Publishing 2013) 165.

19 Mostafa (n 15) 63.

20 Mohamed Elewa Badar, 'The Mens Rea Enigma in the Jurisprudence of the International Criminal Court' in Larissa von der Herik and Carsten Stahn (eds), *The Diversification and Fragmentation of International Criminal Law* (Martinus Nijhoff Publishers 2012) 521.

21 Article 43 of the Egyptian Penal Code. Other jurisdictions have drawn inspiration from Article 43 of the Egyptian Penal Code to include provisions concerning the liability of accomplices acting with *dolus eventualis*. See for example in Kuwait: Article 53 of Law 16 of 1960, in Libya: Article 103 of the Penal Code of 1954, in Iraq: Article 53 of Law 111 of 1969, and in Qatar: Article 45 of the Law 11 of 2004.

22 *Court of Cassation, 25 December 1930, No 1835/47* 164–5.

> secondary uncertain intention on the part of the perpetrator who expects that his act may go beyond the purpose intended to realize another purpose that was not intended initially but nevertheless performs the act and thus appreciates the unintended purpose. As a result of this intention, it becomes irrelevant whether the consequence takes place or not.
>
> The purpose of formulating the definition in this way is to clarify that intention must be present in all circumstances, to include all forms of such intention and to exclude other cases where the intention is not established, in a bid to calling for caution in order not to confuse premeditation with mere error.
>
> The key issue for deciding if *dolus eventualis* is established or not is to ask the following question: while undertaking the intended act, did the perpetrator want to do it even if this act goes beyond its original purpose to perform another criminal consequence that actually happened and was not originally intended? If the answer is in the affirmative, *dolus eventualis* is established. If the answer is negative, then the whole matter is nothing more than an error that may be punishable or not depending on whether the conditions establishing an error are present. Based on the above *dolus eventualis* is not established in the following scenario: X intends to kill Y by poisoning a piece of sweets and offering it to Y. Y keeps the piece of sweets that Z finds, eats and accordingly dies In this case, the accused shall be punished for the attempted murder of Y and shall not be punished for killing Z under the pretext of *dolus eventualis* This is because the secondary intention is not established, only the focused intention is established, and that is fulfilling the original purpose and it does not go beyond to any other criminal purpose.

Badar notes that this judgement 'stirred many scholar[ly] debates given its difference from the conventional opinion widely adopted by the jurisprudence and judiciary in France in viewing *dolus eventualis*'.[23] The controversy arose because the previous Penal Code (the Indigenous Penal Code of 1883) did not include any provision concerning liability for accomplices who acted with *dolus eventualis*. Article 43 (and thereby the legislative inclusion of *dolus eventualis* for accomplices) was only included in the Egyptian Penal Code of 1937. Since then the Court of Cassation has on multiple occasions reiterated its

23 Badar (n 18) 164.

position on the aider and abettor's intent.[24] It has described *dolus eventualis* as the act of foreseeing the criminal result as a possible effect of the assistance and the acceptance of that effect. Thus, if an aider and abettor engages in an act of assistance to achieve a particular criminal result, and that assistance leads to a more serious criminal result than she could have and should have foreseen, she will be liable for acting with *dolus eventualis*.[25]

Scholars have also widely accepted that aiders and abettors can be held liable for acting with *dolus eventualis*. In his work on *dolus eventualis*, Abou El Magd Aly Eisa found that *dolus eventualis* is one of the pillars of criminal liability and constitutes the basis for intentional crime:[26]

> [*D*]*olus eventualis* is the same as the direct criminal intent as they share the same nature and essence. Both are based on the same elements, namely will and knowledge. Knowledge in the *dolus eventualis* is mixed with suspicion and hence it takes the form of inconclusive expectation of the criminal consequence. Will, on the other hand, appears in its weakest form represented in the perpetrator's acceptance of the consequence or his indifference towards it. In fact, indifference towards the criminal consequence means in reality as we see it – accepting this consequence and reconciling oneself with it. The expectation on which the *dolus eventualis* is based on is the actual expectation that cannot be substituted by its probability or necessity or both; otherwise it would be subsumed under unintentional errors. In addition, the criterion governing the *dolus eventualis* is a subjective criterion, in other words, the expected consequence is the one anticipated by the perpetrator according to his own

24 See, for example, *Court of Cassation, 27 January 1959, Digest of Decisions, Year 10, No 23* 91; *Court of Cassation, 26 November 1973, Year 24 No 220* 10072; *Court of Cassation, 6 February 2005, No 56615* 73.

25 *Court of Cassation, 6 February 2005, No. 56615* 73.

26 Abou el Magd Aly Eisa, al Qasr al Gena'i al-Ehtemaly: Derasah Ta'sileyah Tahlileya Mupananah (Conditional Intent: Analytical and Comparative Study) (Dar al-Nahda al-Arabis, 1988) 667, as cited by Badar (n 20) 522, footnote 92. See also Sadiq Reza, 'Egypt' in Kevin Jon Heller and Markus Dubber (eds), *The Handbook of Comparative Criminal Law* (Stanford University Press 2010) 190, footnotes 35–6; citing M Akida, "Criminal Law" in Egypt and its Laws, ed. Nathalie Bernard-Maugiron and Baudouin Dupret (Kluwer Law International, 2002), 45, and W. Mahmoud, "Civil and Criminal Justice" in Egypt and its Laws, ed. Nathalie Bernard-Maugiron and Baudouin Dupret (Kluwer Law International, 2002) 154. According to Akida and Mahmoud, an aider and abettor can be held liable if she foresees the consequences of the principal's intentional actions, which are also referred to as consequences that are "morally linked" to the offender's actions, and if she foresees consequences of act taken with disregard for potential harm to others (*i.e.* recklessness).

> perspective upon attempting to commit the crime even if his perspective was counter to the reality.

In summary, under Egyptian criminal law the aider and abettor must act with active knowledge and at least *dolus eventualis*. The doctrine of wilful blindness does not seem to feature in any scholarly work or judicial decisions.

2.3 *Malawi*

Malawi adopted a common law-based legal system. Under Section 21 of the Malawi Penal Code 'every person who aids or abets another person in committing the offence [...] is deemed to have taken part in committing the offence and to be guilty of the offence'. In the words of Unyolo J in *Makulani v Republic*:[27]

> [A]t law an accomplice is a person who is associated with another in the commission of a criminal offence, whether as a principal or accessory before or after the fact. This includes a person who procures or aids and abets another in the commission of the offence; it also includes a person who receives, in appropriate cases.

To be held liable an accomplice must have acted with the intention to further the perpetration of the principal's crime and with the knowledge that her actions assisted the perpetration of the crime.[28]

Malawi criminal law adopted an expanded definition of 'knowledge'. It recognises that an aider must have 'actual knowledge' (called 'active knowledge' in this work) or 'constructive knowledge' (also referred to as 'wilful blindness').[29] Actual knowledge means the actual awareness of the circumstances of the crime. Wilful blindness is where a person wilfully or deliberately closes her eyes to the obvious and then claims to have had no active knowledge.

Bande, with reference to the English case of *R v Sail*, explains that suspicion and wilful blindness are two different things.[30] The mere fact that a person is suspicious does not automatically imply that she wilfully ignored the facts. To be held liable she must not only have suspected the facts but also have deliberately refrained from making the enquiries she should have made. In the words of Glanville Williams:[31]

---

27 *(1993) 16 (1)* MLR *276 (H.C.) 280*, as cited in Lewis Chezan Bande, *Criminal Law in Malawi* (Kluwer Law International 2012) 122.

28 ibid 125.

29 Lewis Chezan Bande, *Criminal Law in Malawi* (Juta & Company 2017) 193–4.

30 ibid 193 referring to *R v Sail (2006) 2 Cr App R 26.*

31 Glanville Williams, *Criminal Law: The General Part* (2 ed, Stevens & Sons 1961) 157–8.

> [T]he rule is that if a party has his suspicion aroused but then deliberately omits to make further enquiries, because he wished to remain in ignorance, he is deemed to have knowledge. ... In other words, there is a suspicion which the defendant deliberately omits to turn into certain knowledge. This is frequently expressed by saying that he 'shut his eyes' to the fact or that he was 'wilfully blind'. Lord Hewart, C.J., expressed it by saying that 'the respondent deliberately refrained from making inquiries the result of which he might not care to have'.

Thus, in Malawi 'knowledge' includes both active knowledge and wilful blindness.

An aider and abettor must also act with the 'intention' of assisting the perpetrator in the commission of the offence, but the aider and abettor need not intend that the offence be committed. Therefore, an aider and abettor will be liable even though she was indifferent as to whether the crime would be committed or not.[32]

Malawi law recognises two forms of intent: (i) direct intent; and (ii) indirect intent (also referred to as 'oblique intent'),[33] meaning that intent includes not simply deliberate or purposeful conduct but also foreseeable conduct.

Regarding indirect (or oblique) intent, the prohibited conduct or result did not have to have been the aider's main goal, but as Bande notes, 'considering the knowledge he had at the time of doing the act, it was certain that the prohibited act would be done or the result would be brought about if he wanted to achieve his main goal'.[34] In the case of indirect intent the occurrence of the prohibited act or result was certain, based on the facts of the case, even though the aider and abettor did not necessarily desire it; the aider and abettor was aware of the certainty of its occurrence, and nevertheless chose to proceed.

In sum, according to Malawi criminal law the minimum level of intent for the liability of an aider and abettor for her assistance is *dolus indirectus*; *dolus eventualis* is therefore not sufficient. However, for the knowledge requirement wilful blindness could suffice.

2.4 *South Africa*

South Africa is a mixed jurisdiction. Criminal law in South Africa is influenced by Roman-Dutch law,[35] English law,[36] and, to some extent, German criminal

32 Bande (n 27) 125.

33 ibid 83.

34 Bande (n 29) 186.

35 "Roman-Dutch" means Roman law as received and applied in Holland during approximately the sixteenth and seventeenth centuries.

36 The English influence occurred during the nineteenth and twentieth centuries.

law.[37] An important concept in South African criminal law emanating from German criminal law is *dolus eventualis*.[38]

Synman states that in South African criminal law:[39]

> A fair description of accomplices is as follows:
> 1. Persons are guilty of an offence as accomplices if, although they do not satisfy all the requirements for liability contained in the definition of the offence (*Tatbestand*) and although the conduct required for a conviction is not imputed to them by virtue of the principles relating to common purpose, they unlawfully and intentionally engage in conduct whereby they further the commission of an offence by somebody else.
> 2. The word "further" in rule 1 above includes any conduct whereby a person facilitates, assists or encourages the commission of an offence, gives advice concerning its commission, orders its commission or makes it possible for another to commit it.

Thus, an aider and abettor must knowingly associate herself with the commission of the crime and intentionally further its perpetration.[40]

To act knowingly means that the aider and abettor knows that she assists in the perpetration of a crime.[41] It does not matter whether the principal knows that assistance is being given.[42] The doctrine of wilful blindness does not seem to be discussed either in the opinions of the courts or in scholarly work.

---

37 The reason for the German criminal law influence is because of the fact that many scholars studied in Germany and the Netherlands, and incorporated concepts from Europe into South African criminal law. See Carel Rainer Snyman, 'South Africa' in Ulrich Sieber, Hans-Georg Koch and Jan-Michael Simon (eds), *Participation in Crime: Criminal Liability of Leaders of Criminal Groups and Networks* (Duncker & Humblot Publishers 2020) 183–4.

38 ibid 183.

39 ibid 187.

40 Jonathan Burchell, 'South Africa' in Kevin Jon Heller and Markus Dubber (eds), *The Handbook of Comparative Criminal Law* (Stanford University Press 2010) 466.

41 EM Burchell, Jonathan M Burchell and PMA Hunt, *South African Criminal Law and Procedure: General Principles of Criminal Law, Volume 1* (3 ed, Juta & Company 1997) 327. See also *Savoi and Others v National Director of Public Prosecutions and Another* (8006/12) [2013] ZAKZPHC 19; [2013] 3 All SA 548 (KZP) (17 May 2013) 87; *S v Mashaba and Others* (CC216/05) [2005] ZAGPHC 105 (4 October 2005) 19 citing *R v Jackelson* 1920 K 486 490.

42 Burchell, Burchell and Hunt (n 41) 326; *Goldberg v Director of Public Prosecutions: Western Cape* (A446/12) [2013] ZAWCHC 184; 2014 (2) SACR 57 (WCC) (17 December 2013) 78; *Cathay Pacific Airways Ltd and Another v Lin and Another* (260/2016) [2017] ZASCA 35; [2017] 2 All SA 722 (SCA) (29 March 2017) 40.

Regarding the 'intent' requirement, an aider and abettor must intentionally further the commission of a crime committed by somebody else. Negligence is not sufficient,[43] but *dolus eventualis* is.[44] A Draft Criminal Code for South Africa proposed by Snyman states that '[a] person has intention to bring about a result of his conduct if [...] he foresees the possibility of the result flowing from his conduct and reconciles himself to this possibility'.[45] Therefore, an aider and abettor must foresee the possibility that the principal will commit the crime, and, accepting that risk, she must then proceed to assist in the perpetration of the offence.[46] This approach is widely accepted by the courts and academics. In the *Savoi* case, the court held that the test for *dolus eventualis* is twofold: '(a) did the accused subjectively foresee the possibility of his conduct constituting an offence of racketeering? (b) did he reconcile himself with that possibility?'[47]

Hoctor states that:[48]

> Where a consequence (which is the result of an act which the law forbids him to do, or of an omission to do what the law commands) is subjectively foreseen by the actor at the time of the act or omission and he nevertheless proceeds to commit the act or to omit to do what he should do, it is said that, although the actor did not wish or desire to bring about the consequence, he nevertheless intended it and is thus liable.

Thus, according to Kemp: '[I]t is enough if X knew or foresaw that he was assisting Y to commit one or more of a range of possible crimes, which includes the type of crime that Y did in fact commit'.[49]

---

43 Snyman (n 37) 200.

44 Jonathan Burchell, *Principles of Criminal Law* (5 ed, Juta Legal and Academic Publishers 2016) 512. There is general agreement amongst scholars that an aider and abettor can be held liable if she acts with *dolus eventualis*. See also Badar (n 20) 526; Gerhard Kemp, *Criminal Law in South Africa* (Oxford University Press 2012) 292; Burchell, Burchell and Hunt (n 41) 327; Shannon Vaughn Hoctor, *Criminal Law in South Africa* (Wolters Kluwer Law & Business 2017) 60–1.

45 Carel Rainer Snyman, *A Draft Criminal Code for South Africa: With a Commentary* (Juta & Company 1995) 8.

46 Burchell (n 44) 512.

47 *Savoi and Others v National Director of Public Prosecutions and Another (8006/12) [2013] ZAKZPHC 19; [2013] 3 All SA 548 (KZP) (17 May 2013)* 88. The Court also referred to *S v De Oliveira 1993(2) SACR 59(A) 65 i-j*, in discussing the *S v Gwahla 1967(4) SA 566(A) 570* case, stated that 'sometimes the element in (b) is described as "recklessness" as to whether or not he has subjectively foreseen the possibility ensuing'.

48 Hoctor (n 44) 60–1.

49 Kemp (n 44) 292.

In sum, In South Africa an aider and abettor can be held liable if she acts with active knowledge and with *dolus eventualis*.

2.5 *Observations*

None of the countries analysed requires *dolus directus* as the intent requirement for aiding and abetting. Cameroon requires, at a minimum, *dolus indirectus* and active knowledge for the liability of the aider and abettor. Malawi, a common law jurisdiction with many traces of the English legal system, also requires *dolus indirectus*, but, significantly, recognises the wilful blindness

MAP 1 Standards of knowledge in Africa

doctrine. South Africa, a mixed jurisdiction with some German influence in its criminal law, allows for *dolus eventualis* and also requires active knowledge. The modern Egyptian legal system which originated at the time of French colonial occupation, has drawn inspiration from other jurisdictions regarding accomplice liability, and recognises that *dolus eventualis* is sufficient for the liability of an aider and abettor. The Egyptian legal system also demands active knowledge, and it does not address the wilful blindness doctrine. The Criminal Code, which also contains principles of Islamic sharia as an important source of law, has heavily influenced other Muslim jurisdictions, such as

MAP 2 Standards of intent in Africa

Kuwait, Libya, Iraq and Qatar, all of which have adopted the concept of *dolus eventualis* in their respective criminal codes.

3 Asia

This section analyses the knowledge and intent requirements for aiding and abetting in the following jurisdictions in the Asia region: China, India, Israel, Malaysia and Turkey.[50] China and Turkey are civil law jurisdictions, while India, Israel and Malaysia are common law jurisdictions. The main languages spoken in these countries are English, Hindi,[51] Israeli,[52] Malay,[53] Mandarin[54] and Turkish.[55] These countries also represent a combination of economically developed and economically developing states, and they exhibit secular, Hindu, Jewish and Muslim traditions.

3.1 *China*

China's first penal code was adopted in 1979, following the legal reconstruction after the death of Mao Zedong, and it was subsequently revised in 1997.[56] China is a civil law jurisdiction. Under influence of the criminal law of the Soviet Union, four elements are required to establish criminal liability under Chinese criminal law: the object of the crime,[57] the objective side of the

50 The knowledge and intent requirements of aider and abettors is analysed in China, India, Israel, Malaysia and Turkey, because these are the countries where I was able to find the online and print academic texts and judicial decisions necessary for the comparative analysis and where I was able to understand the languages in which the academic texts and judicial decisions where written.

51 In India, even though the main spoken language is Hindi, many publications and judicial decisions are published in English.

52 For Israel, I have referred to texts in English.

53 For Malaysia, I have referred to the limited number of texts I was able to find that were published in English.

54 For China, there seems to be an abundance of literature in Mandarin. I therefore had to refer to the limited number of books I was able to find that were published in English.

55 For Turkey, I was able to work with a translator which allowed me to have access to literature written in Turkish.

56 Marina Aksenova, *Complicity in International Criminal Law* (Hart Publishing 2016) 44.

57 The object of the crime refers to the social relations and interests protected by criminal law, and which are damaged by the criminal actions. In other words, it refers to the social values that are violated by the offence.

crime,[58] the subject of the crime,[59] and the subjective side of the crime. The subjective aspect of the crime (*fanzui zhuguan fangmian*) is comparable to the concept of *mens rea*.[60]

Article 25 of the 1997 Criminal Law of the People's Republic of China stipulates that: 'A joint crime is an intentional crime committed by two or more persons jointly'. According to Article 27, an accomplice plays a secondary or supplementary role in a joint crime. For liability to attach the accomplice must act intentionally and know about the circumstances of the offence committed by the principal.[61]

For aiders and abettors the elements of criminal intent – similar to intent for other crimes – consist of the cognitive element (knowledge) and the volitional element (will).[62] The knowledge element requires firstly, knowledge of the fact that the act is not a single offence, but an offence committed by several persons; secondly, knowledge that the act violates social values; and thirdly, knowledge that each participant anticipates her own as well as others' actions, and the consequences of such actions.[63] The aider and abettor must foresee the possible harmful result of her criminal act.[64] This includes situations in which she clearly realises that the harmful consequence will actually be achieved and circumstances in which there is a justifiable possibility of the occurrence of the harmful results.[65] For example, the knowledge element encompasses knowing whether the life or merely the health of another person will be the target of an attack.[66] However, the aider and abettor does not need to know either the concrete course of action or the exact offence that was committed.[67] Wilful blindness in Chinese criminal law is not discussed by courts and scholars.

---

58 The objective side of the crime refers to the offender's criminal actions, harmful consequences, and the causal link between them.

59 The subject of the crime refers to the natural or legal person who commits the offence.

60 Badar (n 18) 178.

61 Aksenova (n 56) 44.

62 Thomas Richter, 'China' in Ulrich Sieber, Hans-Georg Koch and Jan-Michael Simon (eds), *Participation in Crime: Criminal Liability of Leaders of Criminal Groups and Networks* (Duncker & Humblot Publishers 2020) 10.

63 ibid.

64 Badar (n 18) 183.

65 ibid citing the Commission of Legislative Affairs of the Standing Committee of the NPC: The Chinese Criminal Law of People's Republic of China: Interpretation of the Provisions, Legislative Reasons and Relevant Legal Documents (Peking University Press, 2009) 21.

66 Ulrich Sieber and Karin Cornils, *Nationales Strafrecht in Rechtsvergleichender Darstellung: Allgemeiner Teil, Volume 4* (Duncker & Humboldt 2010) 12.

67 ibid.

The second requirement of criminal intent is the volitional element (will). Article 14 of the Criminal Code of 1997 stipulates that intent is the mental state of intentional crime. Wang comments that:[68]

> Intent refers to the mental state where a person clearly knows that his act will produce socially dangerous consequences but who wishes or allows such consequences to occur.

For the aider and abettor the intent requirement refers to two kinds of mental attitudes towards the harmful consequences of her actions: (i) to hope; and (ii) to allow for.[69] 'To hope' refers to the aider and abettor's pursuit of the harmful results, whereas 'to allow for' means that the aider and abettor does not pursue the results, but she also does not oppose or try to prevent them. Although *dolus eventualis* is not recognised *per se* in the Criminal Code of 1997, this interpretation of intent is similar to the concept of *dolus eventualis*. Direct intent, indirect intent, *dolus eventualis* and even negligence[70] are all recognised in Chinese criminal law.[71] An aider and abettor must act with the hope that her actions will assist in the perpetration of the offence, or she must at least allow for the possibility that her acts could assist the principal.[72]

In sum, because the cognitive element (knowledge) and the volitional element (will) are closely related and must co-exist to establish the intent to commit an intentional crime,[73] an aider and abettor who acts with *dolus eventualis* can only incur liability if she fulfils the strict knowledge requirements. In other words, when she decides to assist the principal perpetrator she considers the result to be acceptable, and the volitional element (will) must be evaluated in light of the resulting consequences.[74]

---

68 Shizhou Wang, *Criminal Law in China* (Kluwer Law International 2017) 77.

69 Badar (n 18) 183.

70 Wang (n 68) 87–88 : there are two kind of negligence recognised in Chinese criminal law: careless negligence, which exists when a person does not realise the harmful consequences of her actions, though she should and would have avoided it if she had foreseen the danger, and negligence with undue assumption, which exists when a person foresees the harmful consequences of her actions but believes, recklessly, that the harmful result will not occur.

71 ibid 87–8.

72 Sieber and Cornils (n 66) 12.

73 Badar (n 18) 184.

74 ibid 185.

3.2 *India*

India is a common law jurisdiction. Macaulay's Indian Penal Code of 1860 was influenced by English criminal law, the French Penal Code, and Edward Livingston's Benthamite draft Louisiana Penal Code.[75] Chapter 5 of the Indian Penal Code is devoted to the crime of abetment and provides for three kinds of abettors: (i) instigators; (ii) conspirators; and (iii) aiders. An aider is a person who:[76]

> [E]ither prior to or at the time of the commission of an act, does anything in order to facilitate the commission of that act, and thereby facilitate the commission thereof.

The aider '[i]ntentionally aids [...] the doing of that thing'.[77]

'Knowledge' in some cases merges with 'intent' and is used to support the inference of intent.[78] It is, however, necessary to distinguish between 'knowledge' and 'intent'. In Indian criminal law knowledge implies an awareness of the consequences of one's conduct.[79] An aider and abettor who intends that the principal carry out the abetted crime is only liable if she knows that such conduct would amount to a crime.[80] The commentary to the Indian Penal Code notes that there is no abetment (in this work referred to as 'aiding and abetting') without knowledge.[81] Simply providing assistance without knowing that an offence is being committed does not amount to intentional assistance.[82] In India neither courts nor scholars engage with the wilful blindness doctrine.

75 Aksenova (n 56) 42.

76 Explanation 2 of section 107 of the Indian Penal Code.

77 Section 107 of the Indian Penal Code.

78 Neha Jain, 'India' in Ulrich Sieber, Susanne Forster and Konstanze Jarvers (eds), *National Criminal Law in a Comparative Legal Context, Defining Criminal Conduct, Volume 3.1* (Schriftenreihe des Max-Planck-Instituts für Ausländisches und Internationales Strafrecht 2011) 379.

79 ibid citing V Palkar, 'India' in *International Encyclopaedia of Laws, Volume 2: Criminal Law* (The Hague 2001) 81.

80 Aksenova (n 56) 43; Stanley Yeo, 'India' in Kevin Jon Heller and Markus Dubber (eds), *The Handbook of Comparative Criminal Law* (Stanford University Press 2010) 296–7 citing *Mohd Jamal v Emperor AIR 1930 Sind 64*. The Supreme Court of India in *Shri Ram v State of U.P, 1975 3 SCC 495*, paragraph 6, stated that the mere act of aiding the accused without any evidences to prove that the accused had sufficient knowledge of the 'nefarious design of the killer and his associates', cannot constitute an 'abatement by intentional aiding'.

81 Aksenova (n 56) 43; VV Raghavan, *Law of Crimes: Exhaustive Commentary on Indian Penal Code, 1860 (Act No. 45 of 1860)* (5 ed, India Law House 1999) sections 1–300 citing *Mahomad Janab, AIR 1930 Sind 64; 30 Cr LJ 1088 269*.

82 Aksenova (n 56) 43 43 citing *Ram Nath, 26 Cr LJ 362; AIR 1925 All 230*.

Concerning the intent requirement of an aider and abettor, commentaries on Indian criminal law identify three principal types of *mens rea*: (i) intention; (ii) recklessness; and (iii) negligence.[83] The general position is that an aider and abettor must have intended that the abetted person carry out the crime.[84] Intent refers to the aim of bringing about a contemplated result or the foresight that certain consequences will result from a particular course of conduct.[85] The Indian Penal Code also provides for cases in which the aided and abetted crime differs from the actual offence committed by the principal,[86] and cases in which the effect caused by the abetted act differs from that intended by the aider and abettor.[87] Sections 111 and 113 of the Indian Penal Code state:[88]

> Section 111: When an act is abetted and a different act is done, the abettor is liable for the act done, in the same manner and to the same extent as if he had directly abetted it: Provided the act done was a probable consequence of the abetment, and was committed under the influence of the instigation, or with the aid or in pursuance of the conspiracy which constituted the abetment.
>
> Section 113: When an act is abetted with the intention on the part of the abettor of causing a particular effect, and an act for which the abettor is liable in consequence of the abetment, causes a different effect from that intended by the abettor, the abettor is liable for the effect caused, in the same manner and to the same extent as if he had abetted the act with the intention of causing that effect, provided he knew that the act abetted was likely to cause that effect.

A person 'intends' the consequences that she foresees and desires and she is presumed to foresee the natural and probable consequences of her acts.[89] Ratanlal and Dhirajlal note:[90]

---

83 Jain (n 78) 379.
84 Yeo (n 80) 296–7 citing *Mohd Jamal v Emperor AIR 1930 Sind 64*.
85 Jain (n 78) 377–8 citing KD Gaur (ed), *Criminal Law and Criminology* (New Delhi 2002) 24.
86 Article 111 of the Indian Penal Code.
87 Article 113 of the Indian Penal Code.
88 Yeo (n 80) 297 notes that 'the test for criminal liability under section 111 is objective, while that under section 113 is subjective'.
89 Jain (n 78) 379 citing KD Gaur (ed), *Criminal Law and Criminology* (New Delhi 2002) 24, and V Palkar, 'India' in *International Encyclopaedia of Laws, Volume 2: Criminal Law* (The Hague 2001) 81.
90 Ratanlal Ranchhoddas and Dhirajlal Keshavlal Thakore, *Ratanlal & Dhirajlal's Law of Crimes: A Commentary on the Indian Penal Code, 1860* (Bharat Law House 2013) 507.

> Sections 111, 112 and 113 make it abundantly clear that if a person abets another in commission of an offence and the principal goes further thereafter and does something more which has a different result from that intended by the abettor and makes the offence an aggravated one, the abettor is liable for the consequences of the acts of his principal. The crux of the problem in an enquiry of this sort is whether the abettor as a reasonable man at the time of his instigation or intentionally aiding the principal would have foreseen the probable consequences of his abetment.

Therefore, it is presumed that the aider and abettor intend the natural consequences of her actions. Moreover, and aider and abettor can be held criminally accountable for the perpetration of a different crime than the one she had aided, provided that it was a probable consequence of her aid and was committed under the influence of her aid.[91] There are a number of cases supporting this view. In one case several people were found to have beaten a man, but one of them had killed the victim. The court decided that since the intention of all the participants was only to beat the victim, they were only liable for grievous hurt.[92] In another case, A ordered B and C to seize and forcibly take D with a view to assaulting him. D was beaten and tortured to the point of death. The court held that A was guilty of at least abetting the commission of voluntarily causing grievous hurt.[93] Also, in two cases dealing with instigation the aiders and abettors were not liable for the aggravated offence where the principal stabbed the victim with a spearhead of which the aider and abettor was unaware,[94] or where the principal gave the deceased a heavy blow with a stick resulting in death while the aider and abettor was unaware of the existence of the stick.[95] The Indian courts' approach to intent is similar to acting with *dolus indirectus*.

In summary, although the line between the knowledge and intent requirements are not always clear, it is clear that an aider and abettor (an 'abettor' or 'intentional aider' in the Indian Penal Code) must act with active knowledge and intent. The intent requirement includes both *dolus directus* and *dolus indirectus*. The knowledge requirement does not include wilful blindness.

---

91 ibid 506–7.

92 ibid 508 citing *Goluck Chung* (1866) 5 WR (Cr) 75.

93 ibid citing *Doorgessur Surmah* (1867) 7 WR (Cr) 61 97.

94 ibid citing *Girja Prasad* AIR 1935 All 346: (1935) 36 Cri LJ 438 (All): (1934) 57 All 717.

95 ibid citing *Nanboo Kedar* AIR 1962 MP 91: (1962)1 Cri LJ 435 (MP).

3.3 *Israel*

Israel is a common law jurisdiction. The liability of aiders and abettors is set forth in Article 31 of the Israeli Penal Law[96] which states that:

> If a person does anything – before an offense is committed or during its commission – to make its commission possible, to support or protect it, or to prevent the perpetrator from being taken or the offense or its loot from being discovered, or if he contributes in any other way to the creation of conditions for the commission of the offense, then he is an accessory.

For liability to attach an aider and abettor must act with knowledge and intent. Gosnell states that 'knowledge' is defined in terms of what a person can predict as the likely effect of her conduct and then consciously proceeding on the basis of that foresight.[97] In a case dealing with the crime of failure to prevent a felony the Supreme Court of Israel declined to apply the doctrine of wilful blindness as a substitute for active knowledge.[98]

As regards the intent requirement, Article 19 states that, '[a] person commits an offense only if he committed it with criminal intent'. Article 20(b), which deals with *dolus indirectus*, stipulates that, '[f]or purposes of the intent, the ability to foresee that a certain consequence is an almost certainly possible occurrence is equivalent to the intent to cause that occurrence'.[99]

Various interpretations of the intent requirement had emerged in the case law. The Supreme Court of Israel finally clarified the issue in the leading case of *Plonit v State of Israel*. The court held that it is sufficient that the aider and abettor foresaw the possibility that the principal *might* perpetrate the crime.

---

96 Article 498(a) of the Special part of the Israeli Penal Law contains a special offense of facilitation, and states that: 'If a person gives another tools, materials, money, information or any other means, knowing that they may directly or indirectly be used for the commission or to facilitate its commission, then he is liable to three years imprisonment.' According to Article 498(a) of the Israeli Penal Law the foreseeability of the possibility that a crime will be committed and that the provision of means that will enable or facilitate the perpetration of the offence, is sufficient for conviction. This offence does not require that the crime be committed or attempted. The crime is completed at the time the means are given.

97 Christopher Gosnell, 'Damned If You Don't: Liability for Omissions in International Criminal Law' in Yvonne McDermott, William A Schabas and Niamh Hayes (eds), *The Ashgate Research Companion to International Criminal Law: Critical Perspectives* (Routledge 2013) 104.

98 *Har-Shefi v State of Israel* (*2001*) *55*(*ii*) *PD 735* 756–68.

99 Israel, *Penal Law 5737–1977* (4 ed, Aryeh Greenfield Publications 2005) 10–11.

The court also stated that the requirement of the Israeli Penal Code that the aider must act with the purpose of facilitating the offence, relates only to her contribution. Thus, the aider must intend that her contribution facilitate the perpetration of the crime.[100] The Supreme Court has also held that oblique intent (referred to in this work as *dolus indirectus*) is sufficient in this regard. Thus, where the aider is almost certain that her contribution would facilitate the commission of a crime, she might be convicted even though she did not wish to facilitate the commission of the crime. Regarding the *Plonit* decision Kugler states:[101]

> The implication of the court's decision is that if the aider believes that the principal will commit the principal offense and acts in order to facilitate the commission of the offence, he or she may be convicted of aiding in spite of the fact that he or she has no interest in the commission of the offence. It seems that in a case where the aider only foresees the possibility of the commission of the principal offense, the aider may be convicted if it is his or her desire that should the offense actually be committed, his or her act will facilitate its commission.

Moreover, in *Gaber v State of Israel* the Supreme Court clarified that to find that an aider and abettor was 'almost certain that his act would facilitate the commission of the offence', the aider needed to be almost certain that the crime would actually be perpetrated.[102] In commenting on this case Kugler notes that when an aider and abettor does not wish to facilitate the perpetration of the crime, conviction depends on finding that the aider and abettor was almost certain both that the crime would be committed *and* that her assistance would facilitate its perpetration.[103]

Therefore, it is not necessary for an aider and abettor to want the conduct that constitutes the principal offence to be performed.[104] It is sufficient that the aider and abettor foresaw the possibility that the principal would perpetrate the offence, provided that the aider and abettor wanted to assist.[105]

100 *Plonit v State of Israel* (CA 320/99 55(3) PD 22 [1999]) 32–39; Gosnell (n 97) 104; Itzhak Kugler, 'Israel' in Kevin Jon Heller and Markus Dubber (eds), *The Handbook of Comparative Criminal Law* (Stanford University Press 2010) 352, 370.

101 Kugler (n 100) 352, 388, footnote 50.

102 ibid 352, 370 citing *C.A. 7580/02 Gaber v State of Israel*.

103 ibid 352, 388, footnote 52.

104 ibid 352, 370.

105 ibid.

The aider and abettor can thus be held liable if she acts with *dolus eventualis* regarding the principal's offense.

In conclusion, under Israeli criminal law an aider and abettor could incur liability for acting with active knowledge and with *dolus eventualis*.

3.4 *Malaysia*

Malaysia is also a common law jurisdiction. The Malaysian Penal Code is very similar in structure regarding the crime of abetment (referred to in this work as aiding and abetting) to the Indian Penal Code and the Singaporean Penal Code.[106] Section 107 of the Malaysian Penal Code describes the crime of abetment. There are four situations in which a person is said to commit an abetment, namely (i) by instigating a person to commit an offence;[107] (ii) by commanding a person to commit an offence;[108] (iii) by engaging in a conspiracy to commit an offence;[109] or (iv) by intentionally aiding a person to commit an offence.[110]

To charge an aider and abettor with abetment, she must have acted with knowledge and intent.[111] In *Public Prosecutor v Datuk Tan Cheng Swee and Ors*, the court stated that:[112]

> Briefly to constitute the offence of aiding and abetting the prosecution must prove intention on the part of the abettor to aid and he must be shown to have known the circumstances constituting the crime at the time when he voluntarily does a positive act of assistance.

An aider and abettor acts with knowledge if she knows that an offence will be committed or is contemplated and that her aid will assist the perpetration of that offence.[113] However, if she did not know that an offence would be

106 Bashir Ahmad Mallal and Andrew Christopher Simon, *Mallal's Penal Law* (Malayan Law Journal 2002) 140.

107 Article 107, paragraph a.

108 Article 107, paragraph aa. In 2012, this limb was inserted under section 107: Act A1430, Penal Code (Amendment Act) 2012.

109 Article 107, paragraph b.

110 Article 107, paragraph c.

111 *Hj Abdul Rahim Hassan & Anor v Public Prosecutor* (1997) MLJU 238.

112 *Public Prosecutor v Datuk Tan Cheng Swee & Ors* (1979) 1 MLJ 166.

113 Kheng Lian Koh, CMV Clarkson and NA Morgan, *Criminal Law in Singapore and Malaysia: Text and Materials* (Malayan Law Journal 1989) 317 citing *Ramabatar Agarwalla v The State* (1983) Cri LJ 122 CL.

committed she cannot be liable.[114] The Malaysian courts and legal scholars are silent on the doctrine of wilful blindness.

A person abets by aiding when, by some act done, she intends to assist the perpetration of the crime by the principal.[115] The court in *Datuk Tan Cheng Swee and Ors* held that '[u]nder the [...] class of abetment by intentional aid there must be evidence to show that by some act done by the abettor he had intended to aid or facilitate the commission of the principle offence'.[116]

The aider and abettor must therefore have intentionally aided the commission of the crime.[117] Importantly, similar to the Indian and Singaporean Penal Codes, Section 111 of the Malaysian Penal Code states that and aider and abettor is liable, notwithstanding the fact that she had abetted one act and the principal committed a different act. Section 111 is based on the principle that 'every man is presumed to intend the natural consequences of his act'.[118] Accordingly, the different act done must have been a probable consequence of the assistance and must have been perpetrated under influence of the aid.[119] Simon states that for Section 111 to apply:[120]

> [T]he evidence must show that (i) the accused abetted the commission of the offence; (ii) the act actually committed was done under the influence of such abetment; and (iii) the act done was the probable consequence of such abetment.

Section 113 of the Malaysian Penal Code, which corresponds to similar sections in the Indian and Singaporean penal codes, stipulates that an aider and abettor is responsible for an offence caused by the abetted act even though it is different from the act intended by her. Sections 111 and 113 must be read together.[121] According to Section 113 when the act done is the same as the abetted act, but the end result is different from that which the aider and abettor had intended, it must be shown that she knew that the act which she aided was likely to cause that result. Mallal and Simon explain that '[t]his is done by showing that

---

114 Mallal and Simon (n 106) 143.

115 Explanation 2, section 107 of the Penal Code. See also ibid citing *Jimina Jacee d/o CD Athananasius v Public Prosecutor* (2000) 1 SLR 205.

116 *Public Prosecutor v Datuk Tan Cheng Swee & Ors* (1979) 1 MLJ 166 171.

117 The language used in section 107 is 'intentionally aids'.

118 Mallal and Simon (n 106) 151.

119 *Daw Aye Aye Mu v Public Prosecutor* (1998) 2 SLR 64.

120 Mallal and Simon (n 106) 152.

121 ibid 153.

a reasonable man would draw an inference that the particular effect was likely to ensue from a particular act'.[122]

An aider and abettor is therefore liable for any aggravated form of crime which results from her assistance. This work describes this form of intent as *dolus indirectus*.

In conclusion, under Malaysian criminal law an aider and abettor could be held liable if she acts with active knowledge and at least *dolus indirectus*.

3.5 *Turkey*

The Turkish Penal Code of 2004 provides in Article 39(2)(b) and (c) that:

> A person is criminally responsible for aiding and abetting a criminal offence if [...] he provides the means used for the commission of the offence [or] he facilitates the execution of an offence by providing assistance before or after the commission of the offence.

To be held liable for aiding and abetting (referred to as *yardim* in Turkish criminal law) the aider and abettor must act with knowledge and intent.[123]

Reed states that 'it is sufficient for the aider to know the important elements of the criminal offence: ignorance of the details is irrelevant'.[124] An aider and abettor must therefore know that the principal will commit an offence and that she is assisting in the perpetration of the crime.[125] The doctrine of wilful blindness does not feature either in judicial decisions or academic work.

Article 21(2) of the Turkish Penal Code stipulates that '[t]here is probable intent when the individual conducts an act while foreseeing that the elements in the legal definition of an offence may occur'.[126] *Dolus eventualis* is sufficient for criminal liability. The intent of an aider and abettor must be two-fold (*çifte kast*): on the one hand, she must intend the perpetration of the offence by the

---

122 ibid 152–3.

123 Article 21(1) of the Turkish Penal Code states that '[t]he existence of a criminal offence depends upon the presence of intent. Intent is defined as knowingly and willingly conducting the elements in the legal definition of an offence.' See also R Murat Önok, 'Turkey' in Alan Reed and Michael Bohlander (eds), *Participation in Crime: Domestic and Comparative Perspectives* (Taylor & Francis 2013) 461; Silvia Tellenbach, 'Turkey' in Ulrich Sieber, Hans-Georg Koch and Jan-Michael Simon (eds), *Participation in Crime: Criminal Liability of Leaders of Criminal Groups and Networks* (Duncker & Humblot Publishers 2020) 1299.

124 Önok (n 123) 461.

125 Tellenbach, 'Turkey' (n 123) 1299.

126 Feridun Yenisey, *Turkey* (Kluwer Law International 2016) 93.

principal; on the other, she must intend to assist the principal in the commission of the crime. It is, however, not necessary for the principal to be aware of the assistance provided by the aider and abettor.[127] Thus, the assistance does not need to be a *conditio sine qua non* for the principal to commit the offence.[128]

It is sufficient for an aider and abettor to act with *dolus eventualis*.[129] When the principal exceeds the intent of the aider and abettor, the aider and abettor will nevertheless be held liable for the consequences if those consequences were foreseeable.[130] It thus follows that the aider and abettor would not be liable if the principal commits a different crime or a crime of increased gravity than the one the aider and abettor had intended to assist in.[131]

In conclusion, an aider and abettor must act with active knowledge and *dolus eventualis* to incur liability.

3.6 *Observations*

There seems to be general agreement among the Asian jurisdictions analysed that for liability to attach an aider and abettor must act with active knowledge. The doctrine of wilful blindness does not seem to be recognised in any of these jurisdictions. Three out of the five jurisdictions (China, Israel, and Turkey) provide that an aider and abettor could be held liable if she acts with *dolus eventualis*. The remaining two (India and Malaysia) recognise *dolus indirectus* as the threshold standard of intent. Like the African jurisdictions analysed *dolus directus* is not the minimum standard of intent required for aiders and abettors. As was seen regarding the intent requirement in Egypt, other nations in the Asia region, such as Kuwait, Iraq and Qatar, have all included a special provision in their respective criminal codes to provide for liability when the aider and abettor acts with *dolus eventualis*.

127 Silvia Tellenbach, 'Tatbeteiligung in Der Türkei' in Ulrich Sieber and Karin Cornils (eds), *Nationales Strafrecht in Rechtsvergleichender Darstellung: Allgemeiner Teil, Volume 4* (Duncker & Humboldt 2010) 331.

128 ibid 334.

129 Tellenbach, 'Turkey' (n 123) 1299; Silvia Tellenbach, 'Parties to Crime in Turkey' in Ulrich Sieber, Konstanze Jarvers and Emily Silverman (eds), *National Criminal Law in a Comparative Legal Context, Defining Criminal Conduct, Volume 4.1* (Duncker and Humblot 2015) 256–7.

130 Önok (n 123) 461. Reed notes that the majority opinion is that the assistance offered must have a causal link to the completion of the crime.

131 Tellenbach, 'Parties to Crime in Turkey' (n 129) 256.

MAP 3 Standards of knowledge in Asia

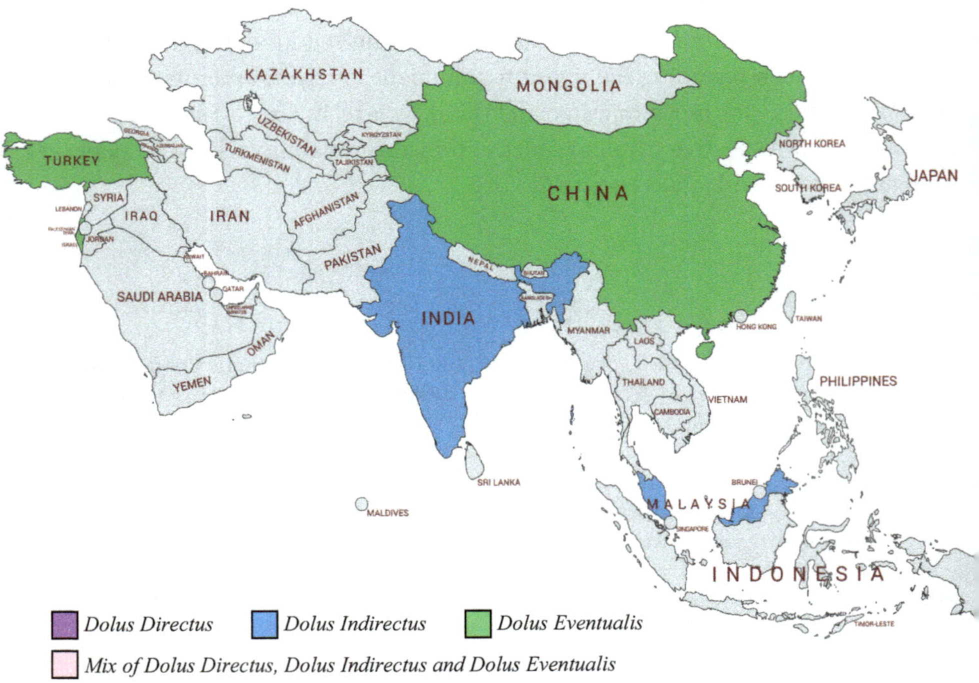

MAP 4 Standards of intent in Asia

4 Europe

In Europe I analyse the knowledge and intent requirements of aiders and abettors in England and Wales, France, Germany, Italy and Russia. The law of France and England and Wales have heavily influenced criminal law in most of their former colonies. German criminal law has also been a source of inspiration for many countries, notably South Africa and many Latin American nations. Russia has influenced Chinese criminal law. The main languages spoken in the European countries analysed are French, English, German, Italian, and Russian.[132]

4.1 *England and Wales*

England and Wales is the only common law jurisdiction analysed in Europe. The jurisprudence of the courts of England and Wales is mired in disagreement over the applicable *mens rea* requirements for particular crimes.

Regarding the knowledge element, in *Johnson v Youden*[133] Lord Goddard CJ stated that '[b]efore a person can be convicted of aiding and abetting the commission of an offence he must at least know the essential matters which constitute the principal offence'. This statement of principle was subsequently approved by the House of Lords in *Churchill*[134] and *Maxwell*.[135] However, the scope of this oft-quoted passage is anything but clear. It appears to include the facts, circumstances and other matters that make up the conduct element of the principal. The extent to which the aider and abettor must know the details of the offence is still unclear. Difficulties arise when the aider and abettor does not know precisely, but only has some general idea, what offence the principal intends to perpetrate.[136]

132 These are all languages that I understand, except for Russian, for which I had recourse to a translator.

133 *Johnson v Youden* [1950] 1 KB 544.

134 *Churchill v Walton* [1967] 2 AC 224.

135 *DPP for Northern Ireland v Maxwell* [1978] 1 WLR 1350.

136 Andrew Ashworth and Jeremy Horder, *Ashworth's Principles of Criminal Law* (8 ed, Oxford University Press 2016) 445.

Sweet v Parsley, a key authority for the proposition that *mens rea* will be required absent very clear provision to the contrary, exhibits the general commitment of English law to establishing culpability in some form by reference to a mental state. Lord Reid explained that:[137]

> [O]ur first duty is to consider the words of the Act: if they show a clear intention to create an absolute offence that is an end of the matter. But such cases are very rare. Sometimes the words of the section which creates a particular offence make it clear that *mens rea* is required in one form or another. Such cases are quite frequent. But in a very large number of cases there is no clear indication either way. In such cases there has for centuries been a presumption that Parliament did not intend to make criminals of persons who were in no way blameworthy in what they did. That means that whenever a section is silent as to *mens rea* there is a presumption that, in order to give effect to the will of Parliament, we must read in words appropriate to require *mens rea*.

In *Brainbridge*[138] the court established that neither mere suspicion nor broad knowledge of some criminal intention is sufficient; the aider and abettor must know what particular offence would be committed. This goes beyond the requirement in *Johnson v Youden*.[139] In *DPP for Northern Ireland v Maxwell*,[140] which was recently confirmed by the Supreme Court of the United Kingdom in *Jogee*,[141] it was finally determined that the aider must at least know the range of possible offences (*i.e.* that the offence committed by the principal must have been within the range of possible offences). As held by Lord Scarman, 'an accessory who leaves it to his principal to choose is liable, provided always the choice is made from the range of offences from which the accessory contemplates the choice will be made'.[142]

It is notable that, although the doctrine of wilful blindness exists in English criminal law,[143] it does not seem to apply to complicity cases. This is because the doctrine would not satisfy the 'awareness of a virtual certainty' standard

137 *Sweet v Parsley* [*1970*] *AC 132* 148.
138 *R v Brainbridge* [*1960*] *1 QB 129*.
139 *Johnson v Youden* [*1950*] *1 K.B. 544*.
140 *DPP for Northern Ireland v Maxwell* [*1978*] *1 W.L.R. 1350*.
141 *R v Jogee* [*2016*] *UKSC 8;* [*2017*] *AC 387* paragraphs 15–16.
142 *DPP for Northern Ireland v Maxwell* [*1978*] *1 W.L.R. 1350*.
143 Ashworth and Horder (n 136) 203.

in *Woollin* (explained below).[144] In sum, the English test for accessorial knowledge is whether the crime committed was within the contemplated range of offences and, if not, whether it was of the same kind as any of the contemplated crimes.[145] Thus, an aider and abettor must act with active knowledge and not merely with wilful blindness.

Regarding intent, English courts have formulated various inconsistent and often contradictory definitions. Over the years two major concepts have developed on the actual meaning of intention.[146] Firstly, there is the concept of 'direct intention', according to which the prohibited consequence is intended when achieving that consequence is the aim or objective of the actor. Put differently, a result cannot be regarded as intended unless it was the actor's purpose.[147] The second concept is that of 'oblique intention', according to which the prohibited consequence is intended when it is foreseen as a virtual, practical or moral certainty.[148] The aider and abettor must intend to do whatever acts of assistance she provides and she must be aware of their ability to assist the principal.[149] *Woollin*[150] emphasized that in criminal law intention does not necessarily have the same meaning in every context. However, *Moloney*[151] and *Hancock*[152] had previously suggested that the test for intention is generally applicable to all crimes.

In *National Coal Board v Gamble*[153] it was held that the aider and abettor's indifference to the consequences was irrelevant, because she had voluntarily done an act that assisted the principal knowing the circumstances that constituted the crime. Devlin J stated:[154]

---

144 Vanessa Reid, Alexander Sarch and Sophie Walker, 'Thinking Like an Accomplice: The Mens Rea for Complicity in US and English Law after Rosemond and Jogee' in Beatrice Krebs (ed), *Accessorial Liability after Jogee* (Hart Publishing 2020) 170. The authors state that they 'have not been able to find English cases allowing wilful ignorance to satisfy the "awareness of a virtual certainty" standard in general - let alone in complicity cases'.

145 KJM Smith, *A Modern Treatise on the Law of Criminal Complicity* (Clarendon Press 1991) 167–9; *DPP for Northern Ireland v Maxwell [1978] 1 W.L.R. 1350; R v Brainbridge [1960] 1 Q.B. 129.*

146 *DPP v Smith [1961] AC 290; Hyam v DPP [1975] AC 55; R v Moloney [1985] 1 AC 905; R v Hancock [1985] UKHL 9.*

147 Ormerod David, *Smith and Hogan Criminal Law* (12 ed, Oxford University Press 2008) 98.

148 CMV Clarkson, HM Keating and SR Cunningham, *Clarkson and Keating Criminal Law: Text and Materials* (6 ed, Sweet & Maxwell 2007) 119.

149 Ashworth and Horder (n 136) 466–7; Smith (n 145) 141.

150 *R v Woollin [1999] AC 82.*

151 *R v Moloney [1985] 1 AC 905.*

152 *R v Hancock [1985] UKHL 9.*

153 *National Coal Board v Gamble [1959] 1 QB 11.*

154 ibid 23.

> But an indifference to the result of the crime does not itself negative abetting. If one man deliberately sells to another a gun to be used for murdering a third, he may be indifferent about whether the third man lives or dies and interested only in the cash profit to be made out of the sale, but he can still be an aider and abettor. To hold otherwise would be to negative the rule that *mens rea* is a matter of intent only and does not depend on desire or motive.

Thus, in most cases it is possible to determine if a person acted with 'direct intention' or 'oblique intention' by determining what her purpose was. However, there is a minority of cases in which the attribution of intent might prove more challenging. In such cases intent could be established based on foresight of the consequences of an act as a 'virtual certainty'.[155]

In *R v Nedrick*[156] the court adopted the concept of 'oblique intention'. The defendant set another woman's house alight. The house burnt down completely and one of the woman's children died in the fire. The Court of Appeal held that 'a man may intend the certain result whilst at the same time not desiring it to come about'.[157] It also stated that intent may be inferred if death or serious bodily harm was a virtual certainty (barring some unforeseen intervention) because of the defendant's actions and the defendant appreciated that such was the case.[158]

The same issue of the applicability of intent arose in *R v Woollin*.[159] The defendant threw his three-month old son across the room which led to the baby's death two days later. In this case Lord Steyn, in an opinion with which the other members of the House of Lords agreed, found it necessary to substitute the word 'infer' with 'find'. An accused could therefore only be held liable if death or seriously bodily harm was at least a virtual certainty.[160]

In the 2016 landmark decision of *Jogee* the Supreme Court clarified the applicable test for accomplice liability. It declared that intent, not mere foresight, was required to find an aider and abettor guilty of a crime such as murder. The court held that:[161]

155 Iryna Marchuk, *The Fundamental Concept of Crime in International Criminal Law: A Comparative Law Analysis* (Springer Science & Business Media 2013) 36.

156 *R v Nedrick* [*1986*] *1 WLR 1025*.

157 ibid 1027.

158 ibid.

159 *R v Woollin* [*1999*] *AC 82*.

160 ibid.

161 *R v Jogee* [*2016*] *UKSC 8;* [*2017*] *A.C. 387* 83.

> [F]oresight of what might happen is ordinarily no more than evidence from which a jury can infer the presence of a requisite intention. It may be strong evidence, but its adoption as a test for the mental element for murder in the case of a secondary party is a serious and anomalous departure from the basic rule, which results in over-extension of the law of murder …

Therefore, the mental element in assisting or encouraging is an intention to assist or encourage the commission of a crime. This requires knowledge of any existing facts necessary for it to be criminal.[162] In addition, '[i]f the crime requires a particular intent, D2 [the aider and abettor] must intend (it may be conditionally) to assist D1 [the principal actor] to act with such intent'.[163]

However, with reference to *Blakeley and Sutton v DPP*[164] and *Maxwell*,[165] Ashworth and Aksenova explains that in English criminal law complicity requires proof of intention, but not necessarily purpose, and that *dolus eventualis* (or 'advertent recklessness') may be sufficient.[166] In *Blakeley and Sutton v DPP*, T wanted to drive home, but the accused did not want him to leave. The accused laced T's drink with vodka intending to tell him before he left that he was now unable to drive because of alcohol consumption. T left for his car before the accused could tell him that alcohol had been added to his drink. T was subsequently charged with drunk driving and the accused was charged with aiding and abetting that offence. McCullough J stated that in cases where the accomplice's conduct preceded the perpetration of the principal crime, it had to be proved that the accomplice's:[167]

> [I]nadvertent recklessness did not suffice to convict a person accused of being an accessory before the fact, and it had to be shown that the person accused contemplated that his act would or might bring about or

162 ibid 8–9.

163 ibid 90. *Jogee* is a significant case which revisited House of Lords and Supreme Court cases on complicity, namely *R v Powell and English* [1999] 1 AC 1; *Regina v Armel Gnango* [2011] UKSC 59; [2012] 1 A.C. 827.

164 *Blakely and Sutton v DPP* [1991] RTR 405.

165 *DPP for Northern Ireland v Maxwell* [1978] 1 W.L.R. 1350.

166 Marina Aksenova, 'The Specific Direction Requirement for Aiding and Abetting: A Call for Revisiting Comparative Criminal Law' (2015) 4 Cambridge Journal of International and Comparative Law 88, 102; Aksenova (n 56) 32; Andrew Ashworth, 'United Kingdom' in Kevin Jon Heller and Markus Dubber (eds), *The Handbook of Comparative Criminal Law* (Stanford University Press 2010) 539.

167 *Blakely and Sutton v DPP* [1991] R.T.R. 405.

> assist the commission of the principal offence and he must have been prepared, nevertheless, to do his own act and must have done that act intentionally.

The judge added that, 'albeit the motive of the defendants was that T should spend the night with B, [the] intention to prevent him from driving was just as real as [the] knowledge that he intended to drink so little that he would be able lawfully to drive'.[168] According to this approach the aider and abettor would only have needed to intentionally assist the principal with foresight that the principal would or might intentionally commit the crime as a strong possibility, a real possibility or as a likelihood.[169] However, in light of *Jogee* this interpretation has become questionable. It is doubtful whether *dolus eventualis* would be sufficient to hold an aider and abettor liable.

In sum, the doctrine of wilful blindness does not seem to apply to complicity cases in England and Wales. Regarding intent, according to the *Woollin* standard oblique intent is sufficient. This means that if the aider and abettor aimed to achieve a consequence other than the prohibited harm, but nevertheless foresaw such harm as a virtual certainty of her actions, she could be held liable. Significantly, some English scholars have argued that *dolus eventualis* might also be sufficient for holding an aider and abettor liable, but since *Jogee* the law on complicity has evolved. Intent, not mere foresight, is now required to establish the liability of an aider and abettor. It is therefore doubtful that *dolus eventualis* would suffice. Thus, for the purpose of the comparative analysis, the minimum standard of intent in England and Wales is taken to be *dolus indirectus* and not *dolus eventualis*.

4.2 *France*

France is a civil law jurisdiction. An 'accomplice' to a felony is described in Article 121–7 of the French Criminal Code as 'the person who knowingly, by

168 ibid. The Court also added: 'To establish secondary liability against the appellant it is important to appreciate that the real question as to the appellant's state of mind is whether he foresaw the likelihood that the driver would drive in a dangerous manner. [...] Further, we must emphasise what the prosecution had to prove in relation to the appellant's state of mind. It accepted that it was not sufficient to prove that the appellant ought to have foreseen that Westbrook would drive dangerously. The prosecution had to prove that the appellant did foresee that Westbrook was likely to drive dangerously when he permitted him to get into the driver's seat'.

169 Janet Loveless, *Criminal Law Text, Cases and Materials* (5 ed, Oxford University Press 2016) 2002.

aiding and abetting, facilitates its preparation or commission'. The accomplice must have furnished the aid with the knowledge that it would support the crime.[170] More precisely, the knowledge element refers to the criminal nature of the intent of the principal[171] and the knowledge that she is participating in the principal's offence.[172] In other words, the act of complicity must have been performed with the knowledge that the act would support the crime and the aider and abettor must have voluntarily participated. Wilful blindness does not seem to be a factor in either statute or case law.

Moreover, the aider and abettor must have acted intentionally – *i.e.* consciously (*sciemment*) – regardless of the intention of the principal.[173] Thus, French criminal law does not provide for the possibility of negligently aiding and abetting an offence.

Legal scholars recognise the concept of *dol éventuel* (*dolus eventualis*).[174] This is where the defendant 'merely foresees the possibility of the result but he does not desire its occurrence'.[175] However, 'this form of *dol* does not amount to *dol spécial* and hence is not a mental state that will support a conviction'.[176] Therefore, *dolus eventualis* would not support the conviction of the aider and abettor in a case of murder, for example. In the *Paemelabre* case the court declined to infer complicity in the unlawful slaughter of animals merely

---

170 Yves Mayaud and Emmanuelle Allain, *Code Pénal* (104 ed, Editions Dalloz 2007) 126. See also Frédéric Debove, François Falletti and Emmanuel Dupic, *Précis de Droit Pénal et de Procédure Pénal* (6 ed, Presses Universitaires de France 2016) 168 stating that 'Pour être punissable, le complice doit avoir adhéré à l'infraction principale de sorte qu'il n'existe pas de complicité par imprudence.'

171 Peggy Pfützner, 'Frankreich' in Ulrich Sieber and Karin Cornils (eds), *Nationales Strafrecht in Rechtsvergleichender Darstellung Allgemeiner Teil. Band 4* (Duncker & Humblot 2010) 281.

172 *Chambre Criminelle, 28 May 1980, Pernot* (*D 1981, IR 137, obs G Roujou de Boubée*) where the court stated: 'le complice doit avoir participé sciemment à l'infraction principale : la notion de complicité apparaît en effet comme inséparable de la conscience chez l'agent, du concours qu'il apporte à la commission d'une infraction.' [...] 'L'intention requise pouvant être définie comme la connaissance du caractère délictueux des actes de l'auteur et la volonté de participer à leur commission.' Significantly, *dolus eventualis* only seems to apply to situations where individuals are endangered because of their failure to conform to the required standards of safety, which is not the case for a person who finances an entity involved in the commission of core crimes.

173 Pfützner (n 171) 84.

174 Badar (n 20) 524.

175 Badar (n 18) 171.

176 ibid.

because the accused had driven a truck containing pigs to a location where they were slaughtered and had removed the dead animals' carcasses.[177]

In conclusion, to be held liable as an aider an abettor under French law one must act with active knowledge and at least *dolus indirectus*.

4.3 *Germany*

German criminal law has had a widespread influence on numerous civil law jurisdictions and on several mixed and common law jurisdictions, such as South Africa and Israel.[178] Article 27(1) of the German Criminal Code defines an aider and abettor as 'any person who intentionally assists another in the intentional commission of an unlawful act'. The intent requirement in the case of aiding and abetting is 'double' (*doppelter*)[179] and is referred to as '*Vorsatz ist Wissen und Wollen*' ('intention is knowledge and wilfulness').[180] This implies that proving intent requires the fulfilment of two distinct elements.

Firstly, '*Wissen*' is the cognitive component. As Badar explains:[181]

> [M]ere potential knowledge is not sufficient. That is not to say that the perpetrator has to make conscious reflections about the material legal elements of the offence; co-consciousness is sufficient. This co-consciousness may be present in two forms: (1) co-consciousness based on awareness; and (2) co-consciousness based on the knowledge of the accompanying circumstances.

Put differently, knowledge means 'awareness' and is required for the liability of the aider and abettor. By contrast, recklessness requires 'conscious disregard',

177 *Chambre Criminelle, 1 December 1944, Paemelabre* (*D 1945 162*) which stated: 'la complicité n'est punissable que si ceux qui ont aidé ou assisté les auteurs de l'action qualifiée crime ou délit, dans les faits qui l'ont préparée ou facilitée, ont agi avec connaissance, ou si ceux qui leur ont procuré le moyen qui a servi à l'action savaient qu'il devait y servir.'

178 Markus Dubber, 'The Promise of German Criminal Law: A Science of Crime and Punishment' (2006) 6 German Law Journal 1049, 1049 states: 'German criminal law theory enjoys widespread influence in the civil law world. Its impact extends from European countries like Spain, Portugal, Croatia, Greece, Turkey, Austria, Switzerland, Finland, and Sweden, to Israel and the Spanish and Portuguese speaking countries of Latin America, and to Asian countries like Taiwan, South Korea, and Japan.'

179 Aksenova (n 166) 101.

180 Badar (n 18) 135 citing the decision *RGSt 51, 305, 311; 58, 247* (Official Collection of the Judgments of the Reichsgericht 'Court of the Reich').

181 ibid.

which is not sufficient to attract liability.[182] The doctrine of wilful blindness also does not feature in German criminal law.

Secondly, the aider and abettor must have the intention to aid the principal in committing the intentional and unlawful crime.[183] Thus the intent must cover the consummation of the principal's offence although the aider and abettor does not need to know every element of the main offence. '*Wollen*' presents the volitional component. It is generally accepted that there are three forms of *Vorsatz*: (i) *Absicht* or *dolus directus* of the first degree; (ii) *dolus indirectus* or *dolus directus* of the second degree (referred to in this work as *dolus indirectus*); and (iii) *bedingter Vorsatz*[184] or *dolus eventualis*.[185] Although the German Criminal Code does not specify which *Vorsatz* is required for the aider and abettor, *dolus eventualis* (also referred to as the concept of conditional intention)[186] seems to be the minimum threshold to ensure an aider and abettor's liability.

As explained by Dubber and Hörnle:[187]

> This volitional element must be distinguished from straightforwardly wanting something to occur (the latter would be purpose, direct intention). ... It is sufficient that, in order to achieve his goal (for example, immobilizing the victim), the offender condones or accepts the harmful outcome or at least comes to terms with it because it is necessary means to his end. An often-mentioned test question asks whether an offender honestly (albeit irrationally) trusted that death (or other harm) would not happen, and so acted only negligently, or if he thought, 'if things go the worst possible way, so be it'. [...] [T]he majority position appears to be that it is enough, for conditional intention, that the defendant considered the result as possible and not entirely unlikely.

182 Markus Dubber and Tatjana Hörnle, *Criminal Law: A Comparative Approach* (Oxford University Press) 236.

183 Badar (n 18) 159.

184 As indicated by Badar (n 18) in footnote 70, 'the term bedingter Vorsatz (conditional intent), is, however misleading, because it is not the intent which is conditional; on the contrary, a conditional intent has not yet reached the threshold of "intent".'

185 Iryna Marchuk, *The Fundamental Concept of Crime in International Criminal Law: A Comparative Law Analysis* (Springer Science & Business Media 2013) 45–6.

186 It is important to distinguish the German criminal law's concept of conditional intent from that of recklessness in United States criminal law.

187 Dubber and Hörnle (n 182) 236, 243.

In sum, under German law an aider and abettor must act with active knowledge and at a minimum *dolus eventualis*.

4.4 *Italy*

Italy is a civil law jurisdiction which has adopted a unitary approach to participation in crime. The Italian Penal Code of 1930 extends liability to all participants of the criminal offence.[188] Article 110 of the Italian Penal Code stipulates that '[w]hen more than one person participates in the same offence, each of them shall be subject to the punishment prescribed, except as provided in the following articles'.

Criminal responsibility for the accomplice arises if she assists the principal intentionally, *i.e.* knowingly and willingly.[189] Article 43 of the Italian Penal Code lays down the mental element of the crime, which is *dolo*, and it states that the prohibited result must be *preveduto* (foreseen) and *voluto* (wanted). *Dolo* equally applies to aiding and abetting.

The aider and abettor must willingly contribute to the perpetration of the crime with general knowledge about the factual situation, and her actions must constitute necessary support for carrying out the crime.[190] Neither the courts nor legal scholars seem to have adopted the wilful blindness doctrine.

Regarding the intent element, the aider must 'want' (also referred to as 'desire') the prohibited result.[191] Significantly, the Court of Cassation has held that a result may be *volute* notwithstanding the fact that it was not desired, if having contemplated the possibility of bringing it about by pursuing a particular course of conduct the aider and abettor is prepared to run the risk of doing so.[192] The doctrine of *dolo eventuale* (*dolus eventualis*) is therefore applicable.[193] Even a small risk may be *volute* if the aider and abettor has reconciled herself with it or accepted it as part of the price she is prepared to pay to secure her objective.[194] In sum, *dolo eventuale* means having the knowledge of the probability that a crime will be committed and accepting the risk. Acceptance

---

188 Astolfo Di Amato and Federica Fucito, *Criminal Law in Italy* (3 ed, Wolters Kluwer Law & Business 2016) 212.

189 ibid 215.

190 Aksenova (n 56) 38; S Beltrani, R Marino and R Petrucci, *Codice Penale: Annotato Con La Giurisprudenza* (Edizioni Giuridiche Simone 2003) 429.

191 McAuley Finbarr and J Paul McCutcheon, *Criminal Liability: A Grammar* (Round Hall Sweet & Maxwell 2000) 301.

192 *Cass, sez I, novembre 24, 1976, La Gioia, Cass Pen Mass Ann 1124, Giust Pen 1977, II, 495.*

193 ibid.

194 Badar (n18) 139; Finbarr and McCutcheon (n 191) 302; *Cass, sez I, 5 luglio 1976, Salvalajo, Cass Pen Mass Ann 1977, 831; Cass, sez I, 30 maggio 1980, Milano, Cass Pen Mass, Ann 1981,*

is equated to wanting. Thus, the crux of *dolo eventuale* is not necessarily the probability of the risk, but rather the fact that the aider and abettor has accepted or reconciled herself with the possibility of a crime being committed. It follows then that the likelihood of the risk occurring does not in itself determine whether it is *voluto*.[195] In other words, it is the acceptance of the risk that makes the individual responsible as if she had wanted to produce the prohibited result. Consequently, it is enough that she had considered the possibility that it would happen and she had accepted it.

In sum, under Italian law liability will attach if an aider and abettor acts with active knowledge and *dolus eventualis*.

4.5 *Russia*

Russia is a civil law jurisdiction. Article 33(5) of the Russian Penal Code describes an aider and abettor (*posobnik*) as 'a person who assisted in the commission of the offence by supplying counsel, directions, information or the means for the commission'.

Regarding the knowledge requirement, foreseeability is required. However, a mere abstract foresight (meaning acting with negligence) does not suffice.[196] The aider and abettor must at least have an idea of the circumstances that constitute the offence.[197] In other words, the aider and abettor must possess the knowledge of the possibility that the unlawful result would occur.[198]

Regarding the intent requirement, according to Article 32 aiding and abetting as a form of accessorial liability requires double intent, namely, (i) intent with regard to crime itself, and (ii) intent with regard to the assistance provided. Regarding the intent of the aider and abettor to assist, it is the prevailing opinion that a crime can be committed with *dolus eventualis* (*kosvennyi umysel*).[199] *Dolus eventualis* is described in Article 25(3) of the Russian Penal Code as follows:

1988, Giust, pen 1982, II, 312; Cass, sez I, 12 febbraio 1982, Bonomo, Cass Pen 1983, Giust Pen 1982, II, 654 Ass Genova 17 febbraio 1978, Levrero, Giur Merito 1980, 167.

195 Finbarr and McCutcheon (n 191) 302.

196 Marchuk (n 185) 58.

197 Peter Rolofs and Ulrike Schittenhelm, 'Russia' in Ulrich Sieber, Hans-Georg Koch and Jan-Michael Simon (eds), *Participation in Crime: Criminal Liability of Leaders of Criminal Groups and Networks* (Duncker & Humblot Publishers 2020) 1007.

198 Badar (n 18) 184.

199 Aksenova (n 56) 39–41; Rolofs and Schittenhelm (n 197) 1007; Caspar Plomp, 'Aiding and Abetting: The Responsibility of Business Leaders under the Rome Statute of the International Criminal Court' (2014) 30 Utrecht Journal of International and European

> A crime shall be considered to be committed with *kosvennyi umysel*, if the person was conscious of the social dangerousness of his actions (omissions), foresaw the possibility of the occurrence of the socially dangerous consequences, did not desire, but consciously allowed these consequences or was indifferent to them.

In other words, a crime is committed with *dolus eventualis* if a person is aware of the danger of her conduct, she foresees the possibility of the harmful consequences occurring, and she does not wish for it but she nevertheless consciously allows those consequences or treats them with indifference.[200] Badar describes it as:[201]

> [A]llowing for the occurrence of the harmful consequence rather than [being] positively in pursuit of it. Furthermore, [the aider and abettor] is ready to commit the act that leads to the consequence. When he determines to commit the act, he considers the consequence as acceptable.

Significantly, although *dolus eventualis* for aiding and abetting is accepted in scholarship there does not seem to be any caselaw of the Supreme Court to confirm that liability attaches to an aider and abettor who acts with *dolus eventualis*.

Active knowledge and *dolus eventualis* are therefore the threshold standard of knowledge and intent that an aider must possess.

4.6 *Observations*

Concerning the knowledge requirement, there is a consensus between France, Germany, Italy and Russia that an aider and abettor must possess active knowledge. Wilful blindness does not seem to be a factor in any of these European nations. In England and Wales the doctrine has been referred to by courts and scholars, but it has ultimately been rejected.

There is no consensus among the European nations analysed regarding the minimum level of intent for aiders and abettors. France is the only civil law jurisdiction that does not seem to provide for liability based on *dolus eventualis*. By contrast, Germany, Italy and Russia do. Significantly, *dolus eventualis* is a civil law concept and with a few exceptions European jurisdictions seem to

---

Law 4; Gennady Esakov, 'R v. Jogee: A Case for Comparative Study' (2018) 6 Russian Law Journal 133, 137–8.

200 Marchuk (n 185) 57–8.

201 Badar (n 18) 184.

MAP 5 Standards of knowledge in Europe

have accepted that it is the minimum standard of intent.[202] In England and Wales it is doubtful whether *dolus eventualis* is sufficient. Thus, I accept for the purpose of this work that the minimum standard of intent required for aiders and abettors in England and Wales is *dolus indirectus*.

202 The Netherlands is amongst the European jurisdictions that accept criminal liability of aiders and abettors who act with *dolus eventualis*. See Elies van Sliedregt, *Individual Criminal Responsibility in International Law* (Oxford University Press 2012) 116–7. A noteworthy case concerning the mental elements of an aider and abettor in the Netherlands is that of *Frans van Anraat*. Van Anraat, who supplied chemicals to the Saddam Hussein regime that were subsequently used in attacks against the civilian populations, was found culpable of aiding and abetting war crimes. The Hague District Court held that Van Anraat must have been aware of the considerable risk that his chemicals would be used to produce chemical weapons, that these weapons would then be deployed against civilian populations, and that he had accepted this risk. *District Court, The Hague, 23 December 2005, LJN: AU8685*, paragraph 7.

MAP 6 Standards of intent in Europe

5 Latina America

In Latin America I analyse the knowledge and intent requirement for aiders and abettors in Argentina, Brazil, and Mexico. These are all civil law jurisdictions as the vast majority of the legal systems in Latin America are based on codified civil law.[203] The main languages spoken in these countries are Spanish and Portuguese.[204] These states all have Christian traditions.

203 The exceptions are Belize (a common law jurisdiction) and Dominica (a mixed jurisdiction).

204 For references in Portuguese I had recourse to a translator.

5.1 *Argentina*

Accomplice liability in Argentine criminal law is regulated by Articles 45 to 49 of the Penal Code. It provides for first-degree accomplices and second-degree accomplices.[205] According to Article 45 first-degree accomplices are '[t]hose who took part in the execution of the act or helped the author by providing assistance or cooperation, and without this assistance, it would not have been committed'.[206] Second-degree accomplices are described in Article 46 as '[t]hose who cooperate [...] with the execution of the crime'.[207] Second-degree accomplices are what this work refers to as aiders and abettors.

An aider and abettor is liable if the principal executed the crime in which the aider and abettor assisted.[208] Also, the aider and abettor is only responsible for the type of crime that she intended to assist with.[209]

An aider an abettor must act with knowledge and intent. Regarding the intent requirement, there is consensus in the academic literature and jurisprudence that supports liability for aiders and abettors who act with *dolus eventualis*.[210]

According to Zaffaroni *dolus eventualis* is when the aider and abettor recognises as possible the perpetration of an offence and despite this recognition does not renounce her plans to assist. She therefore knows that the crime is possible considering the context and she then accepts the risk as a possibility.[211]

The courts have also found that *dolus eventualis* is sufficient. In one case the *Tribunal de Casacion Penal* stated that it is sufficient to show that it was predictable that the actions taken by each participant would result in the perpetration of an offence.[212] In another case the aiders and abettors were found guilty of a homicide that was perpetrated during a robbery. The court determined that

205 Marcelo Ferrante, 'Argentina' in Kevin Jon Heller and Markus Dubber (eds), *The Handbook of Comparative Criminal Law* (Stanford University Press 2010) 31.

206 Unofficial translation by the author.

207 Unofficial translation by the author.

208 Ferrante (n 205) 33.

209 ibid.

210 Eugenio Raúl Zaffaroni, Alejandro Alagia and Alejandro Slokar, *Derecho Penal Parte General* (2 ed, Sociedad Anonima 2006) 797; Carlos Paglieri, *Nueva Teoría Del Delito: Participación Penal* (Azul 2014) 47; Guillermo Julio Fierro, *Teoria de La Participacion Criminal* (2 ed, Astrea 2001) 480.

211 Zaffaroni, Alagia and Slokar (n 210) 524.

212 *Prelis, Gonzalo Alfredo y otros s/Recurso de casación, Tribunal de Casacion Penal Sala IV - La Plata (TC0004 LP), 23/4/2013, RSD-153-13*. The Tribunal de Casacion Penal stated: 'Basta comprobar que el dolo eventual resulte predicable de la acción que preside la actuación de cada uno de los tres intervinientes.'

they acted with *dolus eventualis* by participating in the robbery with guns. By brandishing guns the aiders and abettors had accepted the death of the victims as a possible outcome.[213]

The controversy in Argentine criminal law concerns the knowledge requirement. The discussions have mainly focused on the possibility of holding a principal liable for acting with wilful blindness. Regarding accomplice liability, some authors believe that wilful blindness could be sufficient for an aider and abettor while others do not. On the one hand, Pérez Barberá argues that the wilful blindness doctrine (*ignorancia deliberada*) is compatible with the Argentine Penal Code.[214] Ragués, who also argues that *dolus eventualis* and wilful blindness are sufficent forms of *mens rea* for criminal liablity, maintains that no form of ignorance (such as negligence) is sufficient to impute *dolus eventualis*.[215] He thus considers that knowledge (including active knowledge and wilful blindness) must be proved to establish liability for aiding and abetting with *dolus eventualis*.[216] The mere fact that an aider and abettor acted with *dolus eventualis* does not imply that she also acted with the necessary knowledge requirement.

On the other hand, when discussing the liability of a principal Manrique[217] is not averse to a careful application of the wilful blindness doctrine if it could prevent a principal from using the excuse of the lack of active knowledge to assist in perpetrating crimes without consequences.[218] However, she states that

---

213 *Leiva, Luis s/Recurso de casación, Tribunal de Casacion Penal, Sala III, La Plata (TC0003 LP) cause 20137, 29/11/2007, RSD-862-7.*

214 Gabriel Pérez Barberá, *El Dolo Eventual: Hacia El Abandono de La Idea de Dolo Como Estado Mental* (Hammurabi 2011) 50–52. See also generally the work of Günther Jakobs, in particular 'Indiferencia Como Dolo Indirecto' in José Miguel Zugaldía Espinar and Jacobo López Barja de Quiroga (eds), *Dogmática y Ley Penal: Libro Homenaje a Enrique Bacigalupo* (Marcial Pons 2004) 374, who notes that: 'La indiferencia respecto al derecho, que de ordinario se traduce "sólo" como ignorancia de la ilicitud, puede derivar también en indiferencia sobre los hechos y, en consecuencia, conduce también al desconocimiento de la realización del tipo'.

215 He even proposes that a category such as 'recklessness' (referred to in this work as negligence) be included. If such a category exited, he believes that cases of wilful blindness should be charged as recklessness.

216 Ramón Ragués I Vallès, 'Mejor No Saber: Sobre La Doctrina de La Ignorancia Deliberada En Derecho Penal' in J. Valenzuela (ed), *Discusiones Número XIII: Ignorancia deliberada y Derecho Penal* (EdiUNS 2013) 33.

217 María Laura Manrique, 'Ignorancia Deliberada y Responsabilidad Penal' (2014) 40 Isonomía - Revista de teoría y filosofía del derecho 163, 166 available at <http://www.scielo.org.mx/scielo.php?script=sci_arttext&pid=S1405-02182014000100008> accessed 15 April 2020.

218 ibid 183.

at this time Argentine criminal law has not yet found an adequate response to the normative and conceptual difficulties raised by the wilful blindness doctrine.[219] She argues that acting with wilful blindness is not sufficient to infer liability if the principal is also acting with *dolus eventualis*, because *dolus eventlalis* requires active knowledge and not wilful blindness.[220] This same reasoning seems to be applicable to an aider and abettor. Furthermore, Greco argues that the doctrine of wilful blindness cannot currently be implemented in Argentine criminal law because a legislative reform that acknowledges this doctrine would first have to take place.[221]

There was no precedent for the explicit use of the wilful blindness doctrine by Argentine courts until 2008.[222] Since that time courts have held on a number of occasions that an aider and abettor was criminally liable if she acted with *dolus eventualis* and wilful blindness.[223] On other occasions, however, courts have rejected the application of the wilful blindness doctrine. The Supreme Court of Argentina has not yet expressed itself on the issue.

In conclusion, some scholars argue that wilful blindness is compatible with Argentine criminal law while others argue that it is not. This doctrine has also been adopted by some courts while others have rejected it.

In sum, under Argentine law it is possible to hold aider and abettor liable for acting with *dolus eventualis* and wilful blindness.

---

219 ibid 192.

220 ibid.

221 Luís Greco, 'Comentario Al Artículo de Ramon Ragués' in J. Valenzuela (ed), *Discusiones Número XIII: Ignorancia deliberada y Derecho Penal* (EdiUNS 2013) 76–7.

222 María Victoria Huergo, 'Reflexiones En Torno de La Doctrina de La Willful Blindness y Su Posible Recepción En Argentina' (2010) 5 El Derecho Penal 1, 15 states: 'En nuestro país, hasta el año 2008 no se ha advertido la existencia precedentes en los que se hiciera una referencia expresa a esta doctrina, lo que no significa que no hayan existido resoluciones judiciales en las que se condenara a título de dolo, prescindiendo de la prueba del conocimiento de un elemento del tipo. Como ejemplo arquetípico se encuentra el plenario de la Cámara Nacional de Casación Penal "Iriart, Jorge A. s/recurso de inaplicabilidad de ley" de fecha del 30 de septiembre de 2003'.

223 ibid 4–5 citing the Gerstenkorn, Daniel Enrique s/recurso de casación case, states: 'The tribunal 'no ha hecho uso de esa igualación -ignorancia alegada pero que el sujeto debía superar y conocimiento cierto o probable-, sino que ha argumentado sobre los presupuestos tradicionales del dolo como conocimiento de los elementos constitutivos del tipo objetivo'. Regarding the lack of necessity to prove the knowledge requirement concerning a duty of care, see the Olleac Eduardos case, cited in Hergo 2010, 17 as "Olleac Eduardos/ homicido culposo" de la Cámara de Apelaciones y Garantías en lo Penal de San Isidro, Sala 2a de fecha 19 de mayo de 2008 sobre un caso en el que se le imputó homicidio culposo al titular de la Dirección de Espacios Verdes de la Municipalidad de Pilar, in which it was stated: "ya que de conformidad con lo establecido en el organigrama municipal y

5.2 *Brazil*

Brazil is a Portuguese-speaking civil law nation. The term most often used to indicate complicity is '*cumplicidade*'.[224] The term 'accomplice' appeared in the Criminal Code of the Empire of 1832 (Article 5) in dealing with participation and in Article 18 of the Penal Code of Brazil of 1890 to identify all participants who were not considered authors.[225] The Penal Code of Brazil of 1940 and the 1984 reform of the general part do not refer to the terms 'complicity' or 'accomplice',[226] but rather employ the term '*auxílio*', which can be translated as 'aider'.[227] Article 31 of the Penal Code of 1940 provides for complicity in stating that 'forms of participation (including complicity), where there is at least no attempt at the crime, cannot be punished'.[228]

To incur liability an aider and abettor must act knowingly and both her contribution and the offense in which she participates must be committed intentionally.[229] According to Article 18 of the Penal Code a crime is intentional 'when the agent wanted the result or assumed the risk of producing it'.[230]

en consecuencia no haber observado los reglamentos ni los deberes a su cargo, desde que no se desarrollaron tareas de mantenimiento y control de los juegos colocados en la plaza denominada Don Bosco, ubicada en las calles Aráoz, Salta, Paraná y Perú de la localidad de Pte. Derqui, Partido de Pilar, que debido a esa inactividad negligente de su parte, los mismos se hallaban en un estado deficiente y peligroso para los niños que utilizaban las instalaciones, y que como consecuencia de tal situación el día 30/1/2007, se produjo el desprendimiento de la estructura de la hamaca instalada en aquel predio y su caída sobre el cuerpo de la niña F. M. M. situación que ocasionó su fallecimiento por paro cardiorespiratorio traumático, como consecuencia de traumatismo craneoencefálico dado que parte de la misma produjo el aplastamiento de su cráneo". "Rechazo la idea de que deba excluirse a Olleac de la imputación de lo ocurrido por el simple trámite de sostener que desconocía el contenido del organigrama (…) La 'inconsciencia consciente' o 'voluntaria ignorancia de las obligaciones a su cargo' que pretenden alegarse en el expediente no pueden menos que ser interpretadas como una infracción a su deber objetivo de cuidado. Pensar lo contrario anularía el organigrama que distribuye funciones en un municipio pues cada director se liberaría de sus obligaciones bajo la simple alegación de no haberlo leído. En resumen, quien asume un cargo público asume, consecuentemente, los deberes que dicho cargo impone. Quien ignora los deberes de dicho cargo, lo asume y permanece en él no obstante ello, infringe, por lo menos, una básica norma de cuidado y responde por los resultados lesivos que dicho descuido produce a terceros.' "

224 Ana Luisa Sabadell, 'Brazil' in Ulrich; Sieber, Hans-Georg; Koch and Jan-Michael Simon (eds), *Participation in Crime: Criminal Liability of Leaders of Criminal Groups and Networks* (Duncker & Humblot Publishers 2020) 155.

225 ibid 88.

226 ibid 156.

227 ibid 89.

228 ibid 152–3. Unofficial translation by the author.

229 ibid 156.

230 Unofficial translation by the author.

Article 20 provides that a mistake regarding the material element of a crime excludes *dolus*. Thus, knowledge and intent on the part of the aider and abettor are the two elements required to establish criminally liability for contribution.

Article 18, which deals with the requirement of intent, is interpreted as meaning that a person acts with intent, not only when she intentionally wanted the criminal result (direct intent) but also when she assumed the risk of producing it (*dolus eventualis*).[231] Article 29(2) of the Penal Code also states that if an accomplice 'wanted to participate in a less serious crime, [...] his penalty will be increased up to half, on the hypothesis that the most serious result was predicted'.[232] There also seems to be general consensus among scholars that *dolus eventualis* is sufficient for aider and abettor liability.[233]

The knowledge requirement in Brazilian criminal law has evolved to include wilful blindness.[234] Moro states that:[235]

> Provided that the requirements demanded by the doctrine of wilful blindness are present [...] no legal or moral objection can be seen to not hold him responsible for the criminal result and, therefore, to condemn him for money laundering, given the reprobation of his conduct.

The doctrine of wilful blindness was first used in Brazilian courts in a case of theft from the Central Bank in Fortaleza in the state of Ceará in 2005.[236] The judge found that wilful blindness could replace the active knowledge requirement and that the accused had acted with *dolus eventualis*. The sentence was later changed by the Regional Federal Court, which determined that the crime of money laundering could only be committed with direct intent. However, this case paved the way for the use of wilful blindness by the courts.

In another money laundering case Sergio Fernando Moro J held that a:[237]

---

231 *TRF-4 ACR 5001945-6820134047004 Rapporteur Ricardo Rachid de Oliveira 02/25/2015.*

232 Unofficial translation by the author.

233 Marcelo Andr de Azevedo and Alexandre Salim, *Direito Penal – Parte Geral* (7 ed, Juspodivm 2017) 377–8. See also Rogério Greco, *Curso de Direito Penal* (18 ed, Impetus 2016); Juarez dos Santos Cirino, *Direito Penal – Parte Geral* (5 ed, Conceito Editorial 2012).

234 Sergio Moro, *Crime de Lavagem de Dinheiro* (Saraiva 2010) 69.

235 Moro (n 234). Unofficial translation by the author.

236 *TRF-5 ACR 5520-CE 20058100014586-0 Rapporteur: Rogério Fialho Moreira 07/09/2008.*

237 *TRF- 4 ACR 5004606-3120104047002 Rapporteur: João Pedro Gebran Neto 16/07/2014.* Unofficial translation by the author.

> [P]erson whose conduct constitutes money laundering [...] does not eliminate the willful act and his criminal responsibility if he deliberately chooses to remain ignorant as to the nature of the assets, rights or values involved in the transaction, when he was able to deepen his knowledge about the situation and the facts around the transaction.

In yet another case concerning bank robbery the court held that the accused was not guilty, because he did not act with at least wilful blindness (and therefore not with knowledge) since there were no facts demonstrating that he was aware that the money he received was of illicit origin.[238]

It is noteworthy that Brazilian courts have considered that the wilful blindness doctrine might point to *dolus eventualis*:[239]

> The application of the theory of wilful blindness to the configuration of *dolus eventualis* requires that the agent has been aware of the high probability that he practiced or participated in criminal activity; that the agent was able to deepen his knowledge about the nature of his activity; and that the agent deliberately acted indifferent to that knowledge. [In the present case, the] driver of a stolen vehicle who presents a false [Vehicle Registration and Licensing Certificate] to the federal highway police does not exclude his criminal responsibility by choosing to remain ignorant of the false document, being able to deepen his knowledge and knowing the high probability that he practiced or participated in criminal activity, especially when he had received a considerable amount of money for the task he was going to perform.

Another example of the use of the wilful blindness doctrine as an argument to show *dolus eventualis* is the *Mensalão* case,[240] one of the world's biggest corruption scandals. In this case, Minister Celso de Mello:[241]

> [A]dmitted the possibility of proving the crime of money laundering through eventual intention, supported by the theory of wilful blindness,

---

238 *TRF-5 ACR: 5520 CE 0014586-4020054058100 Rapporteur: Federal Judge Rogério Fialho Moreira 09/09/2008.*

239 *TRF-4. ACR 5001945-68.2013.4.04.7004. Rapporteur Ricardo Rachid de Oliveira. 02/25/2015.* Unofficial translation by the author.

240 *Mensalão case, Informativo STF, AP 470/MG.*

241 *Mensalão case, Informativo STF, AP 470/MG – 142 Min Celso de Mello.* Unofficial translation by the author.

> in which the agent would pretend not to perceive a situation of illegality to, in this position, achieve the desired advantage.

Moreover, as explained by Renato Silveira many of the doctrinal bases of the *Operation Car Wash* (*Lava Jato*) trials related to the acceptance of the wilful blindness theory:[242]

> This thought seems quite opportune when we imagine that a large part of the condemnatory decisions of the judgments derived from Operation Lava Jato (especially with regard to money laundering charges) are based on permissive readings on the use of the deliberate blindness doctrine (wilful blindness) in the Brazilian criminal tribunals, as a substitute or complement to the notion of eventual intent.

Laufer and Silva describe the relationship between wilful blindness and *dolus eventualis* in the following terms:[243]

> The problem of wilful blindness is, in truth, a problem of eventual intent: it is worth investigating whether, according to the national order, one person who acts in the face of suspicious situations, acts in such a way as to possibly perpetrate the crime without caring enough to get to know the circumstances in depth. In this sense, a premise must be established: when it comes to wilful blindness, there must always be perceived 'a certain degree of suspicion about the circumstances in fact'. The participant has some general notion of what surrounds him, coming to suspect the existence of some illegality. Wilful blindness occurs only in relation to any additional knowledge that could be known if the agent undertakes an investigation, albeit a succinct one. It is known that the eventual intention is conceptualized legally from the assumption of the risk of producing the result of the typical action (Article 18, paragraph I, Penal Code). But it is clear that this crime also requires the cognitive element. First, because it is logically impossible to take the risk of producing the result of what is not known, at least minimally. Second, because Article 20 of the Penal Code provides that the error on a constitutive element of the type excludes the *dolus*.

---

242 Renato de Mello Jorge Silveira, 'A Aplicação Da Teoria Da Cegueira Deliberada Nos Julgamentos Da Operação Lava-Jato' (2016) 122 Revista Brasileira de Ciências Criminais 255, 2. Unofficial translation by the author.

243 Christian Laufer and Robson Galvão da Silva, 'A Teoria Da Cegueira Deliberada e o Direito Penal Brasileiro' (2009) 204 Boletim IBCCRIM 1, 10–1. Unofficial translation by the author.

However, a minority of authors, such as Pitombo, Prado, Barros and Silva[244] argue that the doctrine of wilful blindness does not have a place in Brazilian criminal law, as the transposition and application of this American doctrine encounters certain barriers when it is adapted to civil law systems. Pitombo argues that a crime (notably, money laundering) can only be committed with direct intent and, therefore, that both the doctrine of wilful blindness and *dolus eventualis* are not applicable in the Brazilian context.[245] Prado argues that this doctrine creates a risk to legal security because:[246]

> [I]t is absolutely mandatory to take into account that the Brazilian legal system is based on the principle of subjective criminal responsibility, of express legal provision (article 18, CP), without any kind of substitute, distortion or underage. [T]his kind of application gives rise to excessive judicial regulation, and violation of the constitution (article 5, XXXIX, Federal Constitution).

In conclusion, although some authors claim that criminal liability can only follow if one acts with direct intent and knowledge, the courts and the majority of scholars agree that an aider and abettor can be held liable when acting with *dolus eventualis* and that wilful blindness is sufficient to fulfil the knowledge requirement.

5.3 *Mexico*

Mexico is a Spanish-speaking civil law nation. In federal criminal law 'participants' are those who contribute to the criminal offence without executing the action described by the criminal norm.[247] According to federal legislation, jurisprudence and legal doctrine the term 'participant' notably includes the inducer, the helper, the accomplice and the so called '*complicidad correspectiva*'

244 Antônio Sérgio Altieri de Moraes Pitombo, *Lavagem de Dinheiro: A Tipicidade Do Crime Antecedente* (Revista dos Tribunais 2003); Luiz Regis Prado, *Direito Penal Econômico* (Revista dos Tribunais 2016); Marco Antonio de Barros and Thiago Minetti Apostólico Silva, *Lavagem de Ativos: Dolo Direto e a Inaplicabilidade Da Teoria Da Cegueira Deliberada,* (Revista dos Tribunais 2015).

245 Pitombo (n 244) 109, 135–6.

246 Prado (n 244). Unofficial translation by the author.

247 Ricardo Ojeda Bohorquéz, 'Coautoría y Complicidad En El Derecho Mexicano (Doctrina, Jurisprudencia, Elementos Y Criterios de Aplicación)' (2011) 35 Revista Derecho Penal 49, 65–6.

or *'autoría indeterminada'*.[248] *'Complicidad correspectiva'* or *'autoría indeterminada'* corresponds to what I refer to as the aider and abettor. Article 13, Section VI of the Mexican Federal Criminal Code stipulates that accomplices (referred to in this work as aiders and abettors) to a crime are 'those who intentionally help or assist another to commit it',[249] while Section VIII states that accomplices are 'those who without previous agreement, participate with others in the commission of an offence, when the results produced by each participant cannot be specified'.[250]

Regarding the mental elements of a crime, Article 9 of the Mexican Federal Criminal Code states that 'an individual is criminally accountable when, knowing the elements of the crime, or foreseeing the possible results of the crime, he desires or accepts the consequences of the conduct described by the law'.[251] Accordingly, to be liable, one must act knowingly (*conocimiento*) and intentionally (*voluntad*).[252] Regarding the *mens rea* element of the crime of aiding and abetting, Diaz-Aranda states:[253]

> [T]he participant must act with intent; that is, with the knowledge of the circumstances of the event and have the intention of carrying out the conduct. Consequently, imprudent participation will be unpunished. On the other hand, the participants will respond to the extent of their own guilt, and that same will serve to determine the gradation of the penalty imposed to them.

The aider and abettor must act with knowledge of the objective and normative elements of the offence,[254] meaning that she must know the factual circumstances of the crime.[255] Vasconcelos explains that the aider and abettor

248 Enrique Díaz-Aranda, 'Mexico' in Ulrich; Sieber, Hans-Georg; Koch and Jan-Michael Simon (eds), *Participation in Crime: Criminal Liability of Leaders of Criminal Groups and Networks* (Duncker & Humblot Publishers 2020) 620.

249 Unofficial translation by the author.

250 Unofficial translation by the author.

251 Unofficial translation by the author.

252 See generally Simón Pablo Herrera Bazán, 'La Participación Imprudente, Tomo 1' in Miguel Ontiveros Alonso, Mercedes Peláez and Claus Roxin (eds), *Libro Homenaje a Claus Roxin, La Influencia de la Ciencia Penal Alemana en Iberoamérica* (Instituto Nacional de Ciencias Penales 2003) 145–72.

253 Díaz-Aranda (n 248) 620. Unofficial translation by the author.

254 Bohorquéz (n 247) 65–6; Díaz-Aranda (n 248) 621–2.

255 Díaz-Aranda (n 248) 620; Francisco Herberto Pavón Vasconcelos, *Manual de Derecho Penal Mexicano – Parte General* (Porruá 2004) 636; Jiménez de Asúa, *La Ley y El Delito* (2 ed, Hermes 1954) 546.

must know that her actions assisted the principal's crime, and that she must have been aware of the unlawfulness of her conduct as well as that of the principal.[256]

Neither the courts not scholars address the doctrine of wilful blindness in any way. Active knowledge is therefore required for an aider and abettor.

Regarding the intent requirement, the aider and abettor must have the intent to assist the principal.[257] There is consensus among scholars[258] and the courts[259] that *dolus eventualis* is sufficient. The Supreme Court of Justice has held that an aider and abettor acts with *dolus eventualis* if, during one of the preparatory meetings for an assault, the principal proposes to hit the victims and kill them if they resist. Because the aider and abettor attended those meetings he was aware of the principal's readiness to use deadly force and he did not rule out the possibility that the victims might be killed.[260]

Batiaglini and Vasconcelos believe that a person acts with *dolus eventualis* if she foresees the possible consequences of her actions in aiding the principal actor's crime.[261] Díaz-Aranda states that to act with *dolus eventualis* it is sufficient for the aider and abettor to accept, but not necessarily wish, that her actions would assist the principal's crime. In other words, she only needs to know that the principal intends to commit a crime and to want to engage in aiding the criminal consequence, although she does not necessarily wish for this consequence to result.[262]

In sum, an aider and abettor must act with active knowledge and at the very least *dolus eventualis*.

5.4 *Observations*

Regarding the knowledge requirement, both Argentina and Brazil recognise the validity of the wilful blindness doctrine and courts have also applied this standard. However, in Mexico the minimum standard of knowledge is active knowledge.

256 Vasconcelos (n 255) 484.

257 Díaz-Aranda (n 248) 620.

258 Ignacio Villalobos, *Derecho Penal Mexicano* (Porruá 1960); Vasconcelos (n 255); Díaz-Aranda (n 248); Enrique Díaz-Aranda, *Lecciones de Derecho Penal Para El Nuevo Sistema de Justicia Em México* (STRAF 2014).

259 Díaz-Aranda (n 258) 97 citing Semanario Judicial de la Federación, Séptima Época, Primera Sala, vols. 193–8, segunda parte 21.

260 *Supreme Court of Justice, Amparo directo 235/54 MMF. 11 de marzo de 1959 Unanimidad de cuatro votos Ponente: AMA*. See also *Supreme Court of Justice, Amparo directo 856/79 MGM 8 de febrero de 1980 Unanimidad de cuatro votos Ponente: FCT Secretario: FNG*.

261 Vasconcelos (n 255) 487–8.

262 Díaz-Aranda (n 258) 95.

MAP 7 Standards of knowledge in Latin America

MAP 8 Standards of intent in Latin America

Furthermore, all the Latin American jurisdictions analysed allow *dolus eventualis* to be included in the definition of the intent requirement. This can be explained by the fact that most Latin American jurisdictions were inspired by German criminal law and are based on codified civil law.

6 North America

This section analyses the knowledge and intent requirements relating to the aider and abettor in Canada and the United States of America, both at the federal and state levels. Both countries are common law jurisdictions, the main language is English, and the tradition is Christian.

6.1 *Canada*

Pursuant to Section 21(1)(b) of the Criminal Code of Canada every person is a party to an offence who 'does or omits to do anything for the purpose of aiding any person to commit it'. To be liable as a party to an offence by aiding and abetting the accused must intend to assist the principal in the commission of a crime and she must know that she is in fact aiding and abetting.[263]

For the knowledge requirement to be fulfilled the aider and abettor must have been 'aware of the type of crime to be committed' and know 'the circumstances necessary to constitute the offence he is accused of aiding'.[264] This means that the accused must have known of the principal's intention to commit the offence (or a certain type of offence, as the knowledge of the exact crime is not necessary).[265] She must be shown to have acted with 'guilty knowledge'.[266] This classic statement by Lord Goddard CJ in *Johnson v Youden* is illustrative:[267]

> Before a person can be convicted of aiding and abetting the commission of an offence he must at least know the essential matters which constitute that offence. He need not actually know that an offence has been committed, because he may not know that the facts constitute an offence

263 *National Coal Board v Gamble* [1959] 1 Q.B. 11.

264 *R v FW Woolworth co* (1974) 18 CCC (2nd) 23 (*Ont* CA) 32.

265 *R v Dowd* (1899), 4 CCC 170 (*Que Ct Special Sessions*); *R v Hoggan*, [1966] 3 CCC 1, 47 CR 256 (*Alta* CA); *R v Roy* (1900), 3 CCC 472 (*Que* QB).

266 *R v Coy* [1938] 1 WWR 748 (BCSC). See also *R v Russel* (1923), 39 CCC 374 (*Sask* KB).

267 *Johnson v Youden* [1950] 1 K.B. 544.

> and ignorance of the law is not a defence. If a person knows all the facts and is assisting another person to do certain things, and it turns out the doing of those things constitutes an offence, the person who is assisting is guilty of aiding and abetting that offence, because to allow him to say, 'I knew of all those facts but I did not know that an offence was committed,' would be allowing him to set up ignorance of the law as a defence.

The aider and abettor must have active knowledge of the facts constituting the offence committed by the principal.[268] However, the knowledge requirement 'could seemingly be dispensed with if it were shown that the accused intended to help the principal no matter which of a number of crimes he chose to commit'.[269]

Significantly, in *R v Briscoe*,[270] the Supreme Court of Canada held that wilful blindness could substitute the active knowledge requirement and that wilful blindness cannot protect an aider and abettor from liability.[271] Wilful blindness is a form of 'deliberate ignorance' that is distinct from negligence.[272] One cannot, however, incur liability as an aider and abettor because of an honest lack of knowledge.[273]

Regarding the intent requirement, the Ontario Court of Appeal has held that the use of the term 'purpose' in Section 21(1)(b) of the Criminal Code is 'synonymous with intent and does not include recklessness'.[274] It is not enough for the aider and abettor to have intentionally assisted in the perpetration of a crime. She must also have aided for the purpose of assisting the perpetration of the crime.[275] In *R v Hibbert* the court concluded that the term purpose 'does not incorporate the notion of "desire" into the mental state for liability'.[276] This means that intent in the first degree (also referred to as *dolus directus*) is required.

In sum, wilful blindness has been accepted for aider and abettor liability, but *dolus eventualis* has not. Indeed, the aider and abettor must have acted

268 *R v FW Woolworth co* (*1974*) *18 CCC* (*2nd*) *23* (*Ont CA*). See also *R v Hamel* (*1958*), *64 WWR 193* (*BC Co Ct*).

269 V Gordon Rose, *Parties to an Offence* (Carswell 1982). See also *R v Hartford and Frigon* (*1979*), *51 CCC* (*2d*) *462* (*BCCA*).

270 *R v Briscoe* [*2010*] *1 SCR*, *411*.

271 See also *R v McDaid* (*1974*), *19 CCC* (*2d*) *572* (*Ont CA*); Kent Roach, 'Canada' in Kevin Jon Heller and Markus Dubber (eds), *The Handbook of Comparative Criminal Law* (Stanford University Press 2010) 108.

272 *R v Briscoe* [*2010*] *1 SCR*, *411* 22–5.

273 There is in fact no liability unless there is a positive duty. In the case of an individual financing an entity involved in the commission of core crimes, no positive duty exists. See *Callow v Tillstone* (*1900*), *64 JP 823*, *19 Cox CC 576*.

274 *R v Roach* (2004) *192 CCC* (*3d*) *193* (*SCC*) 214.

275 Gordon Rose (n 269) 12.

276 *R v Hibbert* [*1995*] *2 SCR 973* in particular 26–39.

with the purpose of assisting the commission of the offence, *i.e.* she must have acted with *dolus directus*.

6.2 *United States of America*

Aiders and abettors, referred to as 'accomplices' in the United States of America,[277] must intentionally assist or encourage the principal in the commission of a crime.[278] It is commonly agreed that the degree of aid provided by the accomplice to the principal is immaterial, even if the aid was causally unnecessary or played no role in the commission of the offence.[279] It is, however, unclear what degree of *mens rea* is required on the part of an accomplice regarding her assistance and the offence committed by the principal.[280]

Courts and later legislatures have developed criminal law at federal, state and local levels.[281] The United States of America has one federal criminal code (Title 18 of the United States Code) and each state has its own criminal statutes and local ordinances. Federal law applies to criminal cases that cross state lines and to certain conduct (for example, arson, use of chemical weapons, counterfeit and forgery, embezzlement, espionage, genocide, and kidnapping) which is codified in Title 18. Additionally, nowadays almost every state has a criminal code and state courts are charged with the interpretation of those criminal codes.[282] There is thus no uniform criminal code at state level in the United States, but numerous states have introduced or reformed criminal codes based on the 1962 Model Penal Code.[283]

6.2.1 State Law

Regarding the knowledge requirement, Article 2.02(7) of the Model Penal Code[284] states that:[285]

277 Luis E Chiesa, 'United States' in Alan Reed and Michael Bohlander (eds), *Participation in Crime: Domestic and Comparative Perspectives* (Taylor & Francis 2013) 474.

278 Marchuk (n 185) 230.

279 Aksenova (n 166) 99.

280 Marchuk (n 185) 230; Chiesa (n 277) 476.

281 Aksenova (n 56) 34.

282 Paul H Robinson, '[A Brief Comparative Summary of the Criminal Law of the] United States' in Kevin Jon Heller and Markus D Dubber (eds), *The Handbook of Comparative Criminal Law* (Stanford University Press 2010) 564.

283 Aksenova (n 166); Robert Weisberg, 'Reappraising Complicity' (2000) 4 Buffalo Criminal Law Review 217.

284 The Model Penal Code is a proposed criminal code drafted by the American Law Institute. States may choose to adopt the Model Penal Code in its entirety or in part as their criminal law.

285 Emphasis added.

> When knowledge of the existence of a particular fact is an element of an offense, such knowledge is established if a person is aware of a *high probability* of its existence, unless he actually believes that it does not exist.

This approach was followed in the federal case of *US v Jewell*.[286] The court held that proof of wilful ignorance satisfied the requirement of knowledge. Thus, a person has knowledge if she is aware, to a high probability, of the existence of the material facts that constitute an offense, unless she actually believes that these material facts do not exist. This means that if a person is ignorant because of a conscious effort to avoid learning the truth she can be found guilty of knowingly assisting in the commission of an offense. Her avoidance of the truth need not be active; she can be held liable for a failure to take simple, obvious steps to confirm or dispel her suspicions.[287]

Regarding the intent requirement at state level, three major approaches to the mental state of the aider and abettor have been adopted: (i) the 'purposeful intent approach'; (ii) the 'knowledge approach'; and (iii) the '*dolus eventualis* approach'.

6.2.1.1 *The Purposeful Intent Approach*

According to Section 2.06 of the Model Penal Code:[288]

> A person is an accomplice of another person in the commission of an offense if, with the *purpose of promoting or facilitating* the commission of the offense, he aids or agrees or attempts to aid such other person in planning or committing it.

Section 2.02 describes 'acting with purpose' as acting with the conscious objective of causing the prohibited conduct. The accomplice's intent is therefore dual in that she must intend to assist the principal *and* intend for the crime to be committed.[289] The mere knowledge of the offence does not, therefore, satisfy the fault requirement for complicity.[290] The aider and abettor must intend her deliberate act to also assist the principal.[291]

---

286 *United States v Jewell, Court of Appeals for the Ninth Circuit, 532 F 2d 697 (9th Cir 1976) 27 February 1976.*

287 Reid, Sarch and Walker (n 144) 170, who state that wilful blindness suffices.

288 Emphasis added.

289 Aksenova (n 166) 99.

290 ibid 100.

291 Emily Silverman, 'United States' in Ulrich Sieber, Hans-Georg Koch and Jan-Michael Simon (eds), *Participation in Crime: Criminal Liability of Leaders of Criminal Groups and Networks* (Duncker & Humblot Publishers 2020) 63.

The Model Penal Code adopted the so-called 'purposeful intent' approach, the aim of which is to prevent liability from extending to conduct that does not fall within the purposes shared by the accessory.[292] In *US v Peoni* the court held that in order to be an accessory, a defendant must 'in some sort associate himself with the venture, […] participate in it as in something that he wishes to bring about, […] seek by his action to make it succeed'.[293] Under the Model Penal Code, because mere knowledge of the crime is not sufficient to satisfy the *mens rea* requirement of the accomplice, giving a weapon to the principal whom the defendant knew was planning to commit a murder would not trigger liability as an accomplice.[294] However, all states have not accepted this interpretation of the accomplice's *mens rea* in the Model Penal Code.

6.2.1.2 *The Knowledge Approach*

Another position was championed in *Backun v United States* in which Judge Parker held:[295]

> The seller may not ignore the purpose for which the purchase is made if he is advised of that purpose, or wash his hands of the aid that he has given the perpetrator of a felony by the plea that he has merely made a sale of merchandise. One who sells a gun to another knowing that he is buying it to commit a murder, would hardly escape conviction as an accessory to the murder by showing that he received full price for the gun. […] In any such case, not only does the act of the seller assist in the commission of the felony, but his will assents to its commission, since he could refuse to give the assistance by refusing to make the sale.

Moreover, the drafters of the Model Penal Code[296] initially also considered a similar approach, the so-called 'mere knowledge' approach.[297] The scope of liability for accomplices initially was broader than under the current Model Penal Code. Originally it was envisioned to include liability for those who knowingly aided if the aid provided had 'substantially facilitated' the perpetration of the

---

292 ibid 64.

293 *United States v Peoni, Court of Appeals for the Second Circuit, 100 F2d 401 (2d Cir 1938) 12 December 1938.*

294 Chiesa (n 277) 476.

295 *Backun v US, 112 F2d 635 (4th Circuit, 1940)* 637.

296 The draft originally proposed was eventually rejected by the members of the American Law Institute.

297 Silverman (n 291) 64.

crime.[298] Several states followed this approach by criminalising knowing assistance. One noteworthy example is New York, which punishes what is referred to in Section 115.00 of the New York Penal Code as 'criminal facilitation'. It provides that a person is criminally liable when:[299]

> [B]elieving it probable that he is rendering aid to a person who intends to commit a [crime], he engages in conduct which provides such person with means or opportunity for the commission thereof and which in fact aids such person to commit such [crime].

'Criminal facilitation' is not considered a form of accomplice liability in New York[300] and is punished less severely than complicity. Moreover, the knowledge requirement is heightened in comparison to that of accomplice liability. The aid provided, no matter how trivial, is required to provide either the means to commit the crime or the opportunity to do so.[301] A similar approach has been adopted in Kentucky, Arizona and Tennessee.[302]

6.2.1.3 *The Dolus Eventualis Approach*

A handful of states impose liability on accomplices for all reasonably foreseeable crimes committed by the principal rather than just the intended ones. This means that the aider and abettor is liable regardless of whether she acted with the element of intent as foreseen in the definition of the offence for which she has been charged. As explained in the leading state case in support of this approach, *People v Luparello*, the accomplice is criminally responsible for the principal's crime on the basis that she intentionally influenced the underlying nefarious act.[303] In this case the defendant, Luparello, had hired a friend to extract information 'at any cost' about the whereabouts of his former mistress. This resulted in the victim being shot to death. Luparello claimed that his plan was merely to scare the victim and that he did not have the purpose of killing him. The court held that although Luparello was not physically present when

298 Chiesa (n 277) 476, citing in footnote 46 to the *Comments to Model Penal Code*, section 2.06(3)(a), 315–15.

299 New York Penal Law paragraph 115.00.

300 Chiesa (n 277) 476.

301 ibid 477.

302 See Kentucky Penal Code, section 508.080; Arizona Penal Code, section 13-1004; Tennessee Penal Code; regarding the *dolus eventualis* approach, section 39-11-403.

303 *People v Luparello, Court of Appeal of California, 187 Cal App 3d 410, 231 Cal Rptr 832, 25 November 1986.*

the shooting occurred he was nevertheless responsible as an aider and abettor to the crime, because:[304]

> [L]iability is extended to reach the actual crime committed, rather than the planned or 'intended' crime, on the policy [that] aiders and abettors should be responsible for the criminal harms they have naturally, probably and foreseeably put in motion.

Thus, according to this approach, the accomplice's liable includes any reasonably foreseeable offense committed by the person whom she aids.

Although a few states have followed this approach, the majority have rejected it. It has also not been accepted in the Model Penal Code. According to the drafters accomplice liability should only extend to the actions of the principal if these crimes have been 'fairly envisaged for the purposes of the association'.[305] Subsequently, the drafters considered that 'when a wholly different crime has been committed, thus involving conduct not within the conscious objectives of the accomplice, he is not liable for it' and that 'the liability of the accomplice ought not be extended beyond the purpose that he shares'.[306]

In sum, although wilful blindness is widely accepted by state courts, only a small number accept *dolus eventualis*. The minimum level of intent in most states seem to be significantly higher, even to the level of purposeful intent.

6.2.2 Federal Law

At the federal level the 'derivative approach' is applicable. This approach supports an offence-based mental state of the aider and abettor that reflects the mental state required of the principal.[307] The aider and abettor must share the mental element required of the principal. In other words, she must consciously share the principal's knowledge and the principal's criminal intent.[308] Like the principal, the aider and abettor must have knowledge of each element of the offence. Mere suspicion that an offence is likely to occur or is ongoing is not sufficient.[309]

304 ibid.

305 Chiesa (n 277) 478 referring to the *Comments to Model Penal Code*, section 2.06, 310–13.

306 ibid, referring to the *Comments to Model Penal Code*, section 2.06, 310–13.

307 Silverman (n 291) 65.

308 ibid.

309 ibid.

MAP 9 Standards of knowledge in North America

MAP 10 Standards of intent in North America

Thus, at federal level the doctrines of *dolus eventualis* and wilful blindness would only be sufficient for the liability of the aider and abettor to the extent that they are sufficient for the principal.

6.3 *Observations*

In Canada the minimum level of knowledge is wilful blindness. *Dolus eventualis* is not accepted as the intent requirement. Indeed, the aider and abettor must have acted with the purpose of assisting the commission of the offence.

In the United States, because there is no uniform criminal code there are discrepancies, not only between state and federal law but also between states regarding the minimum level of intent required to hold an aider and abettor liable. At the state level wilful blindness is widely accepted, but only a few states accept *dolus eventualis*. The two major approaches are the 'purposeful intent approach' and the 'knowledge approach'. Thus, in most states the minimum level of intent seems to be much higher and might even be purposeful intent (*dolus directus*). At the federal level the aider and abettor must consciously share the principal's knowledge and intent. This means that *dolus eventualis* and wilful blindness would only be applicable if such mental elements would be sufficient for the principal.

In these two common law jurisdictions wilful blindness can replace active knowledge. However, in Canada and in most states in the United States the aider and abettor must, similar to the position under the Rome Statute, act purposefully. This elevated *mens rea* standard excludes the application of *dolus eventualis*.

7 Oceania

In this region I analyse aiders and abettors' knowledge and intent requirements in Australia. Australia is a common law jurisdiction where the main language is English.

7.1 *Australia*

The law on complicity is largely a matter of common law.[310] Although there are different criminal statutes in different states,[311] courts are responsible for

310 Simon Bronitt, 'Australia' in Kevin Jon Heller and Markus Dubber (eds), *The Handbook of Comparative Criminal Law* (Stanford University Press 2010) 61.

311 See the Criminal Code (Cth), the Criminal Code (ACT), the Crimes Act 1900 (NSW), the Criminal Code (NT), the Criminal Code (Qld), the Criminal Law Consolidation Act 1935 (SA), the Criminal Code (Tas), the Crimes Act 1958 (Vic), the Criminal Code (WA).

developing the *actus reus* and *mens rea* requirements for aiders and abettors.[312] The various statutory provisions generally contain only minor differences in terminology and in the tests to determine criminal liability for accessories.[313] In these statutes aiders and abettors are variably described as 'accessories to the commission of an offence', 'principals in the second degree', or 'accessories before the fact'.[314] Section 11.2 of the Criminal Code (Cth) provides that a person who aids, abets, counsels or procures the commission of an offence by another person is taken to have committed that offence and is punishable accordingly.[315]

To establish the *mens rea* of an aider and abettor, the prosecution must prove that the aider and abettor intended to assist in the perpetration of the crime; recklessness does not suffice.[316] It is necessary to show that the accused knew the essential circumstances that established the principal offence and that the accused intentionally assisted or encouraged the primary offender to commit that offence.[317]

Knowledge of the 'essential circumstances' of an offence is required. It is not sufficient for knowledge to be imputed or presumed.[318] In *Giorgianni*, a landmark case in the determination of the *mens rea* elements of aiding and abetting, the aider and abettor procured a vehicle for another person knowing that the vehicle was so defective as to be dangerous. The High Court of Australia found that a mere failure to conduct an inquiry which would yield knowledge about the essential circumstances is not in itself sufficient to hold an aider and abettor liable, because negligent conduct does not make a person an aider or abettor. However, the doctrine of wilful blindness is a significant exception to the general principle that a person cannot be held criminally liable for aiding and abetting unless she has active knowledge.[319] Wilful blindness can replace the active knowledge requirement.[320] In *Antonelli and Barberi*[321] it was found

312 Bronitt (n 310) 61.

313 Mirko Bagaric and Kenneth J Arenson, *Criminal Laws in Australia* (Oxford University Press 2004) 554.

314 ibid 563.

315 Troy Anderson, *Commonwealth Criminal Law* (2 ed, The Federation Press 2018) 56–7.

316 ibid 67.

317 *Giorgianni v R* (1985) 156 CLR 473.

318 ibid.

319 David H Heilpern and Stanley MH Yeo, *Cases on Criminal Law* (The Law Book Company Limited 1995) 280.

320 Mirko Bagaric, 'Australia' in Alan Reed and Michael Bohlander (eds), *Participation in Crime: Domestic and Comparative Perspectives* (Taylor & Francis 2013) 299. However, Bronitt (n 310) 61 states that wilful blindness does not suffice for liability of aiders and abettors.

321 *R v Antonelli and Barberi* (1905) 70 JP 4.

that the deliberate shutting of one's eyes to what is going on is equivalent to knowledge. The principle of equating wilful blindness with knowledge in the case of aiders and abettors has been confirmed in numerous cases.[322] In *Roper v Taylor's Central Garages (Exeter) Ldt* Lord Devlin pointed out that:[323]

> There is a vast distinction between a state of mind which consists of deliberately refraining from making inquiries, the result of which the person does not care to have, and a state of mind which is merely neglecting to make such inquires as a reasonable and prudent person would make.

Criminal liability for aiders and abettors is also restricted to 'the intentional assistance [...] of the doing of those things which go to make up the offence'.[324] The aider and abettor must act with the specific intent (which I refer to as intent in the first degree or *dolus directus*) that the principal commits the crime; oblique intent (also referred to as *dolus indirectus*) in therefore insufficient.[325] In the *Giorgianni* case the High Court stated:[326]

> For the purposes of many offences it may be true to say that if an act is done with foresight of its probable consequences there is sufficient intent in law even if such intent may more properly be described as a form of recklessness. There are, however, offences in which it is not possible to speak of recklessness as constituting sufficient intent. Attempt is one and conspiracy is another. And we think the offences of aiding and abetting [...] are others. Those offences require intentional participation in a crime by lending assistance.

Thus, the assisting acts of an aider and abettor must be intentionally aimed at the perpetration of the actions which make up the principal's crime.[327]

The New South Wales Law Reform Commission has also recommended that an aider and abettor must act with intent and knowledge. It stated that:[328]

---

322 See for example *Gallow v Tillstone (1900) 83 LT 411; R v Glennan (1970) 91 WN (NSW) 609.*

323 *Roper v Taylor's Central Garages [1951] 2 TLR 284 (KBD)* 289.

324 *Giorgianni v R (1985) 156 CLR 473* 482.

325 Simon Bronitt and Bernadette McSherry, *Principles of Criminal Law* (4 ed, Lawbook Company 2017) 410.

326 *Giorgianni v R (1985) 156 CLR 473* 506.

327 ibid.

328 New South Wales Law Reform Commission, 'Complicity, Report No 129' (2010) recommendation 3.1(3).

> For D to be guilty, he or she must have intended to assist or encourage the commission of the offence or an offence of the same type, knowing or believing in the existence of the facts and circumstances that in law constitute respectively the offence or an offence of the same type.

In sum, in Australia an aider and abettor must at the very least act with wilful blindness and intent in the first degree (*dolus directus*).

7.2 *Observations*

Australia, like many other common law jurisdictions analysed in this work, does not seem to recognise *dolus eventualis* as a minimum standard of intent for the aider and abettor. Rather, an aider and abettor must act with *dolus directus*. However, Australia is one of four common law jurisdictions (together with Canada, Malawi, and the United States of America) to have recognised that the doctrine of wilful blindness replaces the active knowledge requirement.

MAP 11 Standards of knowledge in Oceania

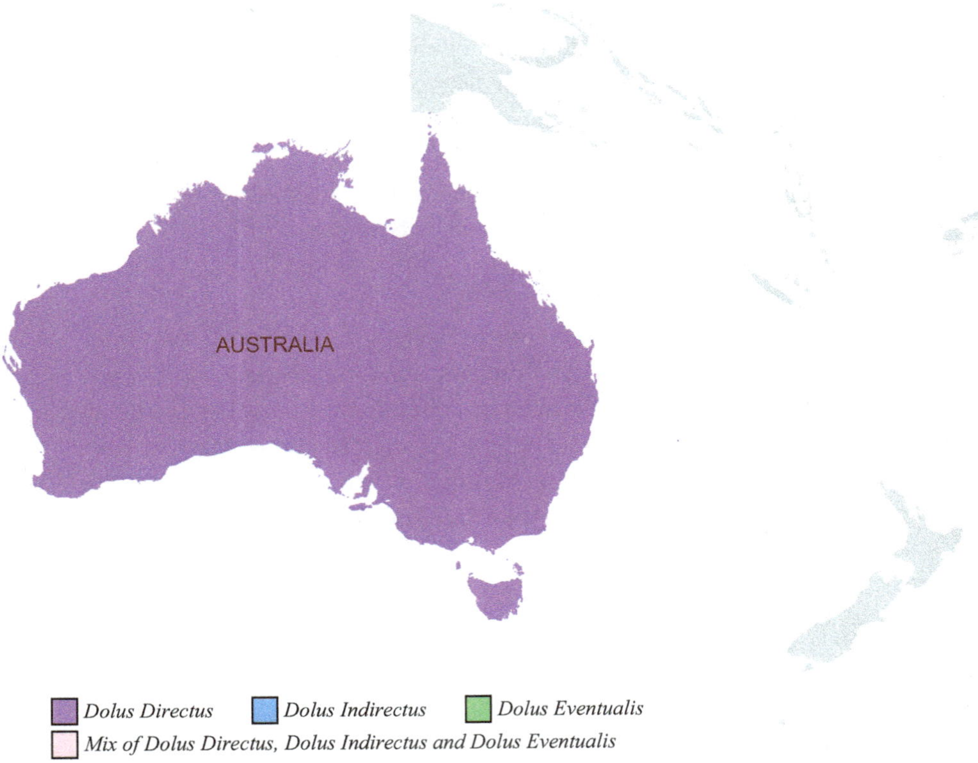

MAP 12 Standards of intent in Oceania

8 Conclusion

Concerning the knowledge requirement, most jurisdictions either do not address the wilful blindness doctrine or have rejected it as the minimum standard of knowledge required for the liability of an aider and abettor.[329] The doctrine of wilful blindness is a common law concept. The only civil law jurisdictions to have accepted wilful blindness are Argentina[330] and Brazil.[331] However, in Argentina the highest court has not had an opportunity to express itself on the acceptance of this doctrine.

329 Namely Cameroon, (see Chapter 5, section 2.1), China (see Chapter 5, section 3.1), Egypt (see Chapter 5, section 2.2), England and Wales (see Chapter 5, section 4.1), France (see Chapter 5, section 4.2), Germany (see Chapter 5, section 4.3), India (see Chapter 5, section 3.2), Italy (see Chapter 5, section 4.4), Israel (see Chapter 5, section 3.3), Malaysia (see Chapter 5, section 3.4), Mexico (see Chapter 5, section 5.3), Turkey (see Chapter 5, section 3.5), and South Africa (see Chapter 5, section 2.4).

330 See Chapter 5, section 5.1.

331 See Chapter 5, section 5.2.

In the common law jurisdictions, four[332] out of nine have recognised that wilful blindness might replace the active knowledge requirement. Viewed in totality, wilful blindness replaces the active knowledge requirement in six[333] out of twenty jurisdictions, all of them common law jurisdictions and Latin American countries.

Furthermore, none of the jurisdictions analysed in Africa, Asia or Latin America seem to have adopted *dolus directus* as a minimum standard of intent. *Dolus directus* only seems to be required in North America and Oceania, all common law jurisdictions. Significantly, in the United States *dolus indirectus* and *dolus eventualis* are also forms of intent recognised in certain states and at the federal level.[334]

In half of the countries analysed in Africa *dolus indirectus* is required[335] and in the other half *dolus eveneutalis* is sufficient.[336] A similar situation presents itself in Asia, where two out of five countries analysed require at least *dolus indirectus*[337] and the other three accept *dolus eventualis*[338] as the minimum standard for the criminal liability of aiders and abettors. In Latin America *dolus eventualis* seems to be widely accepted by all the jurisdictions analysed,[339] as well as by most other countries on the continent (a fact that demonstrates the heavy influence of German criminal law).

Dolus eventualis is a civil law concept which most jurisdictions in Europe seem to have accepted as the minimum standard of intent.[340] Amongst the countries analysed – only England and Wales,[341] a common law jurisdiction, and France,[342] a rare exception among civil law jurisdictions in Europe – have found *dolus eventualis* to be insufficient, and require *dolus indirectus*.

---

332 Namely Australia (see Chapter 5, section 7.1), Canada (see Chapter 5, section 6.1), Malawi (see Chapter 5, section 2.3), the United States of America (see Chapter 5, section 6.2).

333 Namely Argentina (see Chapter 5, section 5.1), Australia (see Chapter 5, section 7.1), Brazil (see Chapter 5, section 5.2), Canada (see Chapter 5, section 6.1), Malawi (see Chapter 5, section 2.3), and the United States of America (see Chapter 5, section 6.2).

334 See Chapter 5, section 6.2.

335 Namely Cameroon (see Chapter 5, section 2.1) and Malawi (see Chapter 5, section 2.3).

336 Namely Egypt (see Chapter 5, section 2.2) and South Africa (see Chapter 5, section 2.4).

337 Namely India (see Chapter 5, section 3.2) and Malaysia (see Chapter 5, section 3.4).

338 Namely China (see Chapter 5, section 3.1), Israel (see Chapter 5, section 3.3) and Turkey (see Chapter 5, section 3.5).

339 Namely Argentina (see Chapter 5, section 5.1), Brazil (see Chapter 5, section 5.2) and Mexico (see Chapter 5, section 5.3).

340 Namely Germany (see Chapter 5, section 4.3), Italy (see Chapter 5, section 4.4) and Russia (see Chapter 5, section 4.5).

341 See Chapter 5, section 4.1.

342 See Chapter 5, section 4.2.

In sum, over half of the countries analysed[343] (most of them civil law jurisdictions) have adopted *dolus eventualis* as the standard for intent. Only one civil law jurisdiction, France, requires a higher standard of intent, namely *dolus indirectus*. Cameroon (a mixed jurisdiction) follows the same approach as France. By contrast, Israel (a common law jurisdiction), South Africa (a mixed jurisdiction) and a minority of states in the United States accept *dolus eventualis* as satisfying the intent requirement.

343 Namely Argentina (see Chapter 5, section 5.1), Brazil (see Chapter 5, section 5.2), China (see Chapter 5, section 3.1), Egypt (see Chapter 5, section 2.2), Germany (see Chapter 5, section 4.3), Italy (see Chapter 5, section 4.4), Israel (see Chapter 5, section 3.3), Mexico (see Chapter 5, section 5.3), Russia (see Chapter 5, section 4.5), South Africa (see Chapter 5, section 2.4), and Turkey (see Chapter 5, section 3.5).

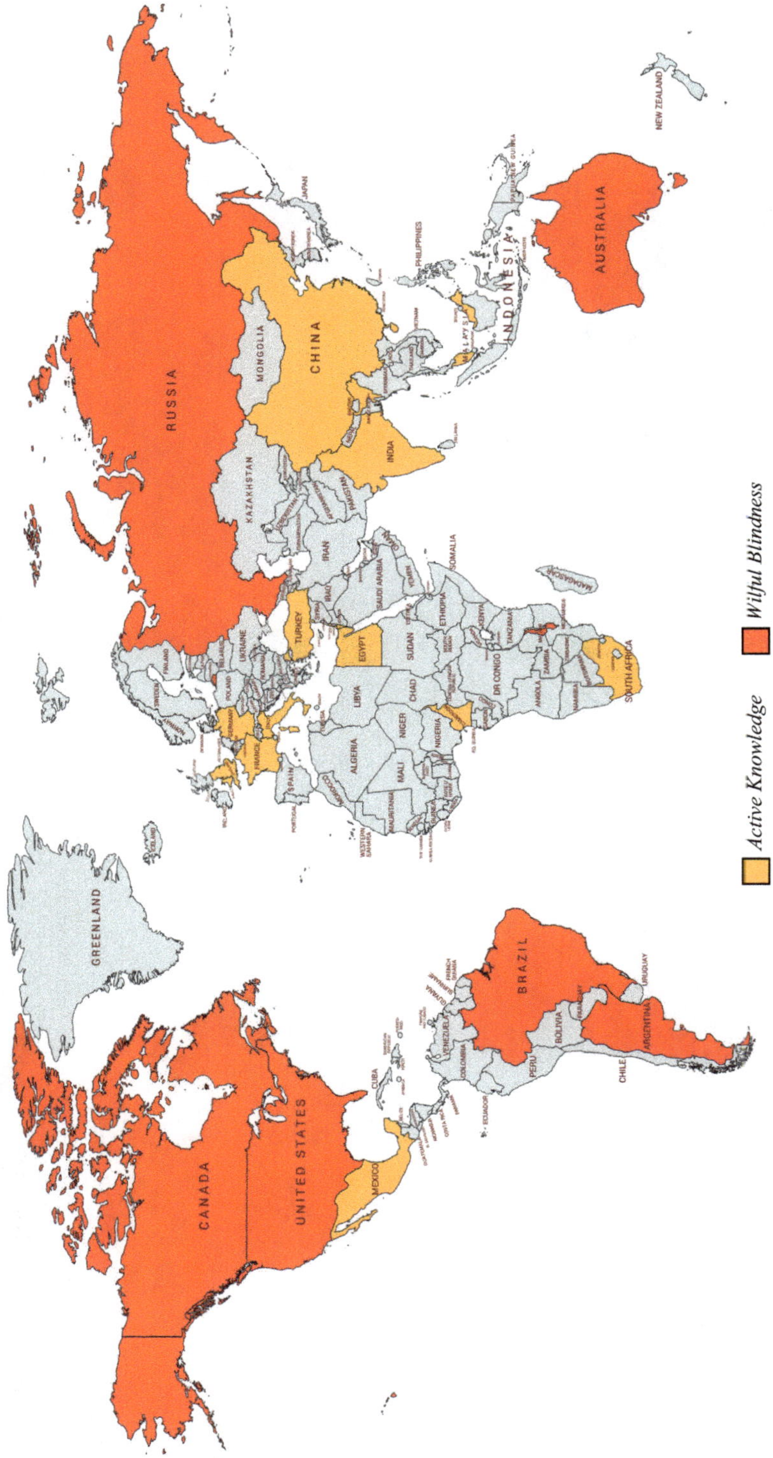

MAP 13 Standards of knowledge worldwide

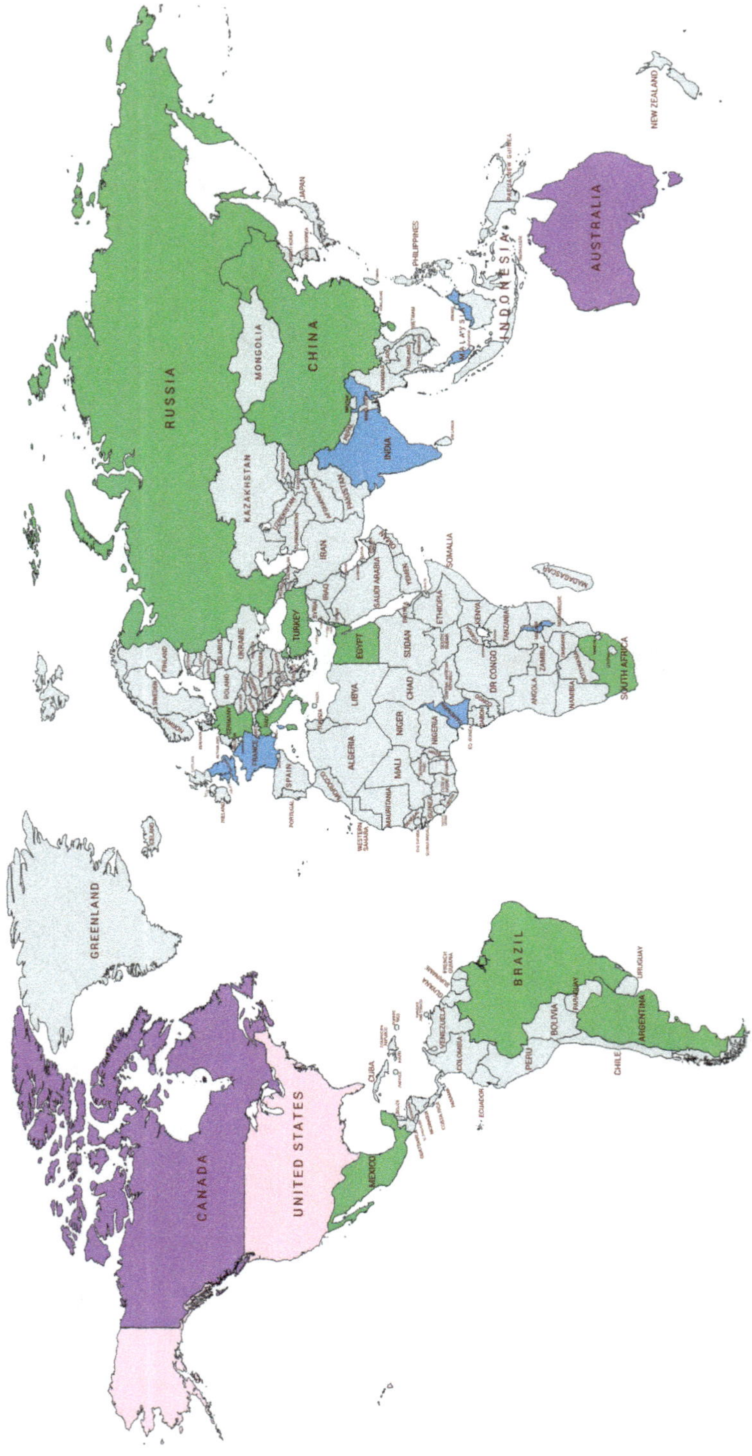

Dolus Directus
Dolus Indirectus
Dolus Eventualis
Mix of Dolus Directus, Dolus Indirectus and Dolus Eventualis

MAP 14 Standards of intent worldwide

PART 3

Determination of the Rules

CHAPTER 6

Application of the Results to International Criminal Law

1 Introduction

To fill the *lacunae* in the primary and supplementary sources of international law regarding the minimum standard of knowledge and intent necessary to hold an aider and abettor liable who finances the commission of core crimes, I firstly undertook an analysis of the applicable law regarding aiding and abetting in international criminal law in Chapter 4. Secondly I conducted a comparative analysis in Chapter V of twenty selected jurisdictions in Africa, Asia, Europe, Latin America, North America and Oceania.

I employ the results of these analyses in this Chapter to determine whether they meet the requirements to be general principles of law recognised by the community of States within the meaning of Article 38(1)(c) of the ICJ Statute. As noted in Chapter 2, section 4.2 above, the existence of a general principle of law applicable in international criminal law is determined by drawing from previous decisions of international and national courts and tribunals. Chapter 4 (at the international level) and Chapter V (at the national level) abstracted legal rules from international and national legal systems with the aim of deriving an underlying principle. Thus, in this Chapter section 2.1 determines that, for wilful blindless, denominators that are common within international law and the different national legal systems across the world do not exist, while section 3.1 finds that such common denominators do exist for *dolus eventualis*. It is important to bear in mind that, of necessity, the content of general principles of law recognised by the community of States is broad. This allows these principles to be flexible enough to serve as a means of dynamic interpretation of legal rules and in the development of the law.

Furthermore, to be elevated to general principles of law in the sense of Article 38(1)(c) the developed general principles of law recognised by the community of States must be compatible with fundamental principles of international criminal law. They are thus tested against the normative framework developed in Part 1 of this work. (Chapter 2, section 4). ILC Special Rapporteur on general principles of law, Vázquez-Bermúdez, notes the following:[1]

1 International Law Commission, 'Second Report of the Special Rapporteur on General Principles of Law, Marcelo Vázquez-Bermúdez, UN Doc. A/CN.4/741' 23.

 | DOI:10.1163/9789004470934_007

> State practice and jurisprudence show that, for a principle common to the principal legal systems of the world to be elevated to a general principle of law in the sense of Article 38, paragraph 1 (c), of the Statute of the International Court of Justice, that principle must be compatible with the fundamental principles of international law.

The compatibility test developed in Chapter 2 section 4, serves to ensure that the developed general principles of law recognised by the community of States are 'not only recognised by the community of States as just, but also as capable of existing within the broader framework of international law'.[2] These compatibility tests are effectuated in section 2.2 for wilful blindness and in section 3.2 for *dolus eventualis*.

2 Wilful Blindness

2.1 *General Principles of Law Recognised by the Community of States*

The wilful blindness doctrine has not been recognised by international courts, tribunals and instruments. Rather, the lowest standard of knowledge they refer to is 'had reason to know' in the context of superior liability, as applied by the ICTY (Article 7(3)) and ICTR (Article 6(3)), and as described in Article 28(a)(i) of the Rome Statute and Article 86(2) of AP I. This standard allows for the criminal liability of military commanders who had information that should have enabled them to conclude that a crime was being committed. This standard is different from the wilful blindness doctrine, which entails that an individual suspected the fact and realised its probability but nevertheless refrained from obtaining the confirmation so as to avoid a conviction. I argue that the 'had reason to know' standard is lower than the wilful blindness standard (as defined in this work). The 'had reason to know' standard is a good indication that a lower standard than active knowledge has in fact been applied by international courts and in international instruments. Therefore, the wilful blindness doctrine should not be dismissed outright.

At the national level, it cannot be argued that the inclusion of the doctrine of wilful blindness as part of the knowledge requirement rises to the level of a general principle of law recognised by the community of States. The reason is simply that this doctrine has not been generally recognised in the jurisdictions

2 ibid.

analysed. Only six out of the twenty States[3] allow for criminal liability to attach when the accused acts with wilful blindness. Moreover, in Argentina, which has theoretically allowed for an extension of the knowledge requirement to include wilful blindness, the highest court has not rendered a definitive decision on this issue. However, as discussed in the following section, these findings should not preclude the future implementation of the wilful blindness doctrine in international criminal law.

I do not argue that there is sufficient evidence internationally and nationally to show that the doctrine of wilful blindness constitutes a general principle of law recognised by the community of States. Rather, my argument is that wilful blindness should be included in the knowledge requirement in international criminal law,[4] because if an individual chooses to deliberately shut her eyes to avoid criminal liability she fulfils the knowledge requirement. Thus, this work claims that the doctrine of wilful blindness, as defined by Glanville Williams, should be adopted as *meaning* knowledge.[5] Therefore, an aider and abettor who provides financial assistance to an entity that commits core crimes should be liable under international criminal law for acting with wilful blindness, because it can be posited that she in fact knew but refrained from obtaining the final confirmation, just to be able to deny active knowledge and thereby avoid criminal liability.

As noted by Blomsma, '[k]nowledge should include only a reasonable degree of certainty',[6] which would be the case with the wilful blindness doctrine. This work approves of Williams' definition of wilful blindness and contends that if it is limited in this way, this doctrine should be regarded as a justified extension of the knowledge requirement. Liability would thus only attach where the aider and abettor either (i) shuts her eyes because she is virtually certain of the answer that her enquiries would provide; or (ii) firmly suspects the veracity of the principal's intent, but she refuses to enquire so as not to know.[7]

---

3 Namely Argentina (see Chapter 5, section 5.1), Australia (see Chapter 5, section 7.1), Brazil (see Chapter 5, section 5.2), Canada (see Chapter 5, section 6.1), Malawi (see Chapter 5, section 2.3), and the United States of America (see Chapter 5, section 6.2).

4 See generally Chapter 5, as well as Kai Ambos, *Treatise on International Criminal Law Volume 1: Foundations and General Part* (Oxford University Press 2013) 276.

5 Glanville Williams, *Criminal Law: The General Part* (2 ed, Stevens & Sons 1961) 159.

6 Jeroen Blomsma, *Mens Rea and Defences in European Criminal Law Book* (Intersentia 2012) 99.

7 AP Simester and others, *Simester and Sullivan's Criminal Law : Theory and Doctrine* (4 ed, Hart 2010) 150.

2.2 General Principles of International Criminal Law

Even though it could not be derived from the analysis of the international and national laws that general principles of law recognised by the community of States could exist regarding the wilful blindness doctrine, this finding should not preclude the future implementation of this doctrine in international criminal law. In fact, if an aider and abettor is virtually certain that her suspicion would be confirmed, but she refuses to take the necessary steps to confirm it in an attempt to avoid criminal liability,[8] international criminal law should include her 'wilful blindness' in the definition of 'knowledge'.

Thus, to ensure that the inclusion of wilful blindness in the definition of 'knowledge' in international criminal law is 'capable of existing within the broader framework of international law',[9] a compatibility test must be conducted. This is done by testing the extension of the knowledge requirement to include wilful blindness against the principles of international criminal law. In fact, this extension of the definition of knowledge to include wilful blindness would only be compatible with the fundamental principles of international criminal law if the principles of legality, specificity, non-retroactivity, *favor rei,* and the prohibition of analogy are respected.

Regarding the principle of legality, it would need to be stipulated in future statutes, *travaux prépartoires*, or in the annexes of the existing statutes of international courts and tribunals that wilful blindness would fulfil the knowledge requirement for aiders and abettors.

To satisfy the principle of specificity, the doctrine of wilful blindness would need to be clearly defined. I suggest the following strict definition of Willams:[10]

> A court can properly find wilful blindness only where it can almost be said that the defendant actually knew. He suspected the fact; he realised its probability; but he refrained from obtaining the final confirmation because he wanted in the event to be able to deny knowledge. This, and this alone, is wilful blindness.

Regarding the principle of non-retroactivity, only a *posterum* application of this doctrine would be lawful. This means that the doctrine of wilful blindness,

---

8 Glanville Williams, 'The Definition of Crime' (1955) 8 Current Legal Problems 127; GR Sullivan and others, *Simester and Sullivan's Criminal Law : Theory and Doctrine* (5 ed, Hart Publishing 2013) 149–50.

9 International Law Commission, 'Second Report of the Special Rapporteur on General Principles of Law, Marcelo Vázquez-Bermúdez, UN Doc. A/CN.4/741' 23.

10 Glanville Williams, *Criminal Law: The General Part* (2 ed, Stevens & Sons 1961) 159.

if adopted by international instruments, would only be applicable to acts of aiding and abetting after the enactment of this doctrine.

The ban on analogy and extensive interpretation would also be respected by the enactment of the wilful blindness doctrine, unless international courts and tribunals give an interpretation to this doctrine that is much broader than the strict definition set forth in the statutes, *travaux prépartoires*, or in the annexes.

Lastly, the principle of *favor rei* would not be implicated unless, for example, an international court or tribunal decided to hold an aider and abettor liable because she acted with wilful blindness before this doctrine was included in the statutes, *travaux prépartoires*, or the annexes.

Most importantly, this work suggests that the doctrine of wilful blindness be recognised and adopted by international criminal courts and tribunals in future. In international criminal law aiding and abetting does not allow for the negligence standard. Currently this means that if an aider and abettor does not finance an entity with active knowledge that her funds would support the commission of the principal's crime, she cannot be held liable. The introduction of the wilful blindness doctrine would allow international courts and tribunals to hold this aider and abettor liable if she chooses not to know.[11] Thus, such inclusion will fill a *lacuna* in legal liability by preventing an aider and abettor from escaping criminal liability simply because she deliberately shut her eyes.

Finally, a transposition of the wilful blindness doctrine into international criminal law would technically be possible because the transposition of nationally derived doctrines into international criminal law is facilitated by the similarities between these two systems. In fact, national and international criminal law are substantially analogous.[12] Although transpositioning into the international setting is not automatic, international criminal courts and tribunals have regularly implemented national legal concepts.[13] The doctrine of wilful blindness should similarly be implemented in international criminal law.

11 Ramon Ragues i Valles, *Ignorancia Deliberada En Derecho Penal* (Atelier Libros Juridicos 2007) 163 is one of the few authors who discusses the wilful blindness doctrine in civil law jurisdictions. He agrees that in cases where negligence is not sufficient for liability, the doctrine of wilful blindness fills the lacunae left by cases in which one decides to shut her eyes to avoid liability.

12 Fabián O Raimondo, *General Principles of Law in the Decisions of International Criminal Courts and Tribunals* (Brill | Nijhoff 2008) 183.

13 ICTY *Prosecutor v Erdemović, Appeals Chamber Judgment* (IT-96-22-A) 2. In Judge Cassese's opinion, ' legal constructs and terms of art upheld in national law should not be automatically applied at the international level. They cannot be mechanically imported into international criminal proceedings'.

3 *Dolus Eventualis*

3.1 *General Principles of Law Recognised by the Community of States*

There are different definitions of *dolus eventualis*. This work supports a strict defintion, according to which an aider and abettor would only be held criminally liable if she consciously accepts that her financial aid could substantially contribute to a crime. Recognising *dolus eventualis* as a form of intent sufficient to lead to an aider and abettor's criminal responsibility would put on equal footing an individual who intentionnally finances an entity involved in the commission of core crimes, and one who *consciously accepts* that her financial assistance could substantially contribute to the perpetration of core crimes but nevertheless *decides* to provide the financial assistance notwithstanding this risk. In other words, the aider and abettor who acts with *dolus eventualis* is aware of the high risk that her financial contribution could be used to commit core crimes and she makes peace with that knowledge. This conscious acceptance of a foreseeable consequence should be sufficient to hold an aider and abettor liable under international criminal law.

Moreover, in jurisdictions where *dolus eventualis* is not recognised such an omission leaves a *lacuna*, since *dolus eventualis* 'is the application of criminal policy to cases, where it is felt that the punishment for the offence committed with negligence [refered to in this work as recklessness] would be too low'.[14] Also, not every intentional crime has a counterpart that criminalises the reckless perpetration of that crime. In fact, aiding and abetting can, in principle, not be committed recklessly. In those cases where an aider and abettor could not be held liable for recklessness, the negation of direct or indirect intent would also completely negate criminal liability.[15] *Dolus eventualis* allows for liability to attach in cases where liability could, despite the accused's guilty mind, not be otherwise imposed.

At the international level there are ample examples of *dolus eventualis* being applied by numerous bodies, although international criminal courts and tribunals, except for the ICC, have not had the opportunity to express themselves on the application of *dolus eventualis* for aiders and abettors.

Dolus eventualis is one of the forms of the volitional element that has been endorsed in the jurisprudence of the *ad hoc* Tribunals.[16] According to *Stakić*, *dolus eventualis* implies that the accused '"reconciles himself" or "makes

14 Blomsma (n 7) 102.

15 ibid.

16 ICTY *Prosecutor v Dusko Tadic, Appeals Chamber Judgment* (IT-94-1-A) 219–20; ICTY *Prosecutor v Milomir Stakic, Trial Chamber Judgment* (IT-97-24-T) 587.

peace" with the likelihood' of the crime being perpetrated.[17] In *Delalic*, the ICTY Trial Chamber held as follows regarding the use of recklessness or *dolus eventualis* to infer intention:[18]

> While different legal systems utilise differing forms of classification of the mental element involved in the crime of murder, it is clear that some form of intention is required. However, this intention may be inferred from the circumstances, whether one approaches the issue from the perspective of the foreseeability of death as a consequence of the acts of the accused, or the taking of an excessive risk which demonstrates recklessness. As has been stated by the Prosecution, the Commentary to the Additional Protocols expressly includes the concept of 'recklessness' within its discussion of the meaning of 'wilful' as a qualifying term in both articles 11 and 85 of Additional Protocol I.

Dolus eventualis has also been recognised as an appropriate *mens rea* standard by the ECCC Judgment in Case 002/01,[19] and by international UN-mandated inquiries into the Sri-Lanka and Gaza conflicts.[20]

Regarding the *dolus eventualis* standard for aiding and abetting at the ICC, I agree with the *Bemba* Pre-Trial Chamber II and the *Lubanga* Trial Chamber in their view that the language of Article 30 of the Rome Statute does not allow for *dolus eventualis* to be considered a sufficient level of intent. The wording of Article 30 – 'means to engage in the conduct' and 'means to cause that consequence or is aware that it will occur in the ordinary course of events' – requires a higher degree of certainty than that required by *dolus eventualis*. In fact, *dolus eventualis* requires the accused to reconcile herself or make peace with the

---

17 ICTY *Prosecutor v Milomir Stakic, Trial Chamber Judgment* (*IT-97-24-T*) 587.

18 ICTY *Prosecutor v Mucić et al, Trial Chamber Judgment* (*IT-96-21-T*) 437.

19 ECCC *Prosecutor v Chea Nuon and Samphan Khieu, Trial Chamber Judgment* (*Case No 002/ 19-09-2007/ECCC/TC*).

20 Sarah Knuckey, 'Murder in Common Article 3' in Andrew Clapham, Paola Gaeta and Marco Sassoli (eds), *The 1949 Geneva Convention : A Commentary* (Oxford University Press 2015) 459 citing the report of the Secretary-General's Panel of Experts on Accountability in Sri Lanka, 31 March 2011, paragraphs 205, 251, which states that the *mens rea* 'encompasses reckless disregard for life' and reporting credible allegations of attacks on hospitals and humanitarian objects as possible murder, whether the targeting was 'direct, or reckless' and the report of the United Nations Fact-Finding Mission on the Gaza Conflict, A/ HRC/12/48, 25 September 2004, paragraph 1433, which refers to an incident as indicting 'an intention, or at least recklessness, to cause harm to civilians, which may amount to wilful killings'.

possible result as a cost of attaining her goal.[21] The intent standard in Article 30 of the Rome Statute is therefore higher than *dolus eventualis*. However, the fact that under the current understanding of the Rome Statute *dolus eventualis* is insufficient to hold an accused liable at the ICC, does not preclude the use of *dolus eventualis* by other tribunals. For example, the statutes of the *ad hoc* Tribunals do not contain a general definition of the *mens rea* element. The judges at the hybrid and *ad hoc* Tribunals are not bound by the statutory wording or the drafting history of the Rome Statute as judges at the ICC are. The refusal to allow a lower *mens rea* standard at the ICC does therefore not preclude the possibility of *dolus eventualis* being used by these other tribunals.

At the national level, *dolus eventualis* is a well-recognised standard of intent in civil law jurisdictions and in some common law and mixed jurisdictions. As seen in the comparative analysis, all civil law countries, expect France, recognise that *dolus eventualis* is sufficient to hold an aider and abettor criminally liable. Additionally, some common law and mixed jurisdictions, such as Israel and South Africa, have also accepted this lower standard of intent.

In conclusion, this standard of *mens rea* is well-accepted by a large number and variety of domestic legal systems. It should be uniformly used and applied in international criminal law, because it fulfils all the requirements to be considered a general principle of law recognised by the community of States as intended by Article 38(1)(c) of the Statute of the ICJ. In fact, international courts, tribunals and instruments have already recognised its validity in international criminal law. Furthermore, most of the jurisdictions analysed have recognised the possible criminal liability of an aider and abettor if she acts with *dolus eventualis*. This is a common denominator in civil law jurisdictions, and amongst common law and mixed jurisdictions more than a third of those analysed[22] have also established liability for aiding and abetting based on *dolus eventualis*. The acceptance of *dolus eventualis* as the minimum standard of intent to hold an aider and abettor liable is thus commonly accepted within numerous and differing national legal systems. Consequently, from the comparative analysis a general principle of law recognised by the community of States – namely, that *dolus eventualis* is sufficient to hold an aider and

---

21 ICTY *Prosecutor v Milomir Stakic, Trial Chamber Judgment* (*IT-97-24-T*) 587; ICTY *Prosecutor v Dusko Tadic, Appeals Chamber Judgment* (*IT-94-1-A*) 219–20; ICC *Prosecutor v Lubanga, Decision on the Confirmation of Charges, Pre-Trial Chamber I* (*ICC-01/04-01/06-803-tEN*) 352; George P Fletcher, *Basic Concepts of Criminal Law* (Oxford University Press 1988) 123, 446.

22 Namely Israel (see Chapter 5, section 3.3), South Africa (see Chapter 5, section 2.4), as well as the minority of states in the United States (see Chapter 5, section 6.2.1.3).

abettor criminally liable – is derived and should be implemented by international courts and tribunals.

3.2 *General Principles of International Criminal Law*

I argue that the acknowledgment of liability for acting with *dolus eventualis* as an aider and abettor in international criminal law amounts to a general principle of law recognised by the community of States. It is also compatible with 'the broader framework of international law',[23] because it respects all principles of international criminal law.

Regarding the principle of legality, it has already been found both internationally and nationally that *dolus eventualis* is a sufficient threshold of intent for the criminal liability of aiders and abettors. Acting with *dolus eventualis* thus violates the prohibition to aid and abet the perpetration of core crimes. This norm is already in existence.

The principle of specificity is fulfilled as *dolus eventualis* has been defined by the *ad hoc* Tribunals. However, I suggest a strict definition of *dolus eventualis*, namely that an aider and abettor who acts with *dolus eventualis* should reconcile herself with the result as a possible cost of attaining her goal. She should be aware of the substantial likelihood that her conduct will result in the realisation of the objective elements of the crime, but, notwithstanding such awareness, she nevertheless decides to carry it out. In other words, with her financial contribution, the aider and abettor should intend to assist the entity in its criminal actions by becoming reconciled with the ultimate consequences, which is that her financial assistance will facilitate the commission of core crimes. She has taken the fact that her financial assistance could be used to commit core crimes into account as a cost of attaining her goal of financially supporting the entity that will commit core crimes, and she has accepted this risk.

The principle of non-retroactivity is respected because international courts and instruments have already recognised the possibility of criminal accountability for acting with *dolus eventualis*. When considering the principle of non-retroactivity, it is also necessary to keep in mind the inherent characteristics of international criminal law. This is a relatively new field of law and is not fully developed. Thus, the evolving legal rules are in continued need of qualification. Since *dolus eventualis* has been used by the *ad hoc* and hybrid Tribunals when dealing with JCE, command responsibility, and the crime of extermination, an

---

23 International Law Commission, 'Second Report of the Special Rapporteur on General Principles of Law, Marcelo Vázquez-Bermúdez, UN Doc. A/CN.4/741' 23.

accused should reasonably expect that she could be held criminally responsible for aiding and abetting when she acts with *dolus eventualis*, even though this lower standard of intent might be detrimental to her.

Moreover, this interpretation does not violate the principle of *favor rei*, because it does not create a new criminal offence with new legal elements. Instead, the relatively 'vague' term 'intent' could foreseeably encompass *dolus directus*, *dolus indirectus* and *dolus eventualis*.

Finally, the ban on analogy and extensive interpretation would be respected, as international courts and tribunals would simply be interpreting the concept of 'intent' and provide clarity on an existing prohibition that had already been laid down, namely the prohibition to aid and abet the perpetration of core crimes.

In sum, in this work I argue that criminal liability for aiders and abettors who act with *dolus eventualis* amounts to a general principle of law recognised by the community of States, and that its application respects the principles of international criminal law.

4 Wilful Blindness and *Dolus Eventualis*

The implementation of the wilful blindness doctrine, together with *dolus eventualis* in the definition of the mental element of aiding and abetting, is not only possible but it is also desirable. The application of the wilful blindness doctrine and *dolus eventualis* for aiders and abettors in international criminal law would avoid the situation where an individual who finances an entity involved in the perpetration of core crimes escapes criminal accountability because she acted neither negligently and recklessly nor with active knowledge and *dolus indirectus*. When discussing the application of *dolus eventualis* in Spanish criminal law, Ragues i Vallès states that when an individual who acts with *dolus eventualis* and decides to maintain her decision not to confirm her suspicions despite the almost immediate availability of the ignored information, she should not be treated differently than an individual who acted with *dolus indirectus* and active knowledge.[24] He also notes that where an individual carries a suitcase filled with drugs:[25]

24 Ragues i Valles (n 12) 202–3.

25 ibid 203. Unofficial translation by the author.

> [I]t does not seem that the subject who, in order to avoid confirming his suspicions, decides not to open the suitcase, despite being able to do so without difficulty, should deserve a more lenient sentence than the individual who knows perfectly well what he is carrying.

Thus, the inclusion of both wilful blindness and *dolus eventualis* in the definition of the mental element of aiding and abetting is legally possible.

Furthermore, a transposition of wilful blindness, a common law concept, and *dolus eventualis*, a civil law concept, within the same framework is not unprecedented. Nationally, Argentina[26] and Brazil[27] have accomplished it. Internationally, the *ad hoc* and hybrid Tribunals and the ICC have implemented numerous civil law and common law concepts within their statutes and jurisprudence. Indeed, the transposition of nationally derived doctrines into international criminal law is possible, since national and international criminal law are substantially analogous.[28] Thus, bringing together a common law concept (wilful blindness) and a civil law concept (*dolus eventualis*) in the definition of the mental element of aiding and abetting is representative of what international criminal law is, namely an integration of national legal concepts from different legal families into international criminal law. The cohabitation of different legal systems is an essential feature of international criminal law.

Finally, one should bear in mind that, even though I argue for the lowering of the knowledge standard to include wilful blindness and the recognition of *dolus eventualis*, criminal liability should *never* follow unless the assistance was substantial. The most efficient way to mitigate concerns of over-inculpation is to place renewed emphasis on the nexus and fault elements.[29] This means that courts must rigorously uphold the substantial contribution requirement for the liability of an individual who finances an entity involved in the perpetration of core crimes.[30] Liability for acting recklessly should not follow in cases of aiding and abetting for individuals who finance entities that commit core

---

26 See Chapter 5, section 5.1.

27 See Chapter 5, section 5.2.

28 Raimondo (n 13) 183.

29 James G Stewart, '"Specific Direction" Is Indefensible: A Response to Heller on Complicity' available at <http://opiniojuris.org/2013/06/12/specific-direction-is-indefensible-a-response-to-heller-on-complicity/> accessed 21 September 2018.

30 James Stewart, 'Overdetermined Atrocities' (2012) 10 Journal of International Criminal Justice 1189.

crimes.[31] Liability should only attach if the individual acts with *dolus directus*, *dolus indirectus* or *dolus eventualis*.

5 Conclusion

This Chapter concluded that the minimum threshold of knowledge necessary to hold an aider and abettor liable in international criminal law is active knowledge. Although in six out of the twenty jurisdictions analysed wilful blindness is sufficient as the minimum standard of knowledge for aiders and abettors, this does not constitute a general principle of law recognised by the community of States. This is because international courts, tribunals and instruments do not recognise wilful blindness as the minimum standard. However, I argue that the rules at the international level should be revised to include wilful blindness.

When measuring the possible extension of the definition of 'knowledge' to include wilful blindness to ascertain its compatibility with the fundamental principles of international criminal law, this work determined that to respect these principles, the inclusion of the wilful blindness doctrine for aiders and abettors would need to be clearly spelled out in future statutes, *travaux prépartoires*, and in the annexes of the existing statutes. It would also have to be clearly defined. I thus argue that, in future, if the concept of wilful blindness is properly implemented in the relevant international instruments, an individual who finances the perpetration of core crimes could be held liable for acting with active knowledge and wilful blindness, provided that the other *actus reus* and *mens rea* elements are fulfilled.

At the international level several international courts, tribunals and institutions have accepted that *dolus eventualis* could be included in the definition of intent. Significantly, the question of whether *dolus eventualis* is sufficient for holding aiders and abettors liable in international criminal law has never arisen, except at the ICC. Discussions concerning *dolus eventualis* have thus far been limited to questions of liability for superiors, JCE, or regarding a particular crime, such as the crime of extermination. At the national level most of the jurisdictions analysed have accepted that an aider and abettor acting with *dolus eventualis* could be held liable. This work therefore concludes that the assessment of international rules, as well as the comparative analysis, reveal

31 Miles Jackson, 'Regional Complementarity: An Interpretation of Article 17(1)(A) of the Rome Statute' (2016) 14 Journal of International Criminal Justice 1061, 85.

that *dolus eventualis* is widely recognised as a sufficient level of intent for aiders and abettors. This constitutes the formation of a general principle of law recognised by the community of States according to Article 38(1)(c) of the ICJ Statute.

Such a general principle also does not violate the principles of international criminal law, because *dolus eventualis* is a standard of intent widely recognised and applied both nationally and internationally. It is also well-defined, although I recommend the implementation of a strict definition. The implementation of a *dolus eventualis* standard for aiders and abettors also respects the principle of *favor rei* because it is foreseeable that the term 'intent' could encompasses *dolus directus*, *dolus indirectus* and *dolus eventualis*.

Finally, an implementation of a common law concept (wilful blindness) and a civil law concept (*dolus eventualis*) in the definition of the mental element of aiding and abetting is not only possible but it is also desirable. Doing so would avoid situations in which liability would be precluded when an individual who finances an entity involved in the perpetration of core crimes acts negligently and recklessly. Moreover, the transposition of wilful blindness and *dolus eventualis* within the same framework has been done nationally in Argentina and Brazil, and internationally by international courts and tribunals which have implemented concepts from different legal families within their governing statutes and jurisprudence. To conclude, international criminal law should include criminal liability for an aider and abettor who acts with wilful blindness and *dolus eventualis*, if her aid substantially contributed to the principal's crime.

CHAPTER 7

Conclusion

The conclusions of this work are as follows: An individual who finances an entity that is involved in the perpetration of core crimes can be held liable under international criminal law as an aider and abettor, except at the ICC, because she does not in principle act purposefully. She must fulfil the material elements of the crime, notably by substantially contributing to the perpetration of the offence. Furthermore, she must possess the mental elements. Regarding the *mens rea* requirement of aiding and abetting, this work resolved the question of the scope of the knowledge and intent requirements required for criminal responsibility by conducting an analysis of the applicable international law and a comparative analysis of twenty national jurisdictions. From these analyses I conclude that, at this time, the minimum standard of knowledge required to hold an aider and abettor liable is active knowledge. However, I argue that this standard should be revised to include wilful blindness. Regarding the intent requirement, the analyses revealed that *dolus directus*, *dolus indirectus*, as well as *dolus eventualis* are included in the definition of 'intent'. An individual who provides money to a mixed organisation that uses these funds to perpetrate core crimes can therefore be criminally accountable for acting with *dolus eventualis*.

Thus, I propose the incorporation of the wilful blindness doctrine in the knowledge requirement and the recognition of the *dolus eventualis* standard for aiders and abettors. These standards should be sufficient to establish liability of an aider and abettor who finances an entity involved in the perpetration of core crimes. If an individual provides financial assistance to an organisation that she knows (or deliberately chooses not to know) could commit core crimes with these funds, she should be deemed to have fulfilled the knowledge requirement of aiding and abetting if she consciously accepted that risk. By the same token, I argue that if an aider and abettor consciously reconciles herself with the likelihood that her financial assistance could be used in the commission of core crimes, and accepts the consequences of her actions, she should be held criminally accountable for acting with *dolus eventualis*. Even though she does not expressly desire the results she nevertheless consciously accepts them. She does not act recklessly, but she acts with the awareness that there is a considerable chance that her financial assistance is facilitating the principal's perpetration of a core crime and she accepts it. However, if she finances an entity that she knows could perpetrate core crimes, but she

 | DOI:10.1163/9789004470934_008

specifically requests that her financial assistance be used for lawful purposes only, she should not be held criminally liable if it later comes to light that her financial assistance was used in the commission of core crimes. This is the case because she lacks intent that her financial assistance should be used in the perpetration of core crimes.

If, in the application of wilful blindness and/or *dolus eventualis*, insubstantial or minimal assistance was viewed as sufficient to satisfy the *actus reus* requirement of aiding and abetting, this outcome would be unjustly harsh. However, when an aider and abettor substantially contributes to the commission of a crime this issue does not arise. She should therefore not be held liable for *any* contribution, but only for a substantial one. Her contribution should not be viewed as a *conditio sine qua non* for the perpetration of the offence, but it should substantially influence it.

In sum, this work concludes that an individual ought to be held criminally liable as an aider and abettor if she, at a minimum, (i) fulfils all of the material elements of aiding and abetting, notably by substantially contributing to the principal's crime with her financial assistance; (ii) strongly suspects that her financial assistance would contribute to the commission of core crimes by the principal, but she nonetheless turns a blind eye to her suspicions in order to escape criminal liability; and (iii) consciously accepts and reconciles herself with the considerable likelihood that her financial assistance could facilitate the perpetration of core crimes. Regarding the mental elements, the minimum threshold for the liability of an aider and abettor should be that the aider and abettor acted with wilful blindness and *dolus eventualis*.

To conclude, both the wrong of the principal *and* the wrong of the individual who substantially contributed to the principal's wrong, matter. Lack of the financial resources necessary to commit core crimes dramatically reduces the probability that these crimes would be committed. International criminal law aims at preventing the perpetration of heinous crimes. This work intends to contribute to this aim by discouraging individuals from financing entities that are involved in the commission of these crimes. The ultimate aim of both international criminal law and this book is the protection of human life.

Bibliography

Books

Aksenova M, *Complicity in International Criminal Law* (Hart Publishing 2016).

Ambos K, *La Parte General Del Derecho Penal Internacional : Bases Para Una Elaboración Dogmática* (Duncker & Humboldt 2005).

Ambos K, *Treatise on International Criminal Law Volume 1: Foundations and General Part* (Oxford University Press 2013).

Anderson T, *Commonwealth Criminal Law* (2 ed, The Federation Press 2018).

Anyangwe C, *Criminal Law: The General Part* (Langaa RPCIG 2015).

Ashworth A and Horder J, *Ashworth's Principles of Criminal Law* (8 ed, Oxford University Press 2016).

Ashworth A and Horder J, *Ashworth's Principles of Criminal Law* (9 ed, Oxford University Press 2019).

Badar ME, *The Concept of Mens Rea in International Criminal Law The Case for a Unified Approach* (Hart Publishing 2013).

Bagaric M and Arenson KJ, *Criminal Laws in Australia* (Oxford University Press 2004).

Bande LC, *Criminal Law in Malawi* (Juta & Company 2017).

Bande LC, *Criminal Law in Malawi* (Kluwer Law International 2012).

Barberis JA, *Formación Del Derecho Internacional* (Editorial Ábaco de Rodolfo Depalma 1994).

Bassiouni MC, *International Criminal Law: Sources, Subjects and Contents, Volume 1* (3 ed, Brill | Nijhoff 2008).

Beltrani S, Marino R and Petrucci R, *Codice Penale: Annotato Con La Giurisprudenza* (Edizioni Giuridiche Simone 2003).

Blomsma J, *Mens Rea and Defences in European Criminal Law Book* (Intersentia 2012).

Bronitt S and McSherry B, *Principles of Criminal Law* (4 ed, Lawbook Company 2017).

Brownlie I, *Oppenheim's International Law: Peace, Volume 1* (Longman 1992).

Burchell EM, Burchell JM and Hunt PMA, *South African Criminal Law and Procedure: General Principles of Criminal Law, Volume 1* (3 ed, Juta & Company 1997).

Burchell, J, *Principles of Criminal Law* (5 ed, Juta Legal and Academic Publishers 2016).

Capotorti F, *Cours Général de Droit International Public, Volume 248* (Brill | Nijhoff 1994).

Casey-Maslen S (ed), *The War Report: Armed Conflict in 2013* (Oxford University Press 2014).

Cassese A and Gaeta P, *Cassese's International Criminal Law* (Oxford University Press 2013).

Cherif M. Bassiouni, *The Legislative History of the International Criminal Court: Introduction, Analysis, and Integrated Text, Volume 1* (Brill | Nijhoff 2005).

Clarkson CMV, Keating HM and Cunningham SR, *Clarkson and Keating Criminal Law: Text and Materials* (6 ed, Sweet & Maxwell 2007).

Crawford J, *Brownlies's Principal of Public International Law* (8 ed, Oxford University Press 2012).

Cryer R, Friman H, Robinson D and Wilmshurst E, *An Introduction to International Criminal Law and Procedure* (3 ed, Cambridge University Press 2014).

Cryer R, *Prosecuting International Crimes: Selectivity and the International Criminal Law Regime* (Cambridge University Press 2005).

David O, *Smith and Hogan Criminal Law* (12 ed, Oxford University Press 2008).

De Asúa J, *La Ley y El Delito* (2 ed, Hermes 1954).

De Azevedo MA and Salim A, *Direito Penal – Parte Geral* (7 ed, Juspodivm 2017).

De Barros MA and Silva TMA, *Lavagem de Ativos: Dolo Direto e a Inaplicabilidade Da Teoria Da Cegueira Deliberada*, (Revista dos Tribunais 2015).

Debove F, Falletti F and Dupic E, *Précis de Droit Pénal et de Procédure Pénal* (6 ed, Presses Universitaires de France 2016).

Di Amato A and Fucito F, *Criminal Law in Italy* (3 ed, Wolters Kluwer Law & Business 2016).

Díaz-Aranda E, *Lecciones de Derecho Penal Para El Nuevo Sistema de Justicia Em México* (STRAF 2014).

Dos Santos Cirino J, *Direito Penal – Parte Geral* (5 ed, Conceito Editorial 2012).

Dubber M and Hörnle T, *Criminal Law: A Comparative Approach* (Oxford University Press).

Dupuy P-M, *L'unité de l'ordre Juridique International, Volume 297* (Brill | Nijhoff 2002).

Einarsen T, *The Concept of Universal Crimes in International Law* (Opsahl Academic EPublisher 2012).

Elliott C, *French Criminal Law* (Willan Publishing 2001).

Fierro GJ, *Teoria de La Participacion Criminal* (2 ed, Astrea 2001).

Finbarr M and McCutcheon JP, *Criminal Liability: A Grammar* (Round Hall Sweet & Maxwell 2000).

Finnin S, *Elements of Accessorial Modes of Liability: Article 25 (3)(b) and (c) of the Rome Statute of the International Criminal Court* (Brill | Nijhoff 2012).

Fletcher GP, *Basic Concepts of Criminal Law* (Oxford University Press 1988).

Fletcher GP, *Rethinking Criminal Law* (Oxford University Press 2000).

Fletcher GP, *The Grammar of Criminal Law: American, Comparative, and International, Volume 1* (Oxford University Press 2007).

Forstner M, *Der Allgemeine Teil Des Ägyptischen Strafrechts* (Nomos 1986).

Garner B, *A Dictionary of Modern Legal Usage* (2 ed, Oxford University Press 1995).

Gordon Rose V, *Parties to an Offence* (Carswell 1982).

Greco R, *Curso de Direito Penal* (18 ed, Impetus 2016).

Heilpern DH and Yeo SMH, *Cases on Criminal Law* (The Law Book Company Limited 1995).
Hoctor SV, *Criminal Law in South Africa* (Wolters Kluwer Law & Business 2017).
Jackson M, *Complicity in International Law* (Oxford University Press 2015).
Kemp G, *Criminal Law in South Africa* (Oxford University Press 2012).
Knoops G-JA, *Mens Rea at the International Criminal Court* (Brill | Nijhoff 2017).
Koh KL, Clarkson CMV and Morgan NA, *Criminal Law in Singapore and Malaysia: Text and Materials* (Malayan Law Journal 1989).
Krey V, *Deutsches Strafrecht, Allgemeiner Teil, Lehrbuch in Deutsch Und Englisch: Teil II* (Kohlhammer ed, 2003).
Lauterpacht H, *Private Law Sources and Analogies of International Law: With Special Reference to International Arbitration* (Longmans, Green and Co 1927).
Loveless J, *Criminal Law Text, Cases and Materials* (5 ed, Oxford University Press 2016).
Mallal BA and Simon AC, *Mallal's Penal Law* (Malayan Law Journal 2002).
Marchuk I, *The Fundamental Concept of Crime in International Criminal Law: A Comparative Law Analysis* (Springer Science & Business Media 2013).
Mayaud Y and Allain E, *Code Pénal* (104 ed, Editions Dalloz 2007).
Moreno Hernández M, *Dogmática penal y Política criminal* (Ubijus Editorial 2018).
Moro S, *Crime de Lavagem de Dinheiro* (Saraiva 2010).
Mostafa MM, *Principes de Droit Pénal Des Pays Arabes* (Librairie Générale de Droit et de Jurispurdence 1972).
Noto F, *Secondary Liability in International Criminal Law: A Study on Aiding and Abetting Or Otherwise Assisting the Commission of International Crimes* (Dike 2013).
Okoth J, *The Crime of Conspiracy in International Criminal Law* (TMC Asser Press 2014).
Oumarou A, *Code de Lois Pénales* (2 ed, Presses Universitaires d'Afrique 2006).
Paglieri C, *Nueva Teoría Del Delito: Participación Penal* (Azul 2014).
Pérez Barberá G, *El Dolo Eventual : Hacia el Abandono de la Idea de Dolo Como Estado Mental* (Hammurabi 2011).
Pitombo ASA de M, *Lavagem de Dinheiro: A Tipicidade Do Crime Antecedente* (Revista dos Tribunais 2003).
Porro S, *Risk and Mental Element: An Analysis of National and International Law on Core Crimes* (Stämpfli 2014).
Prado LR, *Direito Penal Econômico* (Revista dos Tribunais 2016).
Raghavan V V, *Law of Crimes: Exhaustive Commentary on Indian Penal Code, 1860 (Act No. 45 of 1860)* (5 ed, India Law House 1999).
Ragues i Valles R, *Ignorancia Deliberada En Derecho Penal* (Atelier Libros Juridicos 2007).
Raimondo FO, *General Principles of Law in the Decisions of International Criminal Courts and Tribunals* (Brill | Nijhoff 2008).
Ranchhoddas R and Thakore DK, *Ratanlal & Dhirajlal's Law of Crimes: A Commentary on the Indian Penal Code, 1860* (Bharat Law House 2013).

Reuter P, *Droit International Public* (Presses Universitaires de France 1958).

Röling BVA and Cassese A, *The Tokyo Trial and Beyond: Reflections of a Peacemonger* (Polity Press 1993).

Scanlon TM, *Moral Dimensions: Permissibility, Meaning, Blame* (Harvard University Press 2008).

Schabas WA, *The International Criminal Court: A Commentary on the Rome Statute* (2 ed, Oxford University Press 2016).

Sieber U and Cornils K, *Nationales Strafrecht in Rechtsvergleichender Darstellung: Allgemeiner Teil, Volume 4* (Duncker & Humboldt 2010).

Simester AP and others, *Simester and Sullivan's Criminal Law : Theory and Doctrine* (4 ed, Hart 2010).

Smith K, *A Modern Treatise on the Law of Criminal Complicity* (Clarendon Press 1991).

Snyman CR, *A Draft Criminal Code for South Africa: With a Commentary* (Juta & Company 1995).

Sullivan GR, Simester AP, Stark F, Spencer J and Virgo G, *Simester and Sullivan's Criminal Law : Theory and Doctrine* (5 ed, Hart Publishing 2013).

Tomuschat C, *International Law : Ensuring the Survival of Mankind on the Eve of a New Century : General Course on Public International Law, Volume 281* (Brill | Nijhoff 1999).

Traĭnin AN, *Hitlerite Responsibility under Criminal Law* (Hutchinson & Co 1945).

van Sliedregt E, *Individual Criminal Responsibility in International Law* (Oxford University Press 2012).

Vasconcelos FHP, *Manual de Derecho Penal Mexicano – Parte General* (Porruá 2004).

Villalobos I, *Derecho Penal Mexicano* (Porruá 1960).

Villiger ME, *Customary International Law and Treaties: A Manual on the Theory and Practice of the Interrelation of Sources* (2 ed, Kluwer Law International 1997).

Wallace RJ, *Responsibility and the Moral Sentiments* (Harvard University Press 1998).

Wang S, *Criminal Law in China* (Kluwer Law International 2017).

Werle G and Jessberger F, *Principles of International Criminal Law* (3 ed, Oxford University Press 2014).

Williams G, *Criminal Law: The General Part* (2 ed, Stevens & Sons 1961).

Yanev LD, *Theories of Co-Perpetration in International Criminal Law* (Brill | Nijhoff 2018).

Yenisey F, *Turkey* (Kluwer Law International 2016).

Zaffaroni ER, Alagia A and Slokar A, *Derecho Penal Parte General* (2 ed, Sociedad Anonima 2006).

Chapters in Books

Ambos, K, 'Article 25: Individual Criminal Responsibility' in Otto Triffterer and Kai Ambos (eds), *The Rome Statute of the International Criminal Court: A Commentary* (3 ed, Beck/Hart 2016).

Ashworth A, 'United Kingdom' in Kevin Jon Heller and Markus Dubber (eds), *The Handbook of Comparative Criminal Law* (Stanford University Press 2010).

Badar ME, 'The Mens Rea Enigma in the Jurisprudence of the International Criminal Court' in Larissa von der Herik and Carsten Stahn (eds), *The Diversification and Fragmentation of International Criminal Law* (Martinus Nijhoff Publishers 2012).

Bagaric M, 'Australia' in Alan Reed and Michael Bohlander (eds), *Participation in Crime: Domestic and Comparative Perspectives* (Taylor & Francis Ltd 2013).

Bronitt S, 'Australia' in Kevin Jon Heller and Markus Dubber (eds), *The Handbook of Comparative Criminal Law* (Stanford University Press 2010).

Burchell J, 'South Africa' in Kevin Jon Heller and Markus Dubber (eds), *The Handbook of Comparative Criminal Law* (Stanford University Press 2010).

Chiesa LE, 'United States' in Alan Reed and Michael Bohlander (eds), *Participation in Crime: Domestic and Comparative Perspectives* (Taylor & Francis 2013).

Cupido M, 'Group Acting With a Common Purpose' in de Hemptinne Jérôme, Roth Robert and Van Sliedreat Elies (eds), *Modes of Liability in International Criminal Law* (Cambridge University Press 2019).

Czaplinski W, 'Customary International Law as a Basis of an Individual Criminal Responsibility' in Bartlomiej Krzan (ed), *Prosecuting International Crimes: A Multidisciplinary Approach* (Brill | Nijhoff 2019).

Delmas-Marty M, 'Comparative Criminal Law as a Necessary Tool for the Application of International Criminal Law' in A Cassese (ed), *The Oxford Companion to International Criminal Justice* (Oxford University Press 2009).

Díaz-Aranda E, 'Mexico' in Ulrich Sieber, Hans-Georg Koch and Jan-Michael Simon (eds), *Participation in Crime: Criminal Liability of Leaders of Criminal Groups and Networks* (Duncker & Humblot Publishers 2020).

Dschang PK, 'Cameroon' in Ulrich Sieber, Hans-Georg Koch and Jan-Michael Simon (eds), *Participation in Crime: Criminal Liability of Leaders of Criminal Groups and Networks* (Duncker & Humblot Publishers 2020).

Eser A, 'Individual Criminal Responsibility' in Antonio Cassese, Paola Gaeta and John RWD Jones (eds), *The Rome Statute of the International Criminal Court: A Commentary* (Oxford University Press 2002).

Eser A, 'Mental Element - Mistake of Fact and Mistake of Law' in Antonio Cassese, Paola Gaeta and John RWD Jones (eds), *The Rome Statute of the International Criminal Court : A Commentary, Volume 1* (Oxford University Press 2002).

Ferrante M, 'Argentina' in Kevin Jon Heller and Markus Dubber (eds), *The Handbook of Comparative Criminal Law* (Stanford University Press 2010).

Gosnell C, 'Damned If You Don't : Liability for Omissions in International Criminal Law' in Yvonne McDermott, William A Schabas and Niamh Hayes (eds), *The Ashgate Research Companion to International Criminal Law: Critical Perspectives* (Routledge 2013).

Greco L, 'Comentario Al Artículo de Ramon Ragués' in J. Valenzuela (ed), *Discusiones Número XIII: Ignorancia deliberada y Derecho Penal* (EdiUNS 2013).

Herrera Bazán SP, 'La participación imprudente' in Miguel Ontiveros Alonso, Mercedes Peláez and Claus Roxin (eds), *Libro Homenaje a Claus Roxin, La influencia de la ciencia penal alemana en Iberoamérica, Tomo 1* (Instituto Nacional de Ciencias Penales 2003).

Jain N, 'India' in Ulrich Sieber, Susanne Forster and Konstanze Jarvers (eds), *National Criminal Law in a Comparative Legal Context, Defining Criminal Conduct, Volume 3.1* (Schriftenreihe des Max-Planck-Instituts für Ausländisches und Internationales Strafrecht 2011).

Jakobs G, 'Indiferencia Como Dolo Indirecto' in José Miguel Zugaldía Espinar and Jacobo López Barja de Quiroga (eds), *Dogmática y Ley Penal: Libro Homenaje a Enrique Bacigalupo* (Marcial Pons 2004).

Kleffner J, 'The Collective Accountability of Organized Armed Groups for System Crimes' in Andre Nollkaemper and Harmen van der Wilt (eds), *System Criminality in International Law* (Cambridge University Press 2009).

Knuckey S, 'Murder in Common Article 3' in Andrew Clapham, Paola Gaeta and Marco Sassoli (eds), *The 1949 Geneva Convention : A Commentary* (Oxford University Press 2015).

Kugler I, 'Israel' in Kevin Jon Heller and Markus Dubber (eds), *The Handbook of Comparative Criminal Law* (Stanford University Press 2010).

Luo W, 'China' in Kevin Jon Heller and Markus Dubber (eds), *The Handbook of Comparative Criminal Law* (Stanford University Press 2010).

Ohlin J, 'Conspiracy' in A Cassese (ed), *The Oxford Companion to International Criminal Justice* (Oxford University Press 2009).

Olasolo Alonso H and Carnero Rojo E, 'Forms of Accesorial Liability under Article 25(3)(b) and (C)' in Carsten Stahn (ed), *The Law and the Practice of the International Criminal Court* (Oxford University Press 2015).

Önok RM, 'Turkey' in Alan Reed and Michael Bohlander (eds), *Participation in Crime: Domestic and Comparative Perspectives* (Taylor & Francis 2013).

Pfützner P, 'Frankreich' in Ulrich Sieber and Karin Cornils (eds), *Nationales Strafrecht in Rechtsvergleichender Darstellung Allgemeiner Teil. Band 4* (Duncker & Humblot 2010).

Piragoff D and Robinson D, 'Mental Element' in Otto Triffterer (ed), *Commentary on the Rome Statute of the International Criminal Court Observers' Notes, Article by Article* (2 ed, Hart Publishing 2008).

Ragués I Vallès R, 'Mejor No Saber: Sobre La Doctrina de La Ignorancia Deliberada En Derecho Penal' in J. Valenzuela (ed), *Discusiones Número XIII: Ignorancia deliberada y Derecho Penal* (EdiUNS 2013).

Reid V, Sarch A and Walker S, 'Thinking Like an Accomplice: The Mens Rea for Complicity in US and English Law after Rosemond and Jogee' in Beatrice Krebs (ed), *Accessorial Liability after Jogee* (Hart Publishing 2020).

Reza S, 'Egypt' in Kevin Jon Heller and Markus Dubber (eds), *The Handbook of Comparative Criminal Law* (Stanford University Press 2010).

Richter T, 'China' in Ulrich Sieber, Hans-Georg Koch and Jan-Michael Simon (eds), *Participation in Crime: Criminal Liability of Leaders of Criminal Groups and Networks* (Duncker & Humblot Publishers 2020).

Roach K, 'Canada' in Kevin Jon Heller and Markus Dubber (eds), *The Handbook of Comparative Criminal Law* (Stanford University Press 2010).

Robinson PH, '[A Brief Comparative Summary of the Criminal Law of the] United States' in Kevin Jon Heller and Markus D Dubber (eds), *The Handbook of Comparative Criminal Law* (Stanford University Press 2010).

Rolofs P and Schittenhelm U, 'Russia' in Ulrich Sieber, Hans-Georg Koch and Jan-Michael Simon (eds), *Participation in Crime: Criminal Liability of Leaders of Criminal Groups and Networks* (Duncker & Humblot Publishers 2020).

Sabadell AL, 'Brazil' in Ulrich Sieber, Hans-Georg Koch and Jan-Michael Simon (eds), *Participation in Crime: Criminal Liability of Leaders of Criminal Groups and Networks* (Duncker & Humblot Publishers 2020).

Schabas WA and El Zeidy MM, 'Article 17: Issues of Admissibility' in Triffterer Otto and Ambos Kai (eds), *The Rome Statute of the International Criminal Court: A Commentary* (3 ed, CH Beck, Hart, Nomos 2016).

Silverman E, 'United States' in Ulrich Sieber, Hans-Georg Koch and Jan-Michael Simon (eds), *Participation in Crime: Criminal Liability of Leaders of Criminal Groups and Networks* (Duncker & Humblot Publishers 2020).

Simma B and Paulus A, 'Le Rôle Relatif Des Différentes Sources Du Droit International Public: Dont Les Principles Généraux Du Droit' in Hervé Ascensio, Emmanuel Decaux and Alain Pellet, *Droit Pénal International* (11 ed, Pedone 2000).

Snyman CR, 'South Africa' in Ulrich Sieber, Hans-Georg Koch and Jan-Michael Simon (eds), *Participation in Crime: Criminal Liability of Leaders of Criminal Groups and Networks* (Duncker & Humblot Publishers 2020).

Tellenbach S, 'Parties to Crime in Turkey' in Ulrich Sieber, Konstanze Jarvers and Emily Silverman (eds), *National Criminal Law in a Comparative Legal Context, Defining Criminal Conduct, Volume 4.1* (Duncker and Humblot 2015).

Tellenbach S, 'Tatbeteiligung in Der Türkei' in Ulrich Sieber and Karin Cornils (eds), *Nationales Strafrecht in Rechtsvergleichender Darstellung: Allgemeiner Teil, Volume 4* (Duncker & Humboldt 2010).

Tellenbach S, 'Turkey' in Ulrich Sieber, Hans-Georg Koch and Jan-Michael Simon (eds), *Participation in Crime: Criminal Liability of Leaders of Criminal Groups and Networks* (Duncker & Humblot Publishers 2020).

Ventura M, 'Farewell "Specific Direction": Aiding and Abetting War Crimes and Crimes Against Humanity in Perišić, Taylor, Šainović et al, and US Alien Tort Statute

Jurisprudence' in Stuart Casey-Maslen (ed), *The War Report: Armed Conflict in 2013* (Oxford University Press 2014).

Ventura MJ, 'Aiding and Abetting' in Jérôme de Hemptinne, Robert Roth and Elies von Sliedregt (eds), *Modes of Liability in International Criminal Law* (Cambridge University Press 2019).

Von Hirsch A, 'Extending the Harm Principle: "Remote" Harms and Fair Imputation' in Andrew Simester and Anthony Terry Hanmer Smith (eds), *Harm and Culpability* (Oxford University Press 1996).

Yeo S, 'India' in Kevin Jon Heller and Markus Dubber (eds), *The Handbook of Comparative Criminal Law* (Stanford University Press 2010).

Journal Articles

Akehurst M, 'Equity and General Principles of Law' (1976) 25 *International and Comparative Law Quarterly* 801.

Aksenova M, 'The Specific Direction Requirement for Aiding and Abetting: A Call for Revisiting Comparative Criminal Law' (2015) 4 *Cambridge Journal of International and Comparative Law* 88.

Ambos K and Njikam O, 'Charles Taylor's Criminal Responsibility' (2013) 11 *Journal of International Criminal Justice* 789.

Ambos K, 'Remarks on the General Part of International Criminal Law' (2006) 4 *Journal of International Criminal Justice* 660.

Anghie A and Chimni BS, 'Third World Approaches to International Law and Individual Responsibility in Internal Conflicts' (2003) 2 *Chinese Journal of International Law* 77.

Bassiouni CM, 'International Crimes: Jus Cogens and Obligatio Erga Omnes' (1996) 59 Law and Contemporary Problems 63.

Bohorquéz RO, 'Coautoría y Complicidad En El Derecho Mexicano (Doctrina, Jurisprudencia, Elementos Y Criterios de Aplicación)' (2011) 35 *Revista Derecho Penal* 49.

Clapham A, 'Extending International Criminal Law Beyond the Individual to Corporations and Armed Opposition Groups' (2008) 6 *Journal of International Criminal Justice* 899.

Clapham, A, 'The Role of the Individual in International Law' (2010) 21 *European Journal of International Law* 25.

Clark JN, ' "Specific Direction" and the Fragmentation of International Jurisprudence on Aiding and Abetting: Perišić and Beyond" ' (2015) 15 *International Criminal Law Review* 411.

Coco A and Gal T, 'Losing Direction: The ICTY Appeals Chamber's Controversial Approach to Aiding and Abetting in Perišić' (2014) 12 *Journal of International Criminal Justice* 345.

DeFalco RC, 'Contextualizing Actus Reus under Article 25(3)(d) of the ICC Statute: Thresholds of Contribution' (2013) 11 *Journal of International Criminal Justice* 715.

Degan V-D, 'On the Sources of International Criminal Law' (2005) 4 *Chinese Journal of International Law* 45.

Dubber M, 'The Promise of German Criminal Law: A Science of Crime and Punishment' (2006) 6 *German Law Journal* 1049.

Ellis J, 'General Principles and Comparative Law' (2011) 22 *European Journal of International Law* 949.

Esakov G, 'R v. Jogee: A Case for Comparative Study' (2018) 6 *Russian Law Journal* 133.

Fischer JM and Tognazzini NA, 'The Physiognomy of Responsibility' (2011) 82 *Philosophy and Phenomenological Research* 381.

Greenwalt A, 'Foreign Assistance Complicity' (2016) 54 *Columbia Journal of Transnational Law* 531.

Huergo MV, 'Reflexiones En Torno de La Doctrina de La Willful Blindness y Su Posible Recepción En Argentina' (2010) 5 *El Derecho Penal* 1.

Jackson M, 'Regional Complementarity: An Interpretation of Article 17(1)(A) of the Rome Statute' (2016) 14 *Journal of International Criminal Justice* 1061.

Jenks C and Acquaviva G, 'Debate: The Role of International Criminal Justice in Fostering Compliance with International Humanitarian Law' (2014) 96 *International Review of the Red Cross* 775.

Kadish S, 'Complicity, Cause and Blame: A Study in the Interpretation of Doctrine' (1985) 73 *California Law Review* 323.

Kolb R, 'Principles as Sources of International Law: (With Special Reference to Good Faith)' (2006) 53 *Netherlands International Law Review* 1.

Kool RSB, '(Crime) Victims' Compensation: The Emergence of Convergence' (2014) 10 *Utrecht Law Review* 14.

Laufer C and da Silva RG, 'A Teoria Da Cegueira Deliberada e o Direito Penal Brasileiro' (2009) 204 *Boletim IBCCRIM* 1.

Manacorda S and Meloni C, 'Indirect Perpetration versus Joint Criminal Enterprise: Concurring Approaches in the Practice of International Criminal Law?' (2011) 9 *Journal of International Criminal Justice* 159.

Manrique ML, 'Ignorancia Deliberada y Responsabilidad Penal' (2014) 40 *Isonomía - Revista de teoría y filosofía del derecho* 163.

Megret F, 'In Defence of Hybridity: Towards a Representational Theory of International Criminal Justice' (2005) 38 *Cornell International Law Journal* 725.

Murmann U, 'Problems of Causation with Regard to (Potential) Actions of Multiple Protagonists' (2014) 12 *Journal of International Criminal Justice* 283.

Nollkaemper A, 'Concurrence between Individual Responsibility and State Responsibility in International Law' (2003) 52 *The International and Comparative Law Quarterly* 615.

Pilloud C, Pilloud C, Sandoz Y, Swinarski C, Zimmermann B, 'Commentary on the Additional Protocols of 8 June 1977 to the Geneva Conventions of 12 August 1949' (1987) 27 *International Review of the Red Cross* 119.

Seganish WM, 'Criminal Law In Antarctica: Law West Of The Pecos Revisited' (2016) 1 *Journal of Business & Economics Research* 13.

Silveira R de MJ, 'A Aplicação Da Teoria Da Cegueira Deliberada Nos Julgamentos Da Operação Lava-Jato' (2016) 122 *Revista Brasileira de Ciências Criminais* 255.

Spiermann O, 'Twentieth Century Internationalism in Law' (2007) 18 *The European Journal of International Law* 785.

Stewart J, 'Overdetermined Atrocities' (2012) 10 *Journal of International Criminal Justice* 1189.

Timmermann WK, 'Incitement in International Criminal Law' (2006) 88 *International Review of the Red Cross* 823.

Ventura M, 'The "Reasonable Basis to Proceed" Threshold in the Kenya and Côte d'Ivoire Proprio Motu Investigation Decisions: The International Criminal Court's Lowest Evidentiary Standard?' (2012) 12 *The Law and Practice of International Courts and Tribunals* 49.

Von Liszt F, 'Die Deterministischen Gegner Der Zweckstrafe' (1893) 13 *Zeitschrift für die gesamte Strafrechtswissenschaft* 325.

Watson G, 'Two Faces of Responsibility' (1996) 24 *Philosophical Topics* 227.

Weigend T, 'Intent, Mistake of Law, and Co-Perpetration in the Lubanga Decision on Confirmation of Charges' (2008) 6 *Journal of International Criminal Justice* 471.

Weisberg R, 'Reappraising Complicity' (2000) 4 *Buffalo Criminal Law Review* 217.

Werle G, 'Individual Criminal Responsibility in Article 25 ICC Statute' (2007) 5 *Journal of International Criminal Justice* 953.

Williams G, 'The Definition of Crime' (1955) 8 *Current Legal Problems* 107.

International Cases

ECCC

Prosecutor v Kaing Guek Eav, Trial Chamber Judgment (Case No 001/18-07-2007/ECCC/TC).

Prosecutor v Chea Nuon and Samphan Khieu, Trial Chamber Judgment (Case No 002/19-09-2007/ECCC/TC).

ECtHR

Cantoni v France (Judgment of 15 November 1996).
Kononov v Latvia (Judgment of 17 May 2010).

ICC

Prosecutor v Al Mahdi, Decision on the Confirmation of Charges (ICC-01/12-01/15-84-Red).
Prosecutor v Al Mahdi, Trial Chamber Judgment (ICC-01/12-01/15-171).
Prosecutor v Bemba et al, Appeals Chamber Judgment (ICC-01/05-01/08-3636-Red).
Prosecutor v Bemba et al, Corrected Version of Appeal Brief (ICC-01/05-01/13-2143-Corr-Red).
Prosecutor v Bemba et al, Decision on the Confirmation of Charges, Pre-Trial Chamber I (ICC-01/05-01/13-749).
Prosecutor v Bemba et al, Trial Judgment (ICC-01/05-01/13-1989-Red).
Prosecutor v Gombo, Judgment Pursuant to Article 74 of the Statute (ICC-01/05-01/13).
Prosecutor v Goudé, Decision on the Confirmation of Charges (ICC-02/11-02/11-186).
Prosecutor v Katanga and Ngudjolo Chui, Decision on the Confirmation of Charges, Pre-Trial Chamber I (ICC-01/04-01/07-717).
Prosecutor v Katanga, Decision Rransmitting Additional Legal and Factual Material (Regulation 55(2) and 55(3) of the Regulations of the Court) (ICC-01/04-01/07-3371-tENG) (ICC-01/04-01/07-3371-tENG).
Prosecutor v Katanga, Trial Chamber Judgment (ICC-01/04-01/07-3436-tENG).
Prosecutor v Kenyatta, Decision on the Confirmation of Charges (ICC-01/09-02/11-382-Red).
Prosecutor v Lubanga, Appeals Chamber Judgment (ICC-01/04-01/06-3121-Red).
Prosecutor v Lubanga, Decision on the Confirmation of Charges, Pre-Trial Chamber I (ICC-01/04-01/06-803-tEN).
Prosecutor v Lubanga, Trial Chamber Judgment (ICC-01/04-01/06-2842).
Prosecutor v Mbarushimana, Decision on the Confirmation of Charges (ICC-01/04-01/10-465-Red).
Prosecutor v Mbarushimana, Judgment on the Appeal of the Prosecutor against the Confirmation of Charges Decision (ICC-01/04-01/10-514).
Prosecutor v Ongwen, Decision on the Confirmation of Charges (ICC-02/04-01/15-422-Red).
Prosecutor v Ruto et al, Decision on the Confirmation of Charges (ICC-01/09-01/11-373).
Situation on the registered vessels of the Union of the Comoros, the Hellenic Republic and the Kingdom of Cambodia, Decision on the 'Application for Judicial Review by the Government of the Union of Comoros', Pre-Trial Chamber I (ICC-01/13).

ICJ

Case Concerning the Arrest Warrant of 11 April 2000 (*Democratic Republic of the Congo v Belgium*), 14 February 2002.

Case Concerning Application of the Convention on the Prevention and Punishment of the Crime of Genocide (*Croatia v Serbia*), 3 February 2015.

Dispute Regarding Navigational and Related Rights (*Costa Rica v Nicaragua*), Judgment, 13 July 2009.

ICTR

Prosecutor v Ferdinand Nahimana et al, Appeals Chamber Judgment (ICTR-99-52-A).

Prosecutor v Gacumbitsi, Trial Chamber Judgment (ICTR-2001-64-T).

Prosecutor v Jean Baptiste Gatete, Appeals Chamber Judgment (ICTR-00-61-A).

Prosecutor v Jean-Paul Akayesu, Appeals Chamber Judgment (ICTR-96-4-A).

Prosecutor v Karemera et al, Appeals Chamber Judgment (ICTR-98-44-A).

Prosecutor v Karemera et al, Trial Chamber Judgment (ICTR-98-44-T).

Prosecutor v Nyiramasuhuko et al, Appeals Chamber Judgment (ICTR-98-42-A).

Prosecutor v Renzaho, Trial Chamber Judgment (ICTR-97-31-T).

Rukundo v Prosecutor, Appeals Chamber Judgment (ICTR-2001-70-A).

Semanza v The Prosecutor, Appeals Chamber Judgment (ICTR-97-20-A).

Prosecutor v Alfred Musema, Judgment and Sentence (ICTR-96-13-T).

Prosecutor v Ignace Bagilishema, Appeal Judgment: Reasons (ICTR-95-1A-A).

Prosecutor v Ntagerura et al, Appeals Chamber Judgment (ICTR-99-46-A).

Karera v Prosecutor, Appeals Chamber Judgment (ICTR-01-74-A).

Prosecutor v Ntawukuriryayo, Appeals Chamber Judgment (ICTR-05-82-A).

Kalimanzira v Prosecutor, Appeals Chamber Judgment (ICTR-05-88-A).

Prosecutor v Muhimana, Trial Chamber Judgment (ICTR-95-1B-T).

Prosecutor v Jean-Paul Akayesu, Trial Chamber Judgment (ICTR-96-4-T).

Prosecutor v Ntakirutimana, Appeals Chamber Judgment (ICTR-96-10-A & ICTR-96-17-A).

ICTY

Prosecution v Delalic et al, Appeals Chamber Judgment (IT-96-21-A).

Prosecutor v Anto Furundzija, Trial Chamber Judgment (IT-95-17/1-T).

Prosecutor v Brđanin, Appeals Chamber Judgment (IT-99-36-A).

Prosecutor v Dario Kordic, Mario Cerkez, Appeals Chamber Judgment (IT-95-14/2-A).

Prosecutor v Dusko Tadic, Appeals Chamber Judgment (IT-94-1-A).

Prosecutor v Dusko Tadic, Trial Chamber Judgment (IT-94-1-T).

Prosecutor v Erdemović, Appeals Chamber Judgment (IT-96-22-A).

Prosecutor v Goran Jelisic, Trial Chamber Judgment (IT-95-10-T).

Prosecutor v Gotovina and Markac, Appeals Chamber Judgment (IT-06-90-A).
Prosecutor v Hadzihasanovic and Kubura, Appeals Chamber Judgment (IT-01-47-A).
Prosecutor v Haradinaj et al, Appeals Chamber Judgment (IT-04-84-A).
Prosecutor v Krnojelac, Appeals Chamber Judgment (IT-97-25-A).
Prosecutor v Kupreskic et al, Appeals Chamber Judgment (IT-95-16-A).
Prosecutor v Kvočka et al, Appeals Chamber Judgment (IT-98-30/1-A).
Prosecutor v Lukić and Lukić, Appeals Chamber Judgment (IT-98-32/1-T).
Prosecutor v Milomir Stakic, Trial Chamber Judgment (IT-97-24-T).
Prosecutor v Miroslav Kvocka et al, Trial Chamber Judgment (IT-98-30/1-T).
Prosecutor v Vasiljević, Trial Chamber Judgment (IT-98-32-T).
Prosecutor v Mrkšić and Šljivančanin, Appeals Chamber Judgment (IT-95-13/1-A).
Prosecutor v Mrksic et al, Appeals Chamber Judgment (IT-95-13/1-A).
Prosecutor v Orić, Appeals Chamber Judgment (IT-03-68-A).
Prosecutor v Perisic, Appeals Chamber Judgment (IT-04-81-A).
Prosecutor v Perisic, Trial Chamber Judgment (IT-04-81-T).
Prosecutor v Popović et al, Appeals Chamber Judgment (IT-05-88-A).
Prosecutor v Popović et al, Trial Chamber Judgment (IT-05-88-T).
Prosecutor v Radislav Krstic, Appeals Chamber Judgment (IT-98-33-A).
Prosecutor v Sainovic et al, Appeals Chamber Judgment (IT-05-87-A).
Prosecutor v Semanza, Trial Chamber Judgment (ICTR-97-20-T).
Prosecutor v Simić et al, Appeals Chamber Judgment (IT-95-9-A).
Prosecutor v Stanišić and Simatović, Appeals Chamber Judgment (IT-03-69-A).
Prosecutor v Tihomir Blaškić, Appeals Chamber Judgment (IT-95-14-A).
Prosecutor v Tihomir Blaškić, Trial Chamber Judgment (IT-95-14-T).
Prosecutor v Vasiljević, Appeals Chamber Judgment (IT-98-32-A).
Prosecutor v Vidoje Blagojevic and Dragan Jokic, Appeals Chamber Judgment (IT-02-60-A).
Prosecutor v Mucić et al, Trial Chamber Judgment (IT-96-21-T).
Prosecutor v Tolimir, Appeals Chamber Judgment (IT-05-88/2-A).
Prosecutor v Zlatko Aleksovski, Appeals Chamber Judgment (IT-95-14/1-A).
Prosecutor v Zlatko Aleksovski, Trial Chamber Judgment (IT-95-14/1-T).
Prosecutor v Orić, Trial Chamber Judgment (IT-03-68-T).
Prosecutor v Pavle Strugar, Appeals Chamber Judgment (IT-01-42-A).
Prosecutor v Strugar, Trial Chamber Judgment (IT-01-42-T).

IMT

Flick et al, Judgment of 22 December 1947.
France and ors v Göring (Hermann) and ors, Judgment of 1 October 1946.
Trial of the Major War Criminals before the International Military Tribunal, Judgment of 1 October 1946.

MICT

Prosecutor v Vojislav Šešelj, Appeals Chamber Judgment (MICT-16-99-A).

SCSL

Prosecutor v Brima et al, Appeals Chamber Judgment (SCSL-2004-16-A).

Prosecutor v Brima et al, Trial Chamber Judgment (SCSL-04-16-T).

Prosecutor v Charles Ghankay Taylor, Appeals Chamber Judgment (SCSL-03-01-A).

Prosecutor v Moinina Fofana and Allieu Kondewa, Appeals Chamber Judgment (SCSL-04-14-A-829).

STL

Interlocutory Decision on the Applicable Law: Terrorism, Conspiracy, Homicide, Perpetration, Cumulative Charging, Appeals Chamber Judgment (STL-11-01/I/AC/R176bis/F0936).

National Cases

Argentina

Gallow v Tillstone (1900) 83 LT 411.

Leiva, Luis s/Recurso de casación, Tribunal de Casacion Penal, Sala III, La Plata (TC0003 LP) cause 20137, 29/11/2007, RSD-862-7.

Prelis, Gonzalo Alfredo y otros s/Recurso de casación, Tribunal de Casacion Penal Sala IV - La Plata (TC0004 LP), 23/4/2013, RSD-153-13.

Australia

Giorgianni v R (1985) 156 CLR 473.

R v Antonelli and Barberi (1905) 70 JP 4.

R v Glennan (1970) 91 WN (NSW) 609.

Brazil

Mensalão case, Informativo STF, AP 470/MG.

TRF-4 ACR 5004606-3120104047002 *Rapporteur: João Pedro Gebran Neto* 16/07/2014.

TRF-4 ACR 5001945-6820134047004 *Rapporteur Ricardo Rachid de Oliveira* 02/25/2015.

TRF-5 ACR 5520-CE 20058100014586-0 *Rapporteur: Rogério Fialho Moreira* 07/09/2008.

TRF-5 ACR: 5520 CE 0014586-4020054058100 *Rapporteur: Federal Judge Rogério Fialho Moreira* 09/09/2008.

Canada

Callow v Tillstone (1900), 64 JP 823, 19 Cox CC 576.

R v Briscoe [2010] 1 SCR, 411.

R v Coy [1938] 1 WWR 748 (BCSC).
R v Dowd (1899), 4 CCC 170 (Que Ct Special Sessions).
R v Finta [1994] 1 SCR 701.
R v FW Woolworth co (1974) 18 CCC (2nd) 23 (Ont CA).
R v Hamel (1968), 64 WWR 193 (BC Co Ct).
R v Hartford and Frigon (1979), 51 CCC (2d) 462 (BCCA).
R v Hibbert [1995] 2 SCR 973.
R v Hoggan, [1966] 3 CCC 1, 47 CR 256 (Alta CA).
R v McDaid (1974), 19 CCC (2d) 572 (Ont CA).
R v Roach (2004) 192 CCC (3d) 193 (SCC).
R v Roy (1900), 3 CCC 472 (Que QB).
R v Russel (1923), 39 CCC 374 (Sask KB).

Egypt

Court of Cassation, 26 November 1973, Year 24 No 220.
Court of Cassation, 27 January 1959, Digest of Decisions, Year 10, No 23.
Court of Cassation, 6 February 2005, No 56615.
Court of Cassation, 25 December 1930, No 1835/47.

England and Wales

Blakely and Sutton v DPP [1991] RTR 405.
Churchill v Walton [1967] 2 AC 224.
DPP for Northern Ireland v Maxwell [1978] 1 WLR 1350.
DPP v Smith [1961] AC 290.
Hyam v DPP [1975] AC 55.
Johnson v Youden [1950] 1 KB 544.
National Coal Board v Gamble [1959] 1 QB 11.
R v Brainbridge [1960] 1 QB 129.
R v Hancock [1985] UKHL 9.
R v Jogee [2016] UKSC 8; [2017] AC 387.
R v Moloney [1985] 1 AC 905.
R v Nedrick [1986] 1 WLR 1025.
R v Powell and English [1999] 1 AC 1.
R v Woollin [1999] AC 82.
Regina v Armel Gnango [2011] UKSC 59; [2012] 1 AC 827.
Roper v Taylor's Central Garages [1951] 2 TLR 284 (KBD).
Sweet v Parsley [1970] AC 132.

France

Chambre Criminelle, 1 December 1944, *Paemelabre* (D 1945 162).

Chambre Criminelle, 28 May 1980, *Pernot* (D 1981, IR 137, obs G Roujou de Boubée).
Cour de Cassation Criminelle, 30 January 1997, *Mouris Papon* (D, 1997, 147).

Germany

12 August 2009 BGH BeckRS 2009.
30 August 2006 BGH 2 StR 198/06.
7 July 1999 BGH NStZ 1999.

Israel

Har-Shefi v State of Israel (2001) 55(ii) PD 735.
Plonit v State of Israel (CA 320/99 55(3) PD 22 [1999]).

Italy

Cass, sez I, 12 febbraio 1982, Bonomo, Cass Pen 1983, Giust Pen 1982, II, 654 Ass Genova 17 febbraio 1978, Levrero, Giur Merito 1980, 167.
Cass, sez I, 30 maggio 1980, Milano, Cass Pen Mass Ann 1981, 1988, Giust, pen 1982, II, 312.
Cass, sez I, 5 luglio 1976, Salvalajo, Cass Pen Mass Ann 1977, 831.
Cass, sez I, novembre 24, 1976, La Gioia, Cass Pen Mass Ann 1124, Giust Pen 1977, II, 495.

Malaysia

Daw Aye Aye Mu v Public Prosecutor (1998) 2 SLR 64.
Hj Abdul Rahim Hassan & Anor v Public Prosecutor (1997) MLJU 238.
Public Prosecutor v Datuk Tan Cheng Swee & Ors (1979) 1 MLJ 166.

Mexico

Supreme Court of Justice, Amparo directo 235/54 MMF. 11 de marzo de 1959 Unanimidad de cuatro votos Ponente: AMA.
Supreme Court of Justice, Amparo directo 856/79 MGM 8 de febrero de 1980 Unanimidad de cuatro votos Ponente: FCT Secretario: FNG.

South Africa

Cathay Pacific Airways Ltd and Another v Lin and Another (260/2016) [2017] ZASCA 35; [2017] 2 All SA 722 (SCA) (29 March 2017).
Constitutional Court, S v Coetzee and Others (CCT 50/95) [1997] ZACC 2; 1997 (4) BCLR 437; 1997 (3) SA 527.
Goldberg v Director of Public Prosecutions: Western Cape (A446/12) [2013] ZAWCHC 184; 2014 (2) SACR 57 (WCC) (17 December 2013).
S v Mashaba and Others (CCT 216/05) [2005] ZAGPHC 105 (4 October 2005).
Savoi and Others v National Director of Public Prosecutions and Another (8006/12) [2013] ZAKZPHC 19; [2013] 3 All SA 548 (KZP) (17 May 2013).

The Netherlands

District Court, The Hague, 23 December 2005, LJN: AU8685.

United States of America

Backun v US, Court of Appeals for the Fourth Circuit, 112 F2d 635 (4th Circuit, 1940) 10 June 1940.

Doe I v Nestle USA, Inc., Court of Appeals for the Ninth Circuit, 766 F.3d 1013 (9th Cir. 2014) 4 September 2014.

John Doe VI v Exxon Mobil Corporation, Court of Appeals District of Columbia Circuit (2015 WL 5042118) 6 July 2015.

John Doe VIII v Exxon Mobil Corporation, Court of Appeals District of Columbia Circuit (527 Fed. Appx. 7) 26 July 2013.

Khulumani v Barclay National Bank Ltd, Court of Appeals for the Second Circuit, 504 F3d 254 (2d Cir 2007) 10 December 2007.

People v Luparello, Court of Appeal of California, 187 Cal App 3d 410, 231 Cal Rptr 832, 25 November 1986.

United States v Peoni, Court of Appeals for the Second Circuit, 100 F2d 401 (2d Cir. 1938) 12 December 1938.

United States v Jewell, Court of Appeals for the Ninth Circuit, 532 F. 2d 697 (9th Cir. 1976) 27 February 1976.

Blog Posts

Ambos, K, 'Complicity in War Crimes through (Legal) Arms Supplies?' *EJIL:Talk* (20 January 2020) https://www.ejiltalk.org/complicity-in-war-crimes-through-legal-arms-supplies/?fbclid=IwAR1XQ0oWW40nE7NcHt1EhdoXPPtdqbtxvnpvj43UScvU88cNmHVMgxhUHaY.

Fielding A, 'Charles Taylor Appeal: Why Its Rejection of "Specific Direction" Doesn't Matter' *Beyond the Hagne* (September 30, 2013) https://beyondthehague.com/2013/09/30/charles-taylor-appeal-why-its-rejection-of-specific-direction-doesnt-matter/#more-474.

Heller, KJ, 'Two Thoughts on Manuel Ventura's Critique of Specific Direction' *Opinio Juris* (January 10, 2014) http://opiniojuris.org/2014/01/10/two-thoughts-manuel-venturas-critique-specific-direction/.

Milanovic M, 'The Limits of Aiding and Abetting Liability: The ICTY Appeals Chamber Acquits Momcilo Perisic' *EJIL:Talk!* (March 11, 2013) https://www.ejiltalk.org/the-limits-of-aiding-and-abetting-liability-the-icty-appeals-chamber-acquits-momcilo-perisic/.

Stewart JG, '"Specific Direction" Is Indefensible: A Response to Heller on Complicity' *Opinio Juris* (January 10, 2014) http://opiniojuris.org/2013/06/12/specific-direction-is-indefensible-a-response-to-heller-on-complicity/.

Stewart JG, '"Specific Direction" Is Unprecedented: Results from Two Empirical Studies' *EJIL:Talk!* (September 4, 2013) https://www.ejiltalk.org/specific-direction-is-unprecedented-results-from-two-empirical-studies/#more-9258.

Stewart JG, 'An Important New Orthodoxy on Complicity in the ICC Statute?' *MANIFESTO* (January 21, 2015) http://jamesgstewart.com/the-important-new-orthodoxy-on-complicity-in-the-icc-statute/.

Stewart JG, 'Judicial Rejection of "Specific Direction" Is Widespread' *MANIFESTO* (December 23, 2015) http://jamesgstewart.com/judicial-rejection-of-specific-direction-is-widespread/.

Ventura MJ, 'Specific Direction à La Perišić, the Taylor Appeal Judgment and What It Could Mean for the ICTY Appeals Chamber in Šainović et al – Part I' *Spreading the Jam* (January 9, 2014) https://dovjacobs.com/2014/01/09/guest-post-specific-direction-a-la-perisic-the-taylor-appeal-judgment-and-what-it-could-mean-for-the-icty-appeals-chamber-in-sainovic-et-al-part-ii/.

Weigend T, 'How to Interpret Complicity in the ICC Statute' *MANIFESTO* (December 15, 2014) http://jamesgstewart.com/how-to-intepret-complicity-in-the-icc-statute/.

Magazine Articles

Dall E, Keatinge T and Berger A, 'Countering Proliferation Finance: An Introductory Guide for Financial Institutions' *Royal United Services Institute for Defence and Security Studies* (2017) https://rusi.org/sites/default/files/201704_rusi_cpf_guidance_paper.1_0.pdf%0D.

Heller KJ, in *Milestones in International Criminal Justice: Recent Legal Controversies at the UN Yugoslav Tribunal* (Chatham House 2013).

Statutes

Additional Protocol to the Geneva Conventions of 12 August 1949, and Relating to the Protection of Victims of International Armed Conflicts (Protocol I) (1977).

Charter of the International Military Tribunal – Annex to the Agreement for the Prosecution and Punishment of the Major War Criminals of the European Axis ('London Agreement') (1945).

Convention Against Torture and Other Cruel, Inhuman or Degrading Treatment or Punishment (1984).

Convention on the Prevention and Punishment of the Crime of Genocide (1948).

Elements of Crimes of the International Criminal Court (2011).

Extraordinary Chambers in the Courts of Cambodia Law (2001).
International Covenant on Civil and Political Rights (1966).
Israel, *Penal Law 5737-1977* (4 ed, Aryeh Greenfield Publications 2005).
Law on Specialist Chambers and Specialist Prosecutor's Office (Kosovo Tribunal) (2015).
Regulation on Panels with Exclusive Jurisdiction over Serious Criminal Offences (East Timor Tribunal) (2000).
Rome Statute of the International Criminal Court (last amended 2010) (1998).
Statute of the Extraordinary African Chambers (2012).
Statute of the International Court of Justice (1945).
Statute of the International Criminal Tribunal for Rwanda (1994).
Statute of the International Criminal Tribunal for the former Yugoslavia (2002).
Statute of the Special Court for Sierra Leone (2002).
Vienna Convention on the Law of Treaties (1969).

Reports and Others

International Commission of Jurists, 'Report of the ICJ Expert Legal Panel on Corporate Complicity in International Crimes' (2008).
International Committee of the Red Cross Advisory Service on International Humanitarian Law, 'General Principles of International Criminal Law' (2014).
International Conferences (The Hague), Hague Convention (IV) Respecting the Laws and Customs of War on Land and Its Annex: Regulations Concerning the Laws and Customs of War on Land, 18 October 1907.
International Law Association, 'Report of the Study Group on the Use of Domestic Law Principles in the Development of International Law, Report of the Seventy-Eighth Conference' (2018).
International Law Commission, 'Draft Code of Offences against the Peace and Security of Mankind', 1954 (2005).
International Law Commission, 'Draft Conclusions on Identification of Customary International Law, U.N. Doc. A/73/10' (30 April-1 June and 2 July-10 August 2018).
International Law Commission, 'Fourth Report on Crimes against Humanity', Sean D. Murphy, 18 February 2019, A/CN.4/725.
International Law Commission, 'Record on General Principles of Law, A/CN.4/SR.3489, 25 September 2019'.
International Law Commission, 'Record on General Principles of Law, A/CN.4/SR.3489, 25 September 2019'.
International Law Commission, 'Record on General Principles of Law, A/CN.4/SR.3490, 30 September 2019'.

International Law Commission, 'Record on General Principles of Law, A/CN.4/SR.3492, 2 October 2019'.

International Law Commission, 'Record on General Principles of Law, A/CN.4/SR.3493, 31 October 2019'.

International Law Commission, 'Second Report of the Special Rapporteur on General Principles of Law, Marcelo Vázquez-Bermúdez, UN Doc. A/CN.4/741' (2020).

New South Wales Law Reform Commission, 'Complicity, Report No 129' (2010).

Statistics Division of the United Nations Secretariat, *Standard Country or Area Codes for Statistical Use* (United Nations Publications 1999) <https://unstats.un.org/unsd/publication/SeriesM/Series_M49_Rev4(1999)_en.pdf>.

Stewart JG, 'Aiding and Abetting and Specific Direction in International Criminal Law: A Dataset of Incidents' (2013) <https://docs.google.com/spreadsheets/d/1Jb1cirLsSLresUIQaE6V56usj3jvyi6lsbIrKnNKSUY/edit#gid=0> accessed 8 April 2020.

United Nations General Assembly, Report of the International Law Commission, 4 May 1994, A/CN.4/SR.2330.

United Nations Secretary-General, 'Report of the Secretary-General Pursuant to Paragraph 2 of Security Council Resolution 808' (1993).

United Nations Security Council, 'Security Council Resolution 827/1993' (1993).

United Nations Security Council, 'Security Council Resolution 955/1994' (1994).

Index

www.ingramcontent.com/pod-product-compliance
Lightning Source LLC
Chambersburg PA
CBHW071226230926
51849CB00001B/42
* 9 7 8 9 0 0 4 4 7 0 9 2 7 *